STERN COLLEGE FOR WOMEN · YESHIVA UNIVERSITY

The Story of Yeshiva University

THE STORY OF
YESHIVA UNIVERSITY

The First Jewish University

in America

BY GILBERT KLAPERMAN

Introduction by The Honorable Arthur J. Goldberg

THE MACMILLAN COMPANY

COLLIER-MACMILLAN LIMITED : LONDON

To Libby

MY WIFE, MY HELPMEET,

MY DEAREST FRIEND

*The publication of this book was made possible
by a contribution from the
Anna and Louis Feder Charitable Trust.*

FIRST PRINTING

The Macmillan Company
Collier-Macmillan Canada Ltd., Toronto, Ontario

Printed in the United States of America

CONTENTS

CONTENTS

LIST OF ILLUSTRATIONS

(FOLLOWING PAGE 142)

PREFACE

This work is a labor of love and the fulfillment of a self-imposed obligation. I was a student at what is now Yeshiva University from 1933 to 1941. During that period I graduated from the High School, College and Seminary and in 1955 I received my doctorate in the Bernard Revel Graduate School of Yeshiva University. Before and after 1955, I also taught at Yeshiva College. Thus, with the exception of a brief interlude when I studied at Columbia University and at the State University of Iowa, almost all of the formal education that I possess came to me through Yeshiva University.

This is a gift that I treasure most dearly, for it rooted me strongly in the two mainstreams of scholarship which make up my cultural being—the world of the Torah and the heritage of the western world. I cherish it also because it was hard to come by. My parents were poor and could hardly afford my food and transportation needs. But the fear that I might be denied the opportunity to study was never a matter for concern because the administration of the Yeshiva was as liberal as possible with financial aid and scholarships for any one who qualified. And I and most of my fellow students who were in a similar predicament were thus able to continue our studies.

The single-minded dedication of my parents and the generous policy of the school impressed themselves deeply upon me and I have since felt a profound sense of obligation to memorialize in some way the sacrifice of my own parents for Torah and the Jewish legacy as symbols of the sacrifice of countless immigrants like them. Penniless and uprooted though they were, those of my parents' generation refused to allow their children to be disenfranchised or deprived of their cultural and religious heritage.

I also wanted to repay my debt to Yeshiva, which, as a second home, provided me so generously with the materials for spiritual and intellectual life. Thus, perpetuating the history of Yeshiva and the story of its establishment and development seemed a meaningful way in which I could pay tribute to my parents and their generation and to the University as well. Because the University was a product of immigrant effort, my two goals coalesced into one. This loyalty to my Alma Mater is shared by an overwhelming number of my fellow alumni on whom Yeshiva has exercised a unique binding quality. To them and to me it is more than a symbol. It represents the seeding and blossoming of an old tradition and faith in a new soil.

Unearthing Yeshiva's beginnings was a difficult task. It took me back to the founding of Yeshivat Etz Chaim in 1886 and to 1897 and the founding of the Rabbi Isaac Elchanan Theological Seminary, the mother institution from which have sprung the schools and divisions that make up Yeshiva University today. Putting together the account of the immigrants' struggle to preserve the patterns of their religious behavior was fascinating albeit tedious. Mounds of old newspapers had to be scanned and digested, countless interviews had to be conducted, and many stray bits and pieces of information had to be fitted together. What has emerged is not a cold scientific or sociological study—but rather an emotional, sympathetic and evocative appreciation of a heroic generation.

Through the several years of research and writing, I have received much help and encouragement from many individuals. I want to extend special thanks to President Samuel Belkin, whose personal warmth, inspiration and friendship have motivated me in this and in other tasks. I want to thank too, Mr. Samuel Hartstein, Director of Public Relations at Yeshiva, for the facilities he placed at my disposal, Dr. Hyman Grinstein, Director of the James Striar School at Yeshiva, for his many revealing insights and for his personal involvement in my work, Jacob I. Dienstag, Librarian of Yeshiva's Gottesman Library, who made rare research materials available to me, and Dr. Isidore S. Meyer of the American Jewish Historical Society for his encouragement and advice. I also thankfully acknowledge the cooperation of the many graduates, families of founders and others who gave unstintingly of their time and recollections in the countless interviews I conducted.

I proudly thank, too, Justice Arthur J. Goldberg, who at a time when he was in the midst of his many international responsibilities as the then Ambassador of the United States to the United Nations, graciously consented to write the Introduction to this book.

I fondly extend my warm appreciation to the memory of the distinguished and dynamic past president of my synagogue, Henry J. Buchman, Esq., for the magnificent support he generously provided in helping to bring this volume to publication. I take this occasion, too, to express my appreciation to all the members of my congregation for the understanding and encouragement they have offered me through the nineteen years of our warm relationship.

And, finally, to my dear wife Libby goes the greatest thanks; for all that I have accomplished is due to her faith and love.

Gilbert Klaperman

Lawrence, New York
February, 1969

INTRODUCTION

The history of the Jewish Community in America, while it ante-
dates the existence of the United States, parallels the development of
our own country. The first Jews who came to these shores in 1654
from Recife in Brazil fled the religious persecution of the Spanish
Inquisition in the New World. Their parents and grandparents
before them had fled to the Western Hemisphere to escape similar
persecutions in their native Spain and Portugal.

The early years of Colonial America were preoccupied in a large
part with the elimination of bigotry and persecution. In its successful
evolution our country offered an opportunity to various ethnic and
geographic groups to blend with each other in creating a new and
sparkling heritage for its citizens and the world. Our contemporary
concern with material well-being and success may obscure but cannot conceal the fact that cultural achievement is a theme deeply
rooted into the history of our country.

The 3000 or so Jews who were in the United States at the beginning
of the eighteenth century were too involved with the problem of
survival as a minute minority and too much of a minority in absolute numbers to undertake the establishment of colleges and universities. In the middle of that century their numbers were still too
insignificant to be meaningful. But in the 1880's a mass migration
from Eastern Europe brought hundreds of thousands of Jews to
this country. These immigrants were deeply imbued with the love
for learning that was a historic aspect of Jewish life from antiquity.
If many personally were not scholars, they nevertheless believed that
scholarship should occupy a paramount position in their collective
lives; if they themselves were not learned, they were committed to
the fact that their children or grandchildren should be properly
taught.

It is easy to make generalizations about a people. Jews in particular have learned how facilely calumny and hate are propagated
through generalizations from the individual or the stereotype. But

in the case of commitment to learning, even sacrifice and self-deprivation for the purpose of engaging teachers and supporting their young people through the instructional period of their lives, the generalization about Jews is well justified. The founding of Etz Chaim in 1886 followed by the founding of the Rabbi Isaac Elchanan Theological Seminary a decade or so later were giant efforts to create a learning locus in this country to replace the institutions of learning that the Jewish immigrants had left behind.

The growth and expansion of these two meager institutions into the large complex of religious and secular learning facilities that comprise Yeshiva University today, are a tribute to the freedom of America which in making Jews part of its people allowed them to identify their cultural interests with the broad culture of America. Yeshiva University is also a tribute to the dedication of an immigrant minority that had the vision to prepare a foundation upon which to build for the emerging needs of subsequent generations.

At Yeshiva, the Torah of Moses and the words of God are constructively expressed in the application of the medical arts and sciences, in the research into socio-economic problems of our day and in the preparation of rabbis and teachers of our faith. Just as scholarship cannot be meaningful within the ivory tower which contains it, so the Torah had to be taken from the Ark into the market place and the world. Through its different schools and divisions, Yeshiva University has moved the teaching of the Jewish faith into the society which surrounds it.

It is this evolution of Yeshiva University and to some extent the growth of the Jewish Community in the United States that this excellent volume presents. It is exciting, informative and a distinct contribution to the social history of the Jews in America. It also reflects the coming of age of the Jewish Community and its concomitant achievement of security. For through a number of the schools of the University, training in purely secular disciplines are now being made available to students of all faiths, races and ethnic backgrounds. From an immigrant community that very often had to send its sons to study in schools sponsored by denominational branches of other faiths, Jews are now able to return equal hospitality to their fellow Americans.

I am proud of the accomplishments of Yeshiva University and proud also to be an honorary alumnus of this great institution of learning.

Arthur J. Goldberg

New York, New York

The Story of Yeshiva University

CHAPTER 1. THE HEROIC GENERATION

The last eighty years represent a remarkable span in the history of American Jewry. In these fourscore years the American Jewish community in general and the Orthodox Jewish community in particular have undergone a tremendous change. The immigrant flavor that clung to a large segment of the Jewish community has long since worn off. Now there are almost no new Jewish immigrants arriving in the United States. The generation that settled in America before the restrictive Immigration Acts, culminating in the Act of 1924, is by now only an infinitesimal part of the Jewish population; it is gradually declining and meanwhile losing its identity through the process of Americanization.

The average young adult Jew has no recollection of the great masses of Jewish immigration that came to the United States between 1881 and 1914 and at best possesses only a fond nostalgia for them. These earlier immigrants, who were at times awkward and ill at ease because of their foreign languages, habits, and manners, nevertheless left a proud mark of achievement on the American scene. In their restlessness and ambition they created hospitals and old-age homes, religious institutions and schools, newspapers and theaters, industries and great houses of commerce.

Among the legacies that they bequeathed to American Jewry was Yeshiva University, an institution of learning that reflected their innermost identification as Jews and as Americans. In its phenomenal growth Yeshiva University has expressed the quality of Jewish resiliency and adaptability, the capacity to transplant its ancient heritage in new soil and adjust its way of life to new conditions.

Through the founding of this university the traditional Jews who came from Eastern Europe prepared a new vessel in which to preserve and recreate on American soil the old, rich vintage of Judaism. They were unaware of the catastrophic events that were to extinguish organized Jewish life and the teeming academies of Jewish scholarship in Europe. Yet in their compulsion to create a center of Jewish learning in America, they anticipated the staggering loss of these vital communities. Yeshiva University has provided a ready reservoir of Orthodox Jewish scholarship and leadership not only for America but for the entire world. In this respect the founding of Yeshiva University may yet prove to be the most important and lasting contribution of the East European Jewish immigrants to Jewish survival.

The miracle of this achievement merits the interest and attention of the American Jewish community. The growth of Yeshiva University can best be understood and appreciated against the sociological and historical background of the exciting years that marked the end of the nineteenth century and the beginning of the twentieth.

A Formidable Challenge

More than a million Jewish immigrants landed on the shores of the United States between 1881 and 1905.[1] They came from Russia, Poland, Austria-Hungary (especially from the province of Galicia), and from Roumania. The great majority of them were fleeing from Eastern Europe as a result of the intensified Russian pogroms following the vicious discriminatory May Laws of 1881. In America they tended to settle in the big cities of the East—New York, Boston, Philadelphia, Pittsburgh, Baltimore, Rochester, Syracuse—and even in the big inland cities, such as Chicago, Denver, Detroit and Cincinnati.

About half a million of these new immigrants settled in New York City where the great majority of them had landed. This number far exceeded the total Jewish immigration in the two and one-quarter centuries since 1654 when twenty-three Jews from Recife, Brazil landed in New York and established the first Jewish settlement on the soil of the United States.

The immigrants who had been forced to abandon their homes in Eastern Europe were a hardy lot. With rare exceptions, they arrived penniless and inadequately trained in a profession or handicraft.

They did possess, however, indomitable faith in themselves and un-flagging courage to face all difficulties. They dug their roots deep into the alien soil until it became home to them. They founded families and raised children and children's children who enriched America with invaluable contributions. This immigrant generation of the post-1881 decades may be called, indeed, the heroic genera-tion.

The immigrant group was by no means homogeneous. They were socialist intellectuals, fervent Zionists, tired peasants, bearded shoe-makers, skilled artisans and craftsmen, enlightened atheists, dig-nified rabbis, pale yeshiva students—the docile and compliant and the firebrands, men, women, youngsters, and babies. There were broad differences in age and in personal commitment to the different ideologies of the day. They shared in common the task of adjustment that was severe enough to challenge even the hardiest.

For the religious Jews the problem was particularly acute. The initial assumption that they could continue in their accustomed ways, retaining the old traditions of the Eastern European *shtetl,* received a rude jolt immediately upon their landing. Because they came from Jewish communities where religious tradition inter-penetrated every aspect of life, the religious Jews were almost as much in need of religious institutions that would enable them to continue their daily affirmation of identification with God and Israel as they were in need of jobs that would enable them to sur-vive physically. The new environment, however, was not too friendly to the religious Orthodoxy by which they lived. The religion, cul-ture, and way of life in America were very different from and often hostile to their own; even the Jewish community of New York was not favorably disposed toward them. By 1881 German Jewish immi-grants had eclipsed both numerically and culturally the early Sephar-dic group, who were descendants of the Spanish and Portuguese Jews exiled by the Inquisition. They had acquired the speech, the dress, and the habits of thought of the native population, and they had largely embraced Reform Judaism as a less severe faith than Ortho-doxy. They had prospered and were building centers, communal in-stitutions and temples, characterized by dignity and serene beauty and modeled after the houses of worship of their Christian neighbors. They did not relish the intrusion into their placid, well-ordered existence of coreligionists, foreign in speech and dress, poor in economic resources, and fanatically clinging to what they thought were outmoded religious observances. While these German Jews, who financed and virtually dominated Jewish philanthropic institutions, were willing to minister to the physical well-being of the new immigrants, they were not willing to go beyond necessary alms. They were antagonistic and unsympathetic to the East European Jews and not interested in supporting to any significant extent the religious and educational institutions of the Eastern European brand of Orthodox Judaism. They were especially antagonistic to the institutions that continued the use of the Yiddish language, viewing it as an obstacle to proper integration of the immigrants.[2]

To the newcomers, however, it was a matter of utmost urgency to provide for religious education immediately upon landing in the New World. The threat of the spiritual loss of their children was always before them. The lure of the alien environment was proving irresistible for the young. A strange tongue, a strange culture and a strange mode of thought were disturbing the tranquility of the home by undermining the unity of the family. They were upsetting values held as precious as life itself. A chasm was opening up between fathers and sons, mothers and daughters. How was it to be bridged?

Fortunately, these immigrants had absorbed the message of the long history of Jewish migrations; they realized that the survival of Jews and Judaism was contingent upon the successful transmission of traditional ideas and beliefs and practices from the old generation to the new. They knew that education was the central factor in the vitality of Jewish faith and in the consistency of Jewish behavior. In order to assure the continuity of their mode of life in America, therefore, the new immigrants felt impelled to transplant their old traditions, reroot their spiritual values, and thus guarantee the preservation of their religious principles in the New World.

This was a formidable challenge. The transition from East European Jewish life to the American environment was tantamount to a leap from the Middle Ages to the twentieth century. This bridging of centuries within a single generation could not easily be accomplished. Serious maladjustments were inevitable unless a binding link between the two worlds could be forged. The pivotal factor was the education of the Jewish immigrant in the United States.

Unfortunately, the average immigrant was almost penniless upon arrival in the New World. The religious schools established by the older residents were not geared to meet the needs of a more volatile group, and the rabbinate was helpless in the face of the complex problems that now came to the fore.

By far the saddest tragedy of immigrant life was the utter destitution into which the European newcomer was thrust. In Europe abject poverty had dogged their lives and privation, and persecution had been the measure of their lot. Except for their rich hopes and abundant aspirations, they escaped from their ghettos with little more than their poverty, the clothes on their backs, and their meager effects. Coming over in large and unprecedented numbers, the immigrants found difficulty in becoming financially as well as culturally integrated. Generally unable to fend for themselves upon arrival, they had to depend primarily on the facilities for rehabilitation that were available at the time. In this way they overwhelmed and strained every Jewish communal organization and all resources for relief and adjustment. There is no complete record of the assistance they received in the early years following 1881, but in 1892 almost half of the newcomers needed financial assistance.[3]

Furthermore, unlike earlier Jewish arrivals in America and their American-born descendants, who were almost completely of the commercial class and had easily adapted themselves to American conditions, these immigrants from Eastern Europe came with no business background.[4] Until the beginning of the twentieth century, they

> ... consisted of artisans, unskilled workers, and in large measure, of economically declassed elements and unskilled youths who had just left the "cheder" or "yeshiva" and had no experience or training in economic life.[5]

They were compelled to accept any employment that was offered to them. One writer described the situation:

> The opportunities for employment were limited by available places of residence, by linguistic limitations, by vacancies to be filled in

close proximity to the areas of debarkation, by previous occupation, by economic stratification of earlier Jewish settlers. Factory work was the first step.[6]

Thus, men who had been scholars in the "old country" toiled under unbelievable conditions in sweatshops in order to earn a pittance,[7] while others became street vendors with heavy bundles on their backs, and hawkers and pushcart peddlers in order to eke out a meager livelihood.

A segment of the more adventurous, assisted by the Jewish Colonization Association and the Alliance Israélite Universelle, made their way to pioneer country to seek their fortunes. They settled as far west as the Dakotas, Colorado, Kansas, and Oregon, and as far south as Louisiana in order to establish agricultural colonies. Unfortunately, most of the colonies were short-lived. After back-breaking hardships and frustrating disappointments, the colonists returned to the population centers of the East to merge with the mass manpower pool and wait to be assimilated into the trading and working classes.[8]

Dominated by the exacting logic of economics that forced them into the impersonal and highly competitive world of peddling, storekeeping, factories, dingy flats, and long hours of hard work, coupled with the obstacles of a strange language and the foreign customs of a new land, the immigrants found their early years in America neither easy nor pleasant. That they survived and struck roots and became integrated and blossomed forth was almost miraculous. If an epic is the tale of a heroic soul struggling valiantly against hostile forces, then a million epics were lived in those days.

First Steps in Religious Education

For the one million Jewish immigrants of that period the need to find first sustenance and then economic security was the overpowering motive. It must have been a common occurrence for an immigrant to be greeted on the first day of his arrival in New York City, as was an early arrival in 1885, with the following words:

Young man, you have just landed in the great city of New York, where all the opportunities are opened to you, but if you want to succeed, you must forget about God and your religion and especially about the Sabbath and the dietary laws. You must work every day including the Sabbath and eat what you can get, for God has been left on the other side of the ocean.[9]

The injunction to "forget about God and your religion" seemed to be an unavoidable requirement of self-interest. Economic preservation and religious survival appeared at diametrically opposed poles, mutually exclusive as ways of life and geographically separated by the Atlantic Ocean. In the process of finding enough to eat, many an immigrant was forced to leave God "on the other side of the ocean." And most of those who did never sent for Him even later.

The absence of an encouraging climate for Jewish education made it incumbent upon the immigrant to create his own forms of religious instruction, accessible to his dwelling and more in consonance with his traditional orientation. This was the greatest test to which the immigrant was put. Making a living was hard, but in this he was channelled by the driving power of material requirements. Religious training for his children was another matter.

The problem of religious education was much like that of the highly unsatisfactory state of secular education in general that prevailed at the time. The public school system was still young and hovering on the threshhold of popular acceptance and organized service. There were few school buildings, overcrowded facilities, inadequate teachers, and an unsatisfactory curriculum. Although it was compulsory for youngsters to attend school, the requirements were minimum and their enforcement lax. Under the Compulsory Education Act of 1900, for example, only children between eight and twelve years of age were required to attend school full time. Children between six and eight were not required to go to school at all. Scores of thousands of children of compulsory school age never went to school because there was no school census to indicate who was required to attend school, and there were not enough truant officers to round them up. Others were denied admission because there was no room for them. In 1881 the situation was considerably worse.

In the matter of nonattendance at school the parents were almost always knowing, though perhaps unwilling, accessories. Many an immigrant discovered that the inexorable mechanics of life made him shut out of his active conscience all serious consideration of the education of his children. The children were obliged as soon as they could get employment to work in sweatshops or to peddle newspapers on street corners in order to supplement the family income. Often their earnings provided the necessary margin for the family's sustenance. Thus, whatever free time they might have had for Hebrew education, had it been available, was also eliminated.

Whatever time the immigrants, young and old, did voluntarily set aside for education was spent in the pursuit of practical needs at night classes, learning English or a trade. Whether more of the religious immigrants would have continued their Jewish education and their devotion to religious requirements had they the facilities to do so is now an academic question. The truth is that the average immigrant could afford neither the time nor the money to provide suitable Hebrew education for his children.

Thus the immigrant could exert very little personal initiative in the education of his family. The impasse might have been overcome if the Jewish community on its part had created suitable and attractive schools, strategically located and well administered, and with a curriculum designed to serve the needs of the Russian and Polish Jew. The children might then have found some way to acquire a rudimentary Jewish education.

Unfortunately, until well into the year 1900 there were only five communally sponsored schools designed for poor East European Jews in the downtown East Side.[10] From 1883 until 1889 when the Montefiore Talmud Torah was founded, the only Hebrew School formed to serve children of Russian and Polish immigrants in the City of New York was the Machzikei Talmud Torah at 225-227 East Broadway in lower Manhattan.[11] It was not until the turn of the century that the East European Jewish immigrant began to make gradual transition from the factory to trade and commerce and to achieve a broader measure of financial security. Only then was he able to develop in a larger degree the kind of educational facilities that were suitable to his needs.

The void that the immigrant found in Jewish education, therefore, was great. The Christian missionary movement was very active among the Jewish children of the East Side. Mission teachers were constantly luring them into their schools and making other serious inroads. One such school had enrolled two hundred children, a few of whom had actually been baptized.[12] On 50th Street in Manhattan the Church was actively engaged in bringing Jewish children into its Sunday schools.[13] And on Essex Street, missionaries were enticing children of five, six and seven years of age to their school by bribes as late as 1890.[14] So notorious was this action that it became known as the "Essex Street Blot."[15] The Christian missionary schools in New York were rushing in to fill the vacuum in Jewish education with such alarming success that it was feared they were going to "take the place of those schools we have neglected to provide."[16]

Arising from the need to counteract the incipient inroads of the missionary schools—rather than from the positive motive to establish adequate Jewish education—a similar Jewish mission school movement was founded in 1865.[17] One of the organizations that sponsored such schools was known as the Hebrew Free School Association.[18] Its school system was to include from ten to fifteen schools[19] with at least five schools on the East Side[20] before it faded from the scene because of lack of financial support. Unfortunately, the education afforded by the Hebrew Free School was "meager,"[21] for the major efforts expended by the native and established Jews on behalf of their newly arrived brethren were in the areas of relief and benevolence rather than in education.

> They were not motivated by the desire to spread Torah and perpetuate Judaism but [rather] . . . to hurry and ease the process of Americanization, to teach the immigrants and their children the English language and the customs of the land. . . . These were in the main acts of charity but not acts . . . [for the sake of education].[22]

As a result, the aim of these schools was not so much to provide Jewish education as to teach morality and to exert a refining influence upon the children of the East Side.[23] Particular stress was upon the dispensing of charity to the pupils and the furnishing of "a meal of bread, butter and milk, also a bath and clothing to those requiring it."[24] The full extent of the relationship between the sponsors of the schools and the students can be determined from the fact that one of these schools was partly supported by a "Fund contributed every Sunday by the children of Temple Emanuel Sunday School."[25]

During the early years of the East European immigration, the entrenched Jewish community of New York had still not created any facilities for the religious Jewish education of the newcomers with the exception of the Machzikei Talmud Torah. On the whole, Jewish interest in education was very weak at the time, a fact which a contemporary chronicle bemoans!

> That in a city like ours, where Jewish wealth and interest ranks so high, the subject of Hebrew education is so sadly neglected. . . . The Hebrew Free School should be endowed by a Jewish "Peter Cooper." The directors spend all their efforts in collecting [money] rather than [in] managing the school.[26]

Despite its shortcomings, the Hebrew Free School was the only school that specifically served the needs of the immigrant in any way at all. The other schools which had been established by the native and German congregations had already passed their zenith of service. The Polonies Talmud Torah, which was associated with Shearith Israel, had been almost completely transformed into a Sunday school. By 1870, the German congregational schools had likewise been either converted into Sunday schools or Jewish mission schools and, in some cases, had been completely disbanded.[27] None of these schools were originally intended to serve children of East European heritage, nor were any of them except the Jewish Mission Schools even situated in the East Side area, which had become the focal point of immigrant life and activity.[28] In 1889 as a result of a reorganization, the assets of the Jewish Mission Schools were transferred to the newly formed Educational Alliance.[29]

Like the Jewish Mission Schools, the Educational Alliance was a symbol of the kind of cultural assistance that the immigrant could receive in the new land. Although a Hebrew school was still operated within its framework, the aim of the Educational Alliance was not positive Jewish education. Its major effort was to further as much and as quickly as possible the Americanization of the immigrant[30]—

to make him a "good American" without regard to his remaining a "good Jew."[31]

> They were all eager that the immigrant shed his foreign manners. ... None cared a whit that in the hard struggle to adjust himself to his new milieu the immigrant's fine religious attitude to life, his interest in and appreciation of spiritual and esthetic values were being cruelly perverted, and that his intellectual tradition of ... seeking learning for learning's own sake was being replaced by the cash customer's motive for pursuing knowledge. What matter that the immigrant was being drained of his own culture and was becoming in the words of Louis Adamic a "cultural zero."[32]

Problems of Adjustment

The Americanization efforts filled a vital need for the new arrival. The relief work and the technical schools that were developed also served to help the immigrant adjust to his new surroundings. Yet, despite its unchallenged humanitarian aim and sympathetic attitude, the Americanization program missed the mark, for it did not recognize the essential need of the immigrant. He was not seeking to shed his past identity and religious beliefs in order to assume the mold of his precursors in America.[33] His greatest need was to merge with the American scene and not to be totally submerged in it. Instead of emphasizing and encouraging the possibilities of the cultural and spiritual contributions inherent in the life of the immigrant, the program suppressed and negated their value.

It was consistent with this misguided theory of benevolence that teachers in the Hebrew Free Schools were permitted to teach without wearing hats. As a result, Orthodox public opinion considered these schools as dangerous as the Christian Mission Schools in their destructive effect on Jewish tradition.[34] Even the "religious school" and the Sabbath services for children in the Educational Alliance were conducted in a spirit antagonistic to the conception of the immigrant for whom the institution was created.[35] For while courses were being organized in English and civics, the use of the Yiddish language and the teaching of Hebrew were prohibited.[36] Furthermore, the Educational Alliance Synagogue followed a nontraditional pattern with mixed seating of men and women and the use of an organ during religious services.[37] It was not until a later date that a more realistic philosophy of Americanization was evolved, in which the concept of immigrant adjustment did not imply the abandonment of the culture which he cherished and in which he was grounded.[38]

As a result of the theory of uncompromising Americanization, whatever initial success the immigrant may have been able to achieve in adjusting to his new environment was paid for by a corresponding loss in the affirmation of his faith and tradition. The realization of a measure of Americanization was a Pyrrhic victory in the light of the failure to establish Jewish education and the negation or subordination of spiritual values for a generation and more of fathers and sons—a deficiency sorely reflected in the Jewish community to this day.

The lack of preparation for the proper training of the East European Jewish immigrant might have been the result of the great influx of newcomers after 1881, a phenomenon hitherto not experienced in the history of migrations. In 1880, for example, it was estimated that there were 60,000 Jews in the city of New York.[39] Eight years later there were 125,000, and in 1891 there were 225,000.[40] Twenty-five years later, in 1905, there were 672,000 Jews in the city,[41] an increase of more than 600,000. In the years between 1881 and 1898 alone, a little more than half a million Jews arrived in the city of New York.[42]

Even if the Hebrew schools in 1880 had been adequate for the needs of the older Jewish community, they could hardly have been sufficient after the great immigration began. They were not geared for these large numbers, nor were they located in the centers of the immigrants' dwelling area. It was estimated that in the "10th Ward" (bounded by Rivington Street on the north, Division Street on the south, Christie Street on the west, and Clinton Street on the east) there were 330,000 people living in the area of one square mile. "Nowhere in the world," wrote Jacob Riis, "are so many people crowded together in a square mile as here."[43] Yet in this congested area there was not one Hebrew school created by the native-born or established Jewish New Yorkers.

To furnish proper educational facilities would have meant increasing manifold the number of schools through acquiring new locations, raising greater subsidies, and reorganizing the Jewish community to cope with this responsibility. The struggle of the Hebrew Free School to raise its yearly budget, which in 1879 was only $9,000,[44] is an indication of how weak the Jewish community was in this respect.[45]

An organization to provide education on a mass scale would have required a prodigious effort and could not have been prepared in time to serve the immigrants in their early stages of settlement. Unfortunately, the East European Jews of the early eighties lacked the wherewithal, the leadership and the will to finance such a tremendous expansion for themselves. Even if they could have done so, there was no agency to guide and crystallize their efforts. Like others, many times before, these Jews found themselves incapable of decisive action because they were completely unorganized to meet the emergency.[46] The Russian and Polish Jews who came before the eighties were as delinquent as their German-born and native American brethren in anticipating the need for educational facilities.

Sadly enough, the synagogues shared the responsibility for the anarchy in Jewish education. As late as 1906, the congregations had not recognized the challenge. While the Orthodox Jewish congregations on the East Side were really "institutional churches"[47] with many facets of activities, they did not sponsor that which should have been their primary obligation, Hebrew schools. A non-Jewish observer of the East Side came to the regretful conclusion that "the synagogue is not interested in *ḥedarim* (Hebrew schools)."[48]

Thus, the new immigrants who were zealous in their concern for the religious education of their children could find no other instrument for education than the *ḥeder* and the itinerant *melamed* (tutor of religious subjects). In Eastern Europe the *ḥeder* and the *melamed* were held in high regard and subject to high educational standards, but in America this form of education had completely degenerated.[49] Here there were no standards or organized public opinion to condemn the unsatisfactory *ḥedarim* and to separate them from adequate *ḥedarim*.[50] The *ḥeder* was a purely private enterprise undertaken by individuals who were seeking a livelihood. Because unqualified *melamdim* could open a school without any restriction, the *ḥeder* was entirely unsatisfactory in terms of curriculum and physical facilities.

In 1915, the Department of Health of New York City issued a scathing condemnation of the sanitary conditions in these *ḥedarim*.[51] One can only conjecture as to their condition in the eighties and the nineties. Schoolrooms were frequently set up in dark, windowless basements without ventilation,[52] in garrets, behind stores, above stables, over saloons and dance halls,[53] and in many other impossible locations.[54] The antiquated methods of instruction in the *ḥedarim* were as primitive as the locations.[55] The teachers have been described as largely "maladjusted individuals . . . or mercenary dispensers of Hebrew reading who are an obstacle to the progress of Jewish education in America."[56] At best they were depressingly unfit "to be educators of the young Jewish generation in America."[57] Yet, there were as many *ḥedarim* as synagogues on the East Side,[58] a statistical indication of the thirst for education in the immigrant community.

The literature describing this early period often repeats the characterization of Jewish education as being "very meager."[59] This meagerness not only affected the children of that day but cast its shadow on future generations as well. The absence of opportunities for acquiring a good Jewish education was one of the primary causes for the mass defection from Jewish principles of many of the young people and their parents. Not only did they drift from the traditional observances, but in doing so, they set a pattern for the new immigrants, who arrived daily. They found justification and absolution for their aberrations in the fatalism of the current saying that "no one can touch American soil and be what he was."[60]

Nevertheless, Jewish education was not entirely destined to fall victim to the exigencies of a critical transition period. On the contrary, the strangeness of the conditions and immense needs different from those of the stratified and insulated Jewish life of East Europe[61] evoked a new kind of leadership with an aggressiveness that had not been displayed by any other immigrant group. The subsequent complete integration of the Jew into American life and the contributions with which he was to enrich its culture and commerce, its fine arts, its professions and trades, have their roots in the lives of this amazing generation.

Although few in number, the intellectuals among this group[62] were aided in their efforts by the larger numbers who had benefited from the unique Jewish system under which a universal minimum education was almost mandatory in their native lands of Europe.[63] Many had attended not only a good *ḥeder* but also a yeshiva[64] where they studied Talmud and imbibed the religious classics of Judaism.

This hard core of educated Jews, many of whom had already rejected their religious commitment but remained endowed with the acuteness that came of Talmudic study and Jewish energy, refused to be absorbed in America's "melting pot." Instead, they acted as an intellectual leaven among their comrades, not permitting them to lose their identity. Jacob Riis called them "the yeast of any slum." They bombarded the community with ideas and agitated in the midst of their neighbors with the insatiable love for learning, the traditional hatred of injustice and oppression, and the constant hope for social and spiritual improvement that were a cherished Jewish heritage. Their influence was enormous, and they transformed their brethren from undistinguished and anonymous drudges into articulate American citizens with crystallized loyalties and attitudes that were to leave a marked impression on the American scene.

Out of this confusion of aims and attitudes, out of the babel of tongues and the silence of the inarticulate, there evolved slowly and gropingly a Jewish community, alive and vibrant, a part of the American pattern and yet unique in many respects. From these teeming masses, some of whom had been active in the labor *bund* in Czarist Russia, there emerged the founders of unions, the philosophers of the Socialist movement, and the leaders of radical cosmopolitanism. From their midst also appeared a dedicated few who struggled valiantly to maintain the ideal of Torah and of the traditional Jewish life in its ancient form and dignity. Their impetus stemmed from an absolute repudiation of the early belief that Americanization meant the complete surrender of the religious culture and behavior patterns that had shaped and determined their past.

They realized that the Americanization program sponsored by

the Hebrew Free School Association and their German Jewish brethren would leave them without their heritage. They knew, too, that insular, unadapted, and unharmonized life would cause them to remain forever foreigners in the land of their adoption. Some synthesis had to be developed between the religious pattern which was the web and woof of their existence and the new American culture upon which the tapestry of their lives was to be woven. This attempt at synthesis culminated in the birth and evolution of the Rabbi Isaac Elchanan Theological Seminary and Yeshiva University.

CHAPTER 2. YESHIVAT ETZ CHAIM

The history of Yeshiva University can be traced through a number of clearly defined periods of growth. The first stage begins with the formation of Yeshivat Etz Chaim on September 15, 1886, continues through the founding of the Rabbi Isaac Elchanan Theological Seminary [RIETS] in 1897 eleven years later, and comes to an end in 1915 when the two schools merged to form one institution.

Through its part in this chain of events, Yeshivat Etz Chaim, primarily organized to teach Talmud, was destined to bring about the first major educational contribution of the East European Jews in America. Yet there are no records extant of the almost thirty years of the school's existence. There are definite indications that by 1892 a Mr. Lifshitz, the first Secretary of Yeshivat Etz Chaim, was succeeded by Aryeh Leib Rosenthal, a well-known *sofer* (Torah scribe) on the East side. Later Eliezer Lipnick took over the duties of keeping the records of the institution. However, all the minute books have been lost.

Yeshivat Etz Chaim was founded in order to meet the growing need among East European immigrants for expanded facilities for maximum Jewish education.[1] Neither the improvised *hedarim* with their inadequate teachers nor the "*siddur* peddler," who went from house to house to give instructions in reading the prayers, fulfilled this requirement.

Until 1886 the Machzikei Talmud Torah had been the lone institutionalized school of the Russian and Polish Jews in the United States.[2] However, it was an afternoon school for students attending the public schools and provided only elementary religious education for children of pre-elementary and elementary school age. There were no accommodations for older students who had completed the curriculum; no advanced instruction was offered for immigrant children who had already mastered the subjects in their homeland. Because of these shortcomings, a group of supporters of the Machzikei

Talmud Torah broke away and founded the new school known as Yeshivat Etz Chaim.[3]

The organizing meeting of the founders, according to a newspaper announcement a decade later, was held at the Mariampol Synagogue at 44 East Broadway.[4] The Mariampol Synagogue had been the founding place of the Machzikei Talmud Torah and was later to be the scene of the first meeting of the founders of the Rabbi Isaac Elchanan Theological Seminary. The exact place where the first classes of Etz Chaim were held has not been determined, though in 1887 the school was located in a rented room at 47 East Broadway between Market and Pike streets. From 1890 until 1897 the school was located at 1 Canal Street in a small private house, after which it moved to its final site at 85 Henry Street.[5]

A Brave Departure

The limited scope of instruction at the Machzikei Talmud Torah is not the complete explanation for the break. The founders of Etz Chaim were dissatisfied with the philosophy of the Talmud Torah system that sanctioned attendance at public schools. Their unhappiness stemmed from a deep sense of alarm at the specter of "secular" education which possessed a siren-like attraction for the young immigrants who strove desperately to learn the language and culture of the United States in order to become acceptable Americans. The older generation was apprehensive of the undermining effect of the public schools on religious youth, who were compelled to sit bareheaded, study non-Jewish subjects, be exposed to a non-Jewish environment and, despite themselves, be lured from religious practices. They also objected to the implication that religious training was supplementary to secular schooling and might be relegated to the afternoon when the freshness of the morning hours had already worn off. Accordingly no school that compromised with the public school education, as the Machzikei Talmud Torah did, would satisfy them.

To the immigrants steeped in the Torah and religious observance, the only successful defense against alien influence was intensive scholarship and a broad knowledge of the Jewish faith. The Talmud Torah, Mission Schools, ḥedarim and itinerant melamdim could not impart this knowledge or counteract the inroads of secular education. Only a school that offered the many advantages of secular education and incorporated the desired basic religious teachings could solve the problem. This was the blueprint that the founders of Etz Chaim followed. They projected a religious school where secular instruction would be offered as well, thereby obviating the need for its students to attend public schools.

The new school, a brave departure from the hitherto frustrating attempts at Jewish education, was well called Yeshivat Etz Chaim. Etz chaim, meaning "a tree of life," was the term generally applied to Torah, and yeshiva was the name given to the religious academies of Eastern Europe. In adopting this name, the founders clearly expressed as their primary objective the transfer of the religious training methods of Europe to America.

Unlike Yeshivat Minchat Areb, the first day school founded by the Spanish and Portuguese Jews in New York City in 1755,[6] as well as the day schools that flourished under the sponsorship of the German Reform congregations between 1840 and 1870,[7] and the first "mission school" of the Hebrew Free School Association in 1865, Etz Chaim was essentially dedicated to religious instruction. The earlier schools had come into being during the period of American history when there was no universal public school system, or when church and sectarian schools flourished side by side with the public school system. To a significant extent, elementary secular education was acquired at private schools or under private tutors. (It was not until 1897 that the first public high school was established in old New York.) Those who wanted to add the elements of a religious education had to resort to the supplementary instruction of another private teacher in Hebrew subjects.

The Yeshivat Minchat Areb and the German congregational day schools resulted from an artificial joining of both these courses of study under one roof, an arrangement dictated by convenience, not by a philosophy of education. The quality of religious education in these schools was as rudimentary and uninspiring as in the later *hedarim.*[8]

The new Yeshiva was not a congregational school, but an institutional school[9] sponsored by an independent community organization called *Ḥebra Machzikei Yeshivat Etz Chaim,* the "Association of the Supporters of Yeshivat Etz Chaim."[10] It differed from the earlier day schools in that its emphasis was on Talmud and advanced Jewish studies rather than merely the simple rudiments of Judaism.

The founders of Etz Chaim made it a unique school and the only one of its kind in the United States. Its program furnished "instruction to poor children in Talmud, Bible and *Shulḥan Arukh* [The Code of Jewish Law] from 9 A.M. in the morning until 4 in the afternoon . . . from 4 in the afternoon, two hours [were to] be devoted to teaching the native language, English, and one hour to Hebrew . . . and to read and write Jargon [Yiddish]."[11]

It would be inaccurate to state that secular subjects were given equal weight in the school curriculum with religious studies. On the contrary, secular studies were allotted only a fraction of the school day and at the outset were more of an appendage than an integrated part of the work. In fact, the addition of secular subjects to the curriculum was little more than a concession to the demands of the day, but the new educational formula was to pave the way for the integration of the two streams of cultural values that the immigrant Jews in America were called upon to preserve. By providing maximum Jewish education, the institution of the yeshiva was to prove the most practical manner of securing the Jewish heritage.

The establishment of Etz Chaim ended the cycle of the three major approaches to Jewish education which had initially appeared in American Jewish life.[12] The first viewed Jewish education as supplementary to secular education; it was typified by the early day school by the *heder,* the Talmud Torah, and the private Hebrew teacher. The second approach was the Sunday school. Similar to the Christian denominational school, it was a form of additional Jewish education. The yeshiva system, pioneered by Etz Chaim and firmly rooted in American soil today, was the third and last. Not only did it complement the public school education, but it recognized the co-ordinate value of secular and religious subjects and synthesized both cultural patterns into a harmonious curriculum revealing the resiliency of the East European Jew in his adjustment to the intellectual challenge of the New World.

Only generous hindsight would attribute to the founders of Etz Chaim an awareness of the contribution they were making to Jewish education in America. Their sincerity and devotion, however, were heroic; they were obsessed with the idea of insuring a proper Jewish education for their children and they were dedicated to finding a way to achieve it.

The Foundations Are Set

The legal incorporators of Etz Chaim were Morris Bernstein, Samuel Waxman, a clothing dealer; Abraham Rubenowitz, a tailor; Rachmiel Witman, and Henry M. Greenberg, a real estate dealer. The officers were: Julius D. Bernstein, president; Morris Bernstein, first vice-president; Moses Heller, a tailor, second vice-president. Falk Berman, also a tailor, was treasurer, and Louis Shapiro, a peddler, was secretary. The trustees were Elias Ratkowsky, a rabbi, Louis Siegelstein, a peddler, Rachmiel Witman, and Baruch Pinchas Liberman.

Julius D. Bernstein, the first president, was Rabbi Yehuda David Bernstein, who a decade later was to be a founder of the Rabbi Isaac Elchanan Theological Seminary. Rabbi Elias Ratkowsky, who taught in Etz Chaim without pay, made a living as a "customer peddler" and was known fondly as "Reb Elyeh." Baruch P. Liberman was long to be associated with the Rabbi Isaac Elchanan Theological Seminary and was its first vice-president after it merged with Yeshivat Etz Chaim in 1915. Falk Berman was a member of the governing body of the Machzikei Talmud Torah. Among the other founders were Moses Isaac Bernstein, also a founder of Rabbi Isaac Elchanan Theological Seminary; Kasriel Sarasohn, the publisher of the *Jüdisches Tageblatt* and *Jüdische Gazetten;* Jonah Ginsberg; and Joshua Rothstein, its president in 1888.[13]

Rothstein, a cap manufacturer—clever, worldly and tireless in communal work—was actively involved in helping to form the Association of the American Orthodox Hebrew Congregations, in which a number of congregations on the lower East Side joined for the purpose of organizing a *kehillah* (Jewish community) in the City of New York. It was hoped that the *kehillah*, like the Jewish communities of the European centers, would be presided over by a chief rabbi who would supervise *kashrut* (the manufacturing and purveying of kosher food); render binding decisions on matters of Jewish ritual law; establish a court of *dayyanim* (religious judges) to mediate, arbitrate, and try legal disputes, and stimulate the religious education of the youth. It was envisioned that from the importance of the office of chief rabbi, a sense of unity and cooperation would be imparted to the Jews of otherwise unrelated congregations that made up the new union. In 1888, Rabbi Jacob Joseph was brought from Vilna, Russia, to become the first Chief Rabbi in the City of New York. Unfortunately, however, a number of tragic quarrels broke out around the Chief Rabbi, and when he died in 1902 the Association disintegrated and the office was never filled again.[14]

Among others who were active in founding Etz Chaim were Jacob Hecht, its president in 1892 and first president after its merger with RIETS; Nathan Roggen, treasurer from 1895 through the years after the merger with RIETS in 1915; Yechezkael Schlang; Judah D. Eisenstein; Abraham Alexander; and Shamai Rosenthal.[15]

In addition, many lesser known members of the community were drawn into the service of Etz Chaim. A large number of them were peddlers, and almost all were very poor.[46] Despite the heterogeneous composition of the group, however, there was a unity of purpose that welded them into a working organization. Cooperation of this kind was very rare, and an editorial writer for the *Tageblatt,* commenting on the happy situation, wrote:

> There is harmony among the workers for the cause . . . nobody thinks that he is more important because he brings in more money . . . all the workers are scholars and educated in Judaism and do not have to look for glory.[17]

Looking forward with great anticipation to the establishment of the school,[18] the general community expressed its support by accepting charity boxes posted in their homes and synagogues. The neighborhood women showed their devotion by visiting the classes and distributing apples to the children[19] while others organized a *Malbish Arumim* [clothe the poor] Society to provide shoes and clothes for the students as well as a monthly gift of $25 to the school.[20]

The reliance of Etz Chaim on women's groups for such minor contributions testifies to the very sensitive condition of the school's income. The same might be said of RIETS, which was to follow, and of the many other elementary yeshivot of later years. Very often the assistance of the women provided the margin of existence for the schools. At one time, the Malbish Arumim Society was singled out for newspaper praise because "last week they contributed $100 which the Yeshiva needed desperately to pay the interest due on the building."[21]

The Yeshiva was always in dire need of support because its major sponsors were immigrants who were themselves still in the process of becoming settled. Committed ". . . to give free instruction to poor Hebrew children,"[22] the institution carried a large number of nonpaying students. Although this proved very costly, it was considered a virtue, for it made Jewish education available on a democratic basis. Even when parents could afford to pay tuition, the fees, which ranged as low as twenty-five cents per week, were a meager source of income.

Supplementing the inconsequential tuition fees were the collection boxes, a favorite fund-raising technique with most of the institutions that drew upon the East Side Jews. Synagogues, relief organizations, benevolent organizations, and other causes besieged the crowded tenements with various penny boxes of different sizes and colors. Overseas charities and Palestinian religious organizations who had representatives in New York added their boxes to those of the local groups. Every sympathetic home had several boxes in its kitchen, each devoted to a different worthy undertaking. During the week, on special joyous occasions, or on the eve of the Sabbath before lighting the candles, several pennies were dropped into the boxes in the tradition of Jewish philanthropy. At fixed times collectors, often representing more than one charity, made regular rounds on defined routes to empty the boxes into the appropriate sacks.

As Etz Chaim built up a growing and more responsive following, its boxes became heavier. Sometimes collectors for different organizations unintentionally appropriated the Etz Chaim boxes and thereby deprived the Yeshiva of a portion of its anticipated revenue. Ten years after the school was founded, the losses were large enough to justify advertising in the papers that the "collectors who may have taken Yeshiva boxes by mistake should please return them."[23]

Although the collection boxes and tuition fees formed a predictable source of income, it was very limited. So by and large, the school depended on donations. Recorded, for example, was an annual gift of $50 made by the *mohel* (circumcisor) Baruch Isaac Lubelsky of 27 East Broadway, who put aside 25 cents for each circumcision he performed in order to raise this sum. His gift was publicly acknowledged in a paid newspaper advertisement.[24] Some large gifts received by the Yeshiva were properly memorialized by plaques mounted in various classrooms.[25] One marked a donation of $1,500 by Joshua Rothstein; another was dedicated to Baruch Pinchas Liberman, who had made a $500 gift.[26]

The budget was administered by the treasurer, whose duty it was to see that the income from the various sources continued to flow and that the collected monies were turned over to the administration for proper disbursement.[27] The secretary of the institution was the executive and administrator[28] to whom all collectors were directly responsible.[29]

The functioning of the school was attended to by a gentleman who today would be called a principal, and who had a small office in the building. At one time, a Mr. Kaminetsky held this post.[30] It was his duty to pay out the school expenses, to interview new students and to turn them over to one of the teachers for an examination prior to placement in their proper classes.

Educational Structure

Little is known about the composition of the school, the faculty, and the curriculum. The newspapers and the directors were more concerned with publicizing the appeals for financial aid than with describing the operation of the school itself. Only one contemporary account survives of Etz Chaim in its early days. It is found in the autobiography of Abraham Cahan, who was destined to become a prominent journalist, the editor of the *Jewish Daily Forward,* and a commanding figure in the Socialist movement for almost half a century. He was a clever young man whose studies in a European yeshiva had shown great promise. In 1887, immediately after Etz Chaim was organized, Cahan became one of the first teachers in the English Department of the Yeshiva. He may have been attracted to Yeshivat Etz Chaim because of his background, but he was primarily moved by his need for some income while he was pursuing his secular studies. Cahan records that the curriculum was loosely drawn to provide for the study of grammar, arithmetic, reading, and spelling—all within the "English Department." But because the directors of the school had no clear idea of what should be taught, the English Department functioned haphazardly, more out of a perfunctory acknowledgement for these subjects than a sincere desire to "provide the children with a modern education."[31]

The English Department was divided into two classes. The first was taught by a boy about fourteen, who had just graduated from public school and the second was taught by Cahan, who was a little less than twenty-eight years old. The students ranged from the ages of nine or ten to fifteen[32] and many were exposed to the formal study of secular subjects for the first time. One of the native students received his first lessons in the English language when he entered the Yeshiva after passing his thirteenth birthday.[33]

The young immigrants presented an immense challenge to their devoted teachers. The students drank up the instruction with a thirst centuries old. Cahan frequently remained long after the prescribed teaching hours to tutor his pupils, who were uniformly poor in reading and mathematics and who regarded grammar as an exquisite form of torture. On these occasions, the directors would ask Cahan why he "worked so hard," saying that the students "already knew enough English."[34]

This unenthusiastic attitude toward English was typical among the older immigrants who accepted its presence in their lives as inevitable. In the first decade or two following the surge of mass East European immigration, the divergence that was to crystallize later between the religious laymen and the rabbinate in piety, devotion, and religious observances was not even evident. The religious Jew was as traditional in his behavior, practice and thinking as his rabbi, the only difference between them being in professional status. Thus the perspective of the directors toward secular objects was identical with that of the rabbis and the instructors in the Religious Department of the school.

As a result, a conflict of interests often developed between the two departments. The shortage of funds was as effective a limitation on the scope of the English Department as was the reluctance of the directors. The insufficient supply of textbooks led to two or three students using the same English reader while texts in other subjects were not available at all. When Cahan made a request for $50 for new texts, the directors responded only with a smile. "What's the hurry?" was their answer to all his importunities. Cahan whimsically noted that the religious teachers opposed the proposed allotment with even greater vehemence fearing that money needed for their salaries might be spent on textbooks.[35] And, indeed, their apprehensions were well founded. The budget in 1888 was not resilient enough to permit expenditures in one direction without leaving a corresponding vacuum in another. Even without buying history and arithmetic textbooks, the salaries of the teachers were never paid on time, were often doled out in installments, and the teachers barely managed to subsist.

Cahan's "threat" to the financial stability of Etz Chaim was forestalled from yet another quarter. Toward the end of July, 1888, Rabbi Jacob Joseph made an inspection of the school which resulted in a laudatory press report. By this time, however, Cahan's socialistic predilections must have been common knowledge. The *Tageblatt,* in righteous indignation, published a front page story criticizing the directors for concealing from the Chief Rabbi that an ". . . anarchist . . . a sinner and beguiler . . . is teaching Orthodox children."[36]

Several days later an unsigned letter to the editor from one of the directors apologized that the Yeshiva "did not know that there was such an evil-doer on the staff—but he has already been investigated and 'sacked.' "[37] All this interchange apparently referred to Cahan, because none of the rabbis teaching in the Religious Department fell within the category of the *Tageblatt*'s description, nor could Cahan's fourteen-year-old colleague on the English teaching staff possibly have already earned such a choice reputation. Furthermore, the date seems to coincide with Cahan's own recollection of the termination of his association with Etz Chaim.[38]

Cahan's intervention for additional textbooks—which culminated in the classic accusation that he was corrupting the youth of the school while accepting a salary from the institution—ended, therefore, in failure. And so the students who almost had new books were left without, to await the coming of better days.[39]

Despite the financial stringency, the directors spared no effort to maintain a proper course of instruction, showing particular favor to the Religious Department. Dr. Mordecai M. Kaplan, a student of the Yeshiva in the early nineties, remembers that there were four classes for this section, each with its own teacher, so that there were twice as many teachers as for the two classes composing the English Department. Mordecai Kaplan, at the age of nine and a half, transferred from the Machzikei Talmud Torah because there was no Talmud instruction. After an interview to determine his class, he was admitted to the second class. The teacher, Rabbi Elyeh (Elias) Ratkowsky, a saintly person with a long beard, presided over a class of twenty students with love and paternal affection. The class covered about half a folio page of Talmud each week with Rashi's Commentary; the text was *Baba Metziah* (literally the "Middle Gate," one of the tractates of the Talmud dealing with liability, torts, bailments and similar legal problems).[40]

The third class was taught by a Rabbi Shmuel whose affectionate soubriquet for obvious reasons was "long nose." In this class about two full pages of Talmud were covered each week with occasional *Tosafot* (commentary on the Talmud, composed in the Middle Ages).[41] In the highest class, students had accelerated to a speed of four pages per week with *Tosafot*. The instructor, Rabbi Abraham Adelman, was replaced in 1896 by a Rabbi Yechiel.[42]

The first class included the study of Bible in addition to elementary

Talmud and in 1893 was taught by a Rabbi David. Another teacher, remembered only as "butter-nose," was in charge at one time or another of either the second or third class. He was a strict mentor with a jaundiced face and a short beard. During the middle of the nineties, a student revolt broke out against his harsh methods, and the president, Jacob Hecht, had him replaced. Rabbi Yechiel, who came to the teaching staff at this time, may have been involved in the replacement. Among other teachers mentioned in connection with Etz Chaim was Rabbi Eliezer Vishniver, who taught the highest class in 1888.[43]

In the European tradition, no written examinations were given to test the progress of the students. However their training, which was deemed very successful, brought a satisfactory reaction from the directors. They proudly invited the Jewish community to be present at regular intervals in order to witness the public oral examinations of the students: the newspaper invitation asked "all those who wish to have the pleasure of seeing how American boys are proficient in the Tractate Baba Metziah and know all its contents by heart" to attend the examination.[44] Further pride in the students' performance was reflected by a *Tageblatt* editorial writer, who as one of the audience at an oral examination, was so carried away that he wrote: "we forget that we are on American soil. . . . We thought we were in a Polish Beth Hamidrash."[45] When Chief Rabbi Jacob Joseph assumed his position in New York, one of the first things he did was to visit the school and examine the students. Similarly impressed by their training, he expressed his deep gratification with the work being done.[46] The public examinations were usually on Sundays during Hanukkah and between the Passover and Pentecost holidays when parents and friends of the student could attend. To accommodate large audiences, the assemblies took place in synagogues such as the Beth Hamidrash Shaare Torah at 24 Christie Street,[47] or at Kahal Adath Jeshurun at 12-16 Eldridge Street.[48]

The satisfaction with Etz Chaim's progress was prompted by the successful emphasis on Talmud, the primary interest of the school's organizers. The effectiveness of this course of study had enough of a powerful influence on some students to prompt them to continue their studies on their own after graduation. In 1894, one of the early groups of graduates of Etz Chaim formed an intellectual, religious fraternity called *Ḥebra Shoḥarei Tusheya* (Society of the Lovers of Wisdom).[49] They conducted their own weekly Sabbath service in a school room and met daily after work to study Talmud.[50] Within two years they completed the entire Order of *Mo'ed,* a division of the Talmud that deals mainly with the laws of the Sabbath, festivals and holy days. This accomplishment, praiseworthy of any scholar, was celebrated with a *Siyyum,* a ceremony and feast marking the conclusion of a tractate or order of the Talmud. The event was attended by the most prominent rabbis and laymen in the city. Chief Rabbi Jacob Joseph, himself delivered the final lecture in the study of the Order and then participated in the celebration and praise of the group's achievement. Rev. Zvi Hirsch Masliansky, the formidable people's orator, and Gerson Rozenzweig, the well-known journalist and editor of the Hebrew weekly *Ha-Ivri,* were also among the invited speakers.[51]

Among the young men in the *Ḥebra* were Gershon Avner, Chaim Edelman, Hyman Harris, Chaim Lefkowits, Chaim Levinson, Yechiel Michel Libner, and Shlomo Zalman Solovay. Two brothers named Bernstein and Sam Barnett were also in this group.[52] They were the strong nucleus of the alumni. Rabbi Moses Mayer Matlin, whose son was a student at Etz Chaim in the nineties, invited Jacob L. Andron, an energetic and well-versed young immigrant, to assist in supervising the group. Andron, who devoted all his spare time to educational and communal causes, gladly accepted the invitation and threw himself into the work. When Rev. Herschel Green, a *shoḥet* (ritual slaughterer), who had delivered the daily *shiur,* or Talmudic lecture, was gored by a runaway ox in a slaughterhouse, Andron took over this duty as well. Andron, who continued his interest in Jewish education, later became one of the founders of the Rabbi Jacob Joseph School.

The *Ḥebra Shoḥarei Tusheya* continued to meet well into 1905 and possibly after that although there is no later record. Influenced by Andron, their meeting place at this time was 197 Henry Street, the address of the Rabbi Jacob Joseph School.[53] The society later evolved into a social, cultural and religious fraternal organization. Named *Adas B'nai Yisrael* (the Congregation of the Sons of Israel),[54] it was an active religious group on the East Side for many years.

Toward a Merger with RIETS

By contemporary standards, the curriculum of Yeshivat Etz Chaim was eminently satisfactory and its steady growth reflected the community's confidence. At the end of the nineteenth century the school paid $15,500 to acquire its own building at 85 Henry Street between Market and Pike streets.[55] Eighty students were enrolled in the school,[56] and the Religious or Hebrew Department, as it was frequently called, was staffed by four teachers.[57] By 1905 Etz Chaim's annual budget of $5,000 enabled the school to expand to 6 classes serving from 150 to 175 students. The two additional classes absorbed the younger students who had little or no previous training. Their studies concentrated on Pentateuch and Rashi's Commentary while Talmud was the focal subject of the older grades.[58]

The school, however, still had deficiencies, undoubtedly carried over from its European prototypes. Not only were the secular studies relegated to a secondary position, but even the Hebrew language, which according to the Certificate of Incorporation and Constitution deserved a place in the curriculum, was completely neglected as was the study of Yiddish and the subjects of Prophets and Hagiographa. The already overburdened student who wanted to achieve proficiency in this field had to receive private instruction at home after 7:00 P.M. when the regular school session was over. Therefore many a student extended an already long day by taking on additional work under the guidance of a private teacher and the watchful eye of a demanding parent.[59]

The discipline and administration of the classes also left room for improvement. While there were public examinations of the students and occasional classroom tests by prominent rabbis, grade promotion, left entirely to the discretion of the teacher, was haphazard. A student could be promoted at any time of the year all depending on the will of the teacher.

In the years after 1905, however, Yeshivat Etz Chaim began to show remarkable progress and expansion. In order to provide religious training for youngsters attending the public schools, in 1904 the directors opened an afternoon class for students who were able to study Talmud.[60] At the end of 1906, this Talmud Torah division of the school was enlarged to four classes. The program for these supplementary classes, which met from 4:00 to 7:00 P.M., included the Prophets and *Shulḥan Arukh*.[61] The omissions in the curriculum were also being corrected and the books of the Prophets, which were taught in the supplementary classes, became part of the teaching content of the Yeshiva classes. In 1908 there were four Talmud classes, as well as seven lower classes where Prophets, Hebrew grammar, and *Shulḥan Arukh* were taught in addition to Pentateuch and Commentaries.[62] The increased number of classes also marked an enlarged enrollment, and the age level of the students was extended to include children from six to fourteen years.[63] Those from ten to fourteen made up the Talmud classes.[64] By this time the directors were talking about "hundreds" of students in the school.[65]

The English Department, which was also being regulated and improved,[66] established classes along educationally sound lines. As much as possible, they were graded according to the age, knowledge and ability of the students. The first grade, however, was a catch-all for beginning students from the ages of five to thirteen who had had no previous school training. Admission to the first class did not take place at regular intervals according to fixed terms and semesters. Applicants just off the immigrant boat were assigned to this class immediately upon acceptance in the school.

For a short time in 1906, the first class was taught by David Harry Barash, who had been similarly engaged at RIETS a year or two before. It was an unruly and undisciplined group that welcomed this new teacher on the first day of his teaching career at Etz Chaim. The rabbi who introduced him to the class said in Yiddish: *"Kinder, das iss eire nya teacher."* ("Children, this is your new teacher.") Despite these words, the young Mr. Barash was greeted with a barrage of chalk when he turned his back to write his first lesson on the blackboard. After a while, however, he created a sense of discipline and group responsibility. Yet Dr. Barash recalls he remained at Etz Chaim for only three months. Such a short stay was not uncommon, for teachers' salaries, when paid, were at the rate of $5 a week and their hours of instruction were from 4 to 6 or 7 P.M. on the weekdays, as well as Sunday mornings. These factors, in addition to the students' unruliness, were probably reasons for the rapid turnover in teachers.

As time went on, the English Department was frequently examined by the city's Board of Education.[67] Many students of the highest classes were reported to have passed the tests for admission to City College.[68] Several parents of graduates of Etz Chaim published a glowing testimonial to the efficiency of the school. They thanked the directors

> ... from the depths of their hearts ... for the excellent education that the Yeshiva gave their children in Jewish and other subjects. In a short period of four years, these children of less than 12 years of age, completed a course ranging from beginner's Chumash [Pentateuch] through Gemara [Talmud] and Tosafot. Besides they completed the public school curriculum in a short time and entered City College.[69]

Toward the end of the first decade of the twentieth century and the beginning of the second, the men responsible for the maintenance of Etz Chaim were Mr. Spector, who was president in 1906,[70] and Jacob Hecht, who was again president in 1908. Other officers in 1908 were Harry Fischel, first vice-president; Abraham Fine, second vice-president; Nathan Roggen, treasurer. Among the directors were Joseph Olinski, Abraham Rothstein, Aaron Kommel, Moshe Goldberg, Aryeh Leib Rosenthal, and Leib Siegelstein.[71] Moses Sebulun Margolies and Avraham Eliezer Alperstein were two of the prominent rabbis whose devotion to the educational needs of the school lent dignity and prestige to the Yeshiva.[72]

The rabbis were intimately connected with RIETS as well, Rabbi Alperstein having been with RIETS almost from its beginning and Rabbi Margolies, having been president of the rabbinical school at one time. They were members of the Yeshiva Committee of the Agudat ha-Rabbanim (Union of Orthodox Rabbis) and were conversant with the work at both schools. The laymen, too, including Harry

Fischel, Aryeh Leib Rosenthal, and Jacob Hecht were active in RIETS. By 1915 the two schools were drifting closer to each other by virtue of their common goals and common sponsors. It soon appeared feasible to effect a merger that would strengthen the resulting institutions, consolidate the supporters and sources of income, eliminate overlapping expenses, and create a larger, more comprehensive educational structure with classes from the first grade of elementary school through the rabbinical seminary.

CHAPTER 3. EMERGING PATTERNS IN JEWISH EDUCATION

One of the compelling forces leading to the establishment of an American academy of Jewish studies was the great faith possessed by the new immigrants from Eastern Europe.

The source of this faith lay in the two millenia and more of Jewish schools, dating through centuries of European living and through the great academies of Babylonia to the earliest days of the Palestinian period. In these schools were developed a love for Torah and a passion for scholarship that permeated the Jewish climate and impregnated the Jewish soul. In turn, Jewish scholarship became more than a cultural expression. It was a religious excitation, basic to all Jews as the call to worship and belief. For many, scholarship became identifiable with piety and faith itself.

In their own day, the Jews of the end of the nineteenth century had been strengthened by the existence of great academies of learning. These academies, or yeshivot, dotted the East European countryside. The great schools in Vilna, Volozhin, Slobodka, Lomza, Mir, Telshe, and Radun, as well as the smaller yeshivot in the lesser cities and towns were a string of citadels defending the faith, a chain of beacons, guiding and inspiring the Jewish community. They were presided over by sages who attracted thousands of disciples and converted them into perpetual students. It is no wonder that the immigrant in America, coming from this background, could be deprived of all his worldly possessions but never of his membership in that most respected company of all, "the aristocracy of the learned."

This legacy was treasured by the East Europeans, and early in their American adventure they began to dream of recreating in America the glory of a Vilna or a Volozhin and of picking up again the golden thread of Jewish scholarship.

Their dream coincided with the immediate practical problem of the need for traditional rabbis in the United States. The need for American-trained rabbis the Orthodox Jewish community shared with its Reform brethren, for the entire Jewish community in America was expanding through the influx of immigrants.

However, an academy for Jewish studies that would serve as a rabbinical seminary as well could not be brought into being without a well-established and financially resourceful community to support it. In order to be of maximum service, a school of this kind had to be part of an integrated complex involving the many delicate aspects of community organization. The Orthodox immigrants did not develop such an organization until well into the last decade of the nineteenth century. Consequently, the dream of creating an academy for Torah study and for the preparation of Orthodox rabbis was realized neither quickly nor easily.

The Reform Movement

In the beginning, the East European Jewish immigrants, together with the smaller number of Orthodox Jews who arrived before 1881, were isolated both in numbers and religious practices, even among their fellow Jews. Many of their predecessors had adopted the teachings of Reform Judaism as more suited to the American soil. They looked upon their East European coreligionists as the vestigial remains of an ancient communion, as oddities—most often obnoxious, sometimes acceptable, but never to be viewed with respect or to be considered true equals.[1] The numerical inferiority of the East Europeans was soon eliminated by the overwhelming and continued immigration. With numbers, too, came the expansion and firm establishment of Orthodoxy on a broad and lasting basis. In the development of this movement, the East European immigrants learned a great deal from the Reform community as they found it in 1881.

By that year, the Reform movement was already girded with a threefold source of strength: an organized congregational union, a rabbinical seminary, and a forceful publication to disseminate information and serve as an educational force. These three auxiliary arms of the Reform movement could be directly traced to the influence of Isaac Mayer Wise, a dominant force on the American Jewish horizon. In 1854, Wise had launched *The Israelite,* a crusading publication of Reform, to counterbalance the outspokenly Orthodox *The Occident,* founded in 1843 by Isaac Leeser, the minister of Mikveh Israel, a leading Sephardic Congregation in Philadelphia. Wise was a doughty battler, and when *The Occident* ceased publication in 1869, *The Israelite,* which had become his own personal organ as well, remained one of the few exponents of a sectarian Jewish point of view in the English language in the United States.

In 1873, through the initiative of Isaac Wise, the Union of American Hebrew Congregations was formed. The congregational union became an eager sponsor and strong supporter of Wise's proposal for the establishment of a rabbinical college, and in 1875, two years after its inception, the Union was instrumental in founding the Hebrew Union College in Cincinnati, the first rabbinical college still in existence in America. The idea of a rabbinical college had been proposed much earlier by Major Mordecai Emanuel Noah, and indeed, in 1854, Wise, himself, had attempted to found a rabbinical college to be known as the Zion Collegiate Institute. However, this venture collapsed even before the first sessions were held, although a preparatory school was conducted for one year. A similar abortive effort under the aegis of Isaac Leeser was begun in Philadelphia with the organization of Maimonides College in 1867. So it appeared that no rabbinical college could be maintained or sustained independent of a broad base of support like that which the Union of American Hebrew Congregations provided the Hebrew Union College.

Isaac Mayer Wise's interest in establishing a rabbinical seminary was motivated by the simple logic that a European rabbi could not appear in the American pulpit and successfully preach the principles of what Wise considered an American-inspired religious reformation. Only native American rabbis, or at least American-trained rabbis, could speak convincingly in the language of the land of the "*minhag America,*" the new Reform Jewish ritual born out of American needs. One of the purposes of the Hebrew Union College, therefore, became the preparation of such rabbis, and by 1897, for the first time, the student body of the College was made up exclusively of native Americans.[2]

The formation of the Hebrew Union College had another purpose, and that was to create a body of rabbis with recognized status. The greatest outrage of the second half of the nineteenth century as the number of congregations multiplied and the need for rabbis to service them increased, was that anyone, regardless of his qualifications, could pose as a rabbi.[3] Contemporary writers joked bitterly that any man who donned a Prince Albert coat could claim to be a rabbi and occupy the pulpit[4] while the title "Reverend" was to be had for the asking, and the only requirement for the title of "Doctor" was to put on a stovepipe hat.[5]

The Orthodox complained most about "free lance" rabbis because of the varied and technical standards of scholarship they required for ordination. But it was an equally thorny problem with the Reform.[6] It was hoped that the founding of a rabbinical school would create enough rabbis to fill the vacant pulpits and simultaneously create standards by which the unauthorized would be weeded out.

Originally, Wise had envisioned his projected seminary as a non-denominational school whence rabbis would go forth capable of serving any wing of Judaism. At this college, Orthodox as well as Reform rabbis were to have been prepared by studying a mutually suitable curriculum. From the beginning, however, it became apparent that Orthodox and Reform Jews could not find a common meeting ground on the vital issues of theology and ritual that separated rather than united them. The Hebrew Union College finally became an integral part of the Reform movement, the fountainhead of Reform doctrine and the source for the solution of questions on faith and practice. In this sense, a central authority for Reform Judaism was created, and in the end the strength of Reform was established not only in its appeal to its followers, but also in its unified position, trained leadership, and recognized headquarters.

As with the Reform wing, a rabbinical college was of the utmost priority within the traditional community. The need had already been clearly established, and Isaac Leeser's attempt to found a college had been a brief step toward filling the need. However, the founding of the Hebrew Union College, the strengthening of the Reform movement, and the crystallization of its principles in the Pittsburgh Platform, adopted in 1885 by a group of Reform rabbis meeting in that city, renewed the argument for the establishment of a traditional rabbinical college.[7] The Pittsburgh Platform decisively rejected the divine revelation of the Bible, asserted that the beliefs of Judaism were not eternal but subject to "the postulates of reason," and consequently denied that the authority of the Torah was binding in Jewish life. It also proclaimed that Judaism was a religious community and rejected the notion that the Jews were a nation, denying, thereby, any right to hope or pray for a return to Zion. In simple terms it meant that the *mitzvot,* the traditional observance of the Sabbath, the Festivals, the Holy Days, all were to be done away with.

When the extreme liberal position adopted at the Pittsburgh Conference was fully understood by traditional Jews, Reform stood sharply defined as having made its break with traditional beliefs complete. This had the effect of riving the Jewish community neatly, and further, of alerting the Orthodox community to the quarter against which it had to guard and the measures it had to take to strengthen its lines. Obviously Wise's plan to educate Orthodox rabbis at the Hebrew Union College could no longer be taken seriously even by those who once had considered it possible.

Jewish Theological Seminary

As a direct reaction to the threat of Reform, a rabbinical college, named the Jewish Theological Seminary, was founded in 1886 under the leadership of the Rev. Dr. Sabato Morais of Philadelphia with the aid of Drs. Henry Pereira Mendes and Mendola de Sola as well as a number of Polish and German Jews, who were sympathizers of the new Conservative movement.[8] The ideological difference between the Orthodox and Conservative points of view lay primarily in the East Europeans' almost exclusive emphasis on the study of Talmud and the acceptance of the rabbinic interpretation of the Torah culminating in the *Shulḥan Arukh,* the Code of Jewish Law. The Conservative leaders felt that Reform had indeed gone too far in completely rejecting the normative structure of Judaism. On the other hand, the Conservatives felt that the rigid requirements of the *Shulḥan Arukh* practiced by Orthodoxy should be relaxed to conform to the demanding needs of the day. In short, on the one hand, Conservative Judaism accepted in broad terms the validity of Jewish religious tradition which Reform had denied. But, on the other hand, it maintained that Jewish practice and belief were not as fixed as Orthodoxy taught they were. Thus Conservative Judaism adopted the principle of Reform that change was necessary and possible, and retained the belief of Orthodoxy that Jewish historical tradition was nevertheless a major element that had to be conserved.

For the East European Orthodox Jews, Conservative Judaism seemed an anomaly based on an uncrystallized position, and Joseph Blumenthal, the President of the Association of the Jewish Theological Seminary, was himself reported to have declared that his school "was neither Orthodox or Reform."[9] In any case, for the Orthodox anyone not patterned after the great Talmudic masters of the European academies was disqualified for religious leadership. Although Dr. Morais was a deeply respected man, the East European rabbis and the immigrants who were scholars in the old country did not consider the Sephardic minister an authority on Jewish law. And for this reason, Dr. Morais was not deemed as great a Talmudic scholar as was necessary to head a rabbinic school.

Ha-Ivri, one of the organs reflecting the extreme Orthodox immigrant viewpoint, while recognizing the good intentions of the Jewish Theological Seminary, summarized the series of charges against the school which reflected the attitude of the traditional East European Jews. The periodical pointed out that while the purpose of the Jewish Theological Seminary was to combat the Hebrew Union College and Reform with the combined power of faith and Torah, the teachers themselves, with the exception of Dr. Bernard Drachman,[10] were not suitable to produce such students. Even Dr. Solomon Schechter, president of the Jewish Theological Seminary, admitted that Dr. Drachman was the "only Orthodox on [his] staff."[11] The Hebrew Union College, *Ha-Ivri* suggested, had more able teachers, and the newspaper concluded that the rabbis of the Jewish Theological Seminary possessed secular knowledge but no faith.[12]

Ha-Ivri's correspondents claimed that the two students in the highest grade of the Jewish Theological Seminary had studied only 17 pages of Talmud and a few other Halakhic sources in one entire year of schooling[13] and that they could not read even those properly.[14] As for Rashi's Commentary, only selected portions were studied.[15]

Years later the same biting criticism was to be heard. A writer in 1903 expressed himself as follows:

> What kind of rabbis will come forth from there [the Jewish Theological Seminary]? If they will be reform rabbis . . . then we do not need it . . . because a factory for such rabbis . . . is already established in Cincinnati. If the founders mean to train orthodox rabbis in the Seminary, then I cannot understand them either. An orthodox rabbi must know Talmud and Codes . . . and in the Seminary . . . Talmud and the Codes are taught only as much as Hebrew may be taught in the philosophy department of a university.[16]

Greater sympathy for the Jewish Theological Seminary on the part of the traditional East European Jews might have been developed if certain steps had been taken by Morais and his board to understand the attitude of these immigrants in order to enlist their sympathies. The fact that the Jewish Theological Seminary was considered an Orthodox institution[17] formed a potential common bond of interest. This potential, however, was never properly utilized. For example, it was pointed out that while it was common practice for dignitaries and leading rabbis to examine students of rabbinical schools,[18] Russian and Polish rabbis were never invited to visit or to make such examinations at the Jewish Theological Seminary. This was either a gratuitous slight or evidence that the Seminary did not recognize the East European rabbis and the people they represented. In either case, the sensitive immigrant community considered it as a reflection on their status.[19]

The occasional appeal for funds, as presented in the press, also casts additional light on the directors' lack of understanding of the

Seminary. A particular request to set aside the Sabbath of *Hanukkah*
1897 for sermons and fund raising on behalf of the Jewish Theological Seminary was published in the *Jüdische Gazetten*. Directed to
the Yiddish-speaking and -reading public, this appeal should have
been made in the language they understood best. Yet, it was published in English with only a short introduction in Yiddish, which
the newspaper found necessary to write for the edification of its
readers.[20]

Dr. Morais, a traditionalist rabbi himself, was well aware of the
Eastern European attitude on this subject. A rabbi who was not ade-
quately prepared in Torah, Talmud, *Shulhan Arukh* and Commentaries could not be considered a qualified leader. Therefore Dr.
Morais, in addition to issuing frequent calls for financial assistance,
made an appeal for instructors who could teach Talmud and Codes
in English. Despite this effort, the East European teachers were
reluctant to become affiliated with the Jewish Theological Seminary.
Expressing their feelings, *Ha-Ivri* commented: "There are many who
can and will not" fulfill the first requirement and as for the second
qualification, there are "many who will and cannot."[21] A few months
later Dr. Morais repeated his plea: "Give us better teachers and
we'll take them." But when he was told that such instructors were
available, he had to respond "But they don't know English."[22] This
comment typifies the rift between Dr. Morais and the East European
immigrant. The latter could hardly sympathize with Dr. Morais'
greater concern with the relatively inconsequential question of the
language of instruction.[23] They considered the lack of fluency in
English a technical inadequacy that could hardly disqualify an otherwise able teacher. The displeasing inference—although not entirely
justifiable—was that Morais was prepared to sacrifice the quality of
subject matter on the altar of proper English.

As a result, the instructors at the Jewish Theological Seminary
became known to the East European Jews as "professors" rather
than rabbis and were held to be identical with ignoramuses or
heretics. "The Jewish Theological Seminary has no rabbinical
scholars," the immigrants concluded, "but, God save us, only professors."[24]

Ha-Ivri was perhaps the most outspoken critic of the Jewish

Theological Seminary. The other traditional-minded Yiddish newspapers, the *Jüdische Gazetten, Jüdisches Tageblatt* and the *Jüdische Welt,* more understanding of the direction which the Seminary was taking, were prepared to view the Seminary's deviations with greater leniency.

Nevertheless, even the *Welt* (whose publisher, Rev. Zvi Hirsch Masliansky, the famous Yiddish orator, was later to become a member of the Jewish Theological Seminary Board[25]) was forced to comment adversely. One of their reporters, who covered the graduation ceremonies in 1902, was outraged that "professors of the school sat with uncovered heads . . . and Professor [Abraham Joshua] Jaffe, who delivered a major address in Hebrew was also bareheaded and mentioned the name of God without covering his head."[26] The newspaper voiced disproval in its observation "that there is naturally a great difference between rabbis who graduate from a Volozhin Yeshiva and those who graduate from a Jewish Theological Seminary."[27]

All this seemed to justify *Ha-Ivri's* earlier judgment that the Seminary was as "empty as" and "similar to the Hebrew Union College" with the only difference that it still had foreign students, whereas the Hebrew Union College had only native students.[28] As late as 1908, the efforts of the friendly Yiddish papers and the Seminary leadership were unsuccessful in attracting the East Europeans. The *Tageblatt* editorial writer, forced to admit defeat, stated:

> What is the use of lying? The Seminary is not popular among the people. The great Jewish masses look upon this rabbinical school as upon some rich man's "uptown" institution. Among many, and in many congregations, the students of the Seminary are not considered as real rabbis although this rabbinical school calls itself orthodox and was organized to combat the principles on which the rabbinical school in Cincinnati stands.[29]

The very character of the East Side may have presented an additional obstacle to the Jewish Theological Seminary by preventing it from penetrating the immigrants and therefore making an effective impact upon them. The turbulent East Side, exciting and dynamic, was nevertheless an insular, self-contained community for the immigrants. They traveled infrequently and knew little about the happenings around them other than what was published in the Yiddish press, which they read avidly. They ate, slept, worked, and relaxed all within the borders of that fantastic city within a city. The climate of the East Side was so prevailingly East European that the immigrants were not impressed by the native American character of the Reform movement, nor did they react favorably to the Jewish Theological Seminary, which was initiated by the Sephardic ministers Sabato Morais, Henry Pereira Mendes, and Mendola de Sola, and was supported by the "uptown Jews."[30] They had nothing but scorn for the "Reformers"[31] and rejected their movement which bore the stamp "made in Germany" and had its origin in far-removed Cincinnati.[32] Nor could they follow the Sephardic ministers, who were much closer to Orthodoxy, but equally alien to the East Europeans. They responded more readily to the Socialist preachers and Ethical Culture teachers of their own national origins, who were indigenous to the East Side.

Groping Toward Fulfillment

Although direct appeals for cooperation with the Jewish Theological Seminary were addressed to the Russian rabbis[33] and their congregants, the latter remained untouched. The Orthodoxy of the Eastern Europeans was of a fundamentalist nature and too recently removed from its European origin to be aware of even a possible need for religious adjustment. They were convinced that whatever future problems might confront them could be solved by a continuing and unswerving loyalty to their historical religious pattern of behavior. The Jewish Theological Seminary, however, especially after its reorganization in 1902, reflected an increasing impatience with the traditional and dogmatic aspects of Jewish belief. Its leaders wanted a system more flattering to the new way of living, and consequently they were most susceptible to the relaxation of their religious norms and most tolerant of changes that could be justified as flowing from the needs of modern existence. This relatively easy acceptance of free alteration in Jewish substantive law made it possible for the Jewish Theological Seminary to accept and follow the teachings of Morais' successor, Professor Solomon Schechter and finally, to become completely identified with the Conservative movement. Thus, while the Seminary leaders, faculty and East European immigrants hovered momentarily on common ground, they were being irrevocably drawn toward different goals. The indifference and even the antagonism of the Eastern Europeans to what the Seminary represented was not always understood by the Seminary leaders,[34] and the East European indifference to appeals of Morais, Mendes, and others, which frequently found their way into the Yiddish press,[35] earned them only rebuke and public chastisement. It became increasingly obvious that the graduates of neither the Hebrew Union College nor the Jewish Theological Seminary were acceptable as spiritual leaders of the Orthodox community. However, the problems which faced the other groups plagued Orthodox Jews even more seriously, and their need for American-trained leadership was even more desperate.

Reform was catering to the slowly evolving needs of a homogeneous class of Jews, already established in the United States. The resiliency of their code of religious practices made them amenable to change and encouraged them to welcome identification with the American culture. Because their advocacy of change was not prompted as a defense against external pressures or as a compulsory yielding to circumstances, they felt no threat to their religious existence in the liberalizing tendencies of the day. Where desirable, they merely assimilated new practices and justified the acceptance of them by the inherent liberalism of Reform.

The East European Jew, however, from the moment of his arrival to the United States, was faced with an immediate need for guidance and leadership in bolstering his faith. Although his faith was strong, having been encouraged by centuries of tradition and belief, his acceptance as a free and dignified human being in America without the fetters of the Russian Pale of Settlement, created new and bewildering problems. He was like an unprotected aviator suddenly thrust into space where the atmospheric pressure lessens until he is about to burst. Conditions of living were such as to encourage the abandonment of certain religious practices difficult to fulfill. This new life was upsetting to the immigrant. His faith was threatened; his children were tempted to drift from tradition; and his economic requirements absorbed all his time and energy. He felt subject to "a deadly, disintegrating effect."[36] What the Orthodox Jew needed most was guidance towards a reorientation of values and an adequate rabbinate that could address itself to his children in the American language, win his confidence and loyalty and lead him and his family in the path of traditional Judaism.[37]

Unfortunately, there were no such leaders in America. In the beginning of the second half of the nineteenth century, Rabbi Bernard Illowy was the only Orthodox rabbi in the United States who possessed a thorough university training and spoke English fluently.[38] In 1896, twenty-five years after Rabbi Illowy died, there was not one East European rabbi of the Orthodox rabbis in the City of New York[39] who could claim a similar distinction.[40] This simple but undeniable fact brought home to the East European Jews that they could not continually import rabbis from their native lands. Lacking American leadership from within and facing strong nontraditional agitation from without, the East European community had its survival at stake.

At first the early East European immigrants did not attach too much significance to the Reform movement. They considered Reform a wanton aberration from tradition that, because of its invalidation on religious grounds, was doomed to failure from its inception. Nevertheless, the established Orthodox community did not entirely ignore the growth and development of the movement. Dr. Henry Pereira Mendes issued a newspaper call as early as 1888 to the Orthodox Jews of New York City, emphasizing that they were neglecting the education of their children against the threat of Reform. He pointed out that Reform rabbis were well grounded in secular subjects, while the Orthodox rabbis were not, and it was imperative that preachers with an American background be assured for the Orthodox rabbinate.[41] Although many of these "calls" alerting Orthodox Jews to the dangers of Reform were inspired by the financial needs of the Jewish Theological Seminary, they neverthe-less emphasized the obvious point that Orthodoxy was in great need of American-trained leadership. In subsequent years, these "calls" became more frequent and were issued from the East European immigrant group itself.[42]

Unfortunately, three negative forces retarded the founding of an Orthodox rabbinical college. First in importance was the low prestige and the lack of power and economic security which plagued the East European Orthodox rabbis in America, largely a result of the poverty of their congregations. The rabbis were so harried with maintaining their positions that they lacked the time, energy and vision to create a uniting force. Because of their own personal in-security, they were more critical than constructive and most hesitant to merge forces where the yielding of individual sovereignty was involved. The dissension that characterized their relationships was described by a prominent East European Orthodox rabbi in the following manner: "There is no unity and no agreement among them as to how and by what means to raise the prestige of religion. ... Each decides and acts as if he were the only one in the world."[43] Their jealousies and competitive spirit were noted and commented on even in the European press.[44] The tragic failure of the dream of having a chief rabbi for the City of New York serves as a classical illustration of the result of such conflict.[45]

The sorry position of the Orthodox rabbinate was further aggra-vated by a lack of aggressive, and imaginative leadership to rise above the sordid conditions of the day. There was no Orthodox rabbi with the perseverance and consecration to inspire a following, to create a movement, to evaluate a problem, and to devote his life to improving the status of his fellow immigrants. Unfortunately, on the East Side horizon there was no figure of stature comparable to Isaac M. Wise in missionary zeal and tireless service.

The second factor was the absence of an upper class that had the means and the leisure to sponsor a rabbinical seminary. Such a school could not spring full-grown from the East European immigrant masses at a time when their primary problem was to become es-tablished in the new land. Almost a score of years was to elapse from the start of the great mass immigrations of the eighties before the new immigrants could undertake this great and costly, time-consuming effort.

The main obstacle, however, was the absence of a proper organization and structure to sponsor and support such a school. The moral of the Reform group's experience remained plain: as Isaac M. Wise's attempt to create the Zion Collegiate Institute in 1854 failed for lack of organizational sponsorship and support, so the Hebrew Union College, a later effort, met better fortune because it was sponsored, guided, and nourished by a full-fledged union of congregations. To sum up, therefore, the efforts of East European Jews to create a rabbinical school were hampered initially by the weak position of its rabbinate, by the limited and undeveloped financial resources, and by the absence of a congregational union to sponsor and support such an effort.

It is ironical that Orthodox Jews, who were the greatest admirers of scholarship and who had established schools of learning even before they ministered to their physical comforts during the long history of Jewish migrations, were the last to create a rabbinical college in the United States. All of the previously stated causes, plus the fact that they were the last to arrive in large numbers on the American scene, contributed to their tardiness. The surging need for an Orthodox rabbinical school was not to be gainsaid, however, and with the very dawn of the calendar year 1897, a Certificate of Incorporation was filed by the Rabbi Isaac Elchanan Theological Seminary Association for the founding of a rabbinical school, to be known as the Rabbi Isaac Elchanan Theological Seminary.

CHAPTER 4. THE FOUNDING AND FINANCING OF RIETS

The beginnings of the Rabbi Isaac Elchanan Theological Seminary have been long forgotten, buried with the founders of the school. The recollection of their descendants has been distorted by the passage of time and obscured by events more important in their own lives. There are no records extant of the Seminary from its inception in 1897 to its merger with Yeshivat Etz Chaim in 1915. Only the Certificate of Incorporation, scattered newspaper accounts, one or two contemporary citations and passing references in the memoir literature of the time remain as silent witnesses to the great vision and determination of a few men, who in poverty, without a founding board, congregational union, or experienced leadership, created the first Orthodox rabbinical seminary in America.

The articulation of the need for an Orthodox rabbinical school on American soil in the tradition of the Jews of Russia and Poland marked the coming of age for the Orthodox East European immigrant community. To the East European immigrant this was significant because at this time two other distinct Orthodox communities existed in the United States: the German Orthodox Jews, who showed little warmth and friendship to their East European brethren, and a native American Orthodox group led by ministers like Dr. Henry Pereira Mendes and Rabbi Bernard Drachman. These two Orthodox groups constituted, in part, what the East Siders called the "Uptown Jews," and were among the supporters of the Jewish Theological Seminary of America. Both exhibited a paternal philanthropic and condescending interest in the East European immigrants and were active with other Jews in sponsoring an Americanization program for them.

The East European Jewish immigrants represented the third Orthodox segment in America. They were, by turns, patronized and condoned, derided and condemned, uplifted and improved as they became established on the East Side.[1] It was time for them to assert their individuality by creating the institutions which were indigenous to the area and representative of their interests. The formation of RIETS marked a bold beginning in this direction, as well as a determined attack at the lines of benevolence and dependence that stretched from the "Uptown Jews" to the lower East Side. It was the new immigrants' declaration of independence from the German and the early Polish Jewish settlers in America.

Formation of RIETS

RIETS was incorporated in 1897. A lone newspaper article announcing the formation of the school is the earliest published document about the event. It reads, in part:

> Congregation Anshei Emes of Mariampol at 44 East Broadway, announces that just as the Yeshiva Etz Chaim and the Machzikei Talmud Torah were organized in this Synagogue years ago so, too, the Yeshiva of the great "Gaon," Rabbi Isaac Elchanan, may his memory be a blessing, is being organized now. The purpose of the Yeshiva is [to enroll] children who can study a page of Talmud with Tosafot. A daily "shiur" will be taught by a Rosh Yeshiva [teacher of advanced Talmudic subjects] and a teacher will give instructions in the language of the land. The founder of the Yeshiva is Rabbi Yehuda David Bernstein, the founder of Yeshivat Etz Chaim.[2]

The name of Mr. David Abramowitz, bearing the title Secretary, is signed to the announcement. A decade later, a short historical article revealing the names of two other founders, points out: "RIETS was founded by three lovers of Torah—Rabbi Moses Mayer Matlin, Rabbi Yehuda David Bernstein, and Mr. David Abramowitz."[3] These three "founders," and eight other men who signed the Certificate of Incorporation of RIETS (Samuel Schatzkin, Jehuda Solomon, Asher L. Germansky, Max Lewis, Mendel Zuckerman, Julius Braunstein, Samuel Silberstein and Moses H. Bernstein), represented the founding board of the college.

Of the eleven, Moses Mayer Matlin and Yehuda David Bernstein were rabbis. Rabbi Matlin was born in 1885 in Slutsk, Lithuania where he received his rabbinical training. Later he studied at the famous yeshiva in Kovno and was ordained by the great Rabbi Isaac Elchanan himself. He came to America in the 1890's when he accepted a call from Chief Rabbi Jacob Joseph to serve as one of the *dayyanim,* or judges of religious problems in the Chief Rabbi's Court in New York City. His specific function was to be the supervisor of all *shohatim* under Rabbi Jacob Joseph's direction. He was also a *mashgiah* (supervisor of kosher food preparation) for the California Wine Association of New York.

When the Chief Rabbi died, Rabbi Matlin continued to serve as *mashgiah* under Dr. Philip Hillel Klein. In describing Rabbi Matlin, Dr. Klein wrote that he "is one to whom no one can compare in nobility of character and piety . . ."[4] Rabbi Klein's characterization was well founded, for one of the students who remembered Rabbi Matlin well said he was a complete *tzaddik* (saint or saintly person).[5] Indeed, Rabbi Matlin was a sincere scholar who refused to use his rabbinical profession as a "spade to dig with." He never presided over weddings or funerals, and he refused to issue divorces, or to take any fee for a rabbinical service. With the Chief Rabbi gone and Rabbi Matlin's employment as *dayyan* at an end, he confined himself exclusively to *kashrut* supervision,[6] feeling that it was the only gainful work he could perform that was consistent with his training.

In 1914 he found the opportunity which he hoped would make it possible for him to withdraw from any form of rabbinical occupation. On his way back to New York City from an inspection trip to the wineries in California, he visited some of his European friends and relatives in Sioux City, Iowa. They talked excitedly about the tranquility of life and good climate of the West. Rabbi Matlin was so carried away with their enthusiasm that he applied for and received a government land grant in Montana. There he hoped to create a model Jewish community and earn his living as a farmer. Unfortunately, his Kovno background had made no provision for farming, and soon Rabbi Matlin was forced to give up his land. He returned to Sioux City, where he assumed a rabbinical pulpit and earned the respect of the entire community. Rabbi Matlin died in Sioux City in 1927 at the age of seventy-two.

Rabbi Yehuda David Bernstein was also born in Lithuania, near Kovno, in 1863, and at fourteen was already known to be a prodigy in Talmudic scholarship, an excellent student in mathematics, and an authority on the Code of Maimonides. His date of arrival in the United States is not established. Like Rabbi Matlin, Rabbi Bernstein, we are told, refused to accept a pulpit in order not to use his ordination as a professional instrument for profit. Instead, he tried to make his living in commercial enterprises, apparently failing.[7] Finally he had to become a *mashgiah* in one of the East Side wineries.[8] When RIETS moved to its first permanent quarters at 156 Henry Street, he was so impoverished that he was forced to live in the basement of the building.

Despite his financial difficulties, early students of RIETS knew Rabbi Bernstein as a cheerful, generous man with a sparkling sense of humor. Often he would brighten the long midnight vigils of the Yeshiva *bahurim* (students or youths) at their studies by bringing them bags of candy and fresh fruit. To the more alert students he presented gifts of scholarly volumes and Talmudic commentaries. All who remember him carry the impression of his deep piety and great scholarship.[9]

Of the other founders, Asher L. Germansky had an agency for the sale of steamship tickets, sold *etrogim* (citrons used in the ritual observance of the Festival of Tabernacles) and conducted a book shop.[10] Mendel Zuckerman was a *shohet*.[11] We have no record of the occupations of Moses H. Bernstein, Julius Braunstein, Max Lewis, Samuel Schatzkin, Jehuda Solomon and Samuel Silberstein, or of Joseph Goldenson and Jacob H. Selikowitz, whose names appeared on the petition as added signatures. But it is certain they were not men of great affluence. The founders had no personal resources of accumulated wealth; they had no great influence; they were not backed by any synagogue union; they were confined, in their activities and support, to the East Side, receiving no assistance from the Orthodox Jews of the "uptown" area.

In truth, their strength was not in their influence and power, but

rather in their vision for the future, and in the overwhelming consecration that possessed them as "lovers of Torah." These founders
of RIETS were among those for whom "All Jews . . . have pro-
foundest respect . . . who have great treasures of Torah concealed
under the baskets which they drag on their backs and under the
sewing machines by which they work. More than one of these
Jews who carries apples for sale, is a great scholar and possesses the
degree of [rabbinical] ordination . . ."[12]

As "lovers of Torah," they found no challenge too great and no
task too menial. They went out into the streets to find students and
to interest them in continuing to study. Finally, "they assembled
several lads who wanted to improve themselves in the study of the
Torah,"[13] and with them created the first class of the school.

The specific purpose of the school, according to the initial newspaper announcement, was to provide further education for "children
who could study a page of Talmud with Tosafot." This was necessary since there was no school for advanced Hebrew and religious
studies in the city of New York, or indeed in the entire United States.
There were many young men who were trained in Europe and
wanted to continue their studies on a more advanced level but could
not. Even Yeshivat Etz Chaim was only an elementary school, and
graduates of that school had no place to continue their formal higher
Jewish studies.

The Certificate of Incorporation in which the purposes of the
school were formally presented expressed an additional objective of
the school. The pertinent section reads, "The particular objects for
which the corporation was formed are to promote the study of the
Talmud and to assist in educating and preparing students of the
Hebrew faith for the Hebrew Orthodox Ministry."[14] It is interesting to note that the reference to the preparation for the ministry,
while included in the certificate which was prepared on February
11, 1897, was not even mentioned in the announcement of January 15,
only a month prior, despite the obvious need for a rabbinical school.

Rabbi Bernstein and Mr. Abramowitz may not have considered it
necessary to describe the complete nature of the proposed school in
the brief preliminary newspaper announcement. This would ex-

plain the discrepancy between the press release and the certificate. However, the curriculum of the school as well as later events point conclusively to the fact that even after it was established, RIETS was not designed as a rabbinical seminary in the modern and professional sense of the term. In making provisions for advanced study, the founders were actually following the design of the European yeshiva, which aimed to create scholars who would study for the sake of Torah alone. Since proficiency in Talmud and related fields could lead to ordination, it was implicit that RIETS would also prepare students "for the Hebrew Orthodox Ministry." Thus, for the newspaper reader, the important message was conveyed that a new school for the teaching of "a page of Talmud with Tosafot" had been formed. In petitioning for a charter, the facts had to be spelled out more clearly.

This definition of the rabbinate as a professional application of theoretical scholarship was again a historical attitude implicit in the European yeshivot and in their American protagonists. For the East European Jews the distinction between study for its own sake and study for the purpose of entering the rabbinate was very tenuous. They viewed the rabbinical vocation only as an extension of the avocation of scholarship. They had always equated rabbinical training with an overwhelming knowledge of Torah. For them there was no clearly marked learned estate, not because there were no scholars, but because the people themselves were a nation of scholars.

RIETS was envisioned by the founders as not merely a school with a yeshiva course of study presented to its students, but a movement, an ideal; the ideal to restore the knowledge of the Torah to American Jewry, to arouse vital interest in such study, and to bring about a higher level of spiritual leadership and of Jewish education in general. Consequently, in its early period the school emerged primarily as a center for the study of Torah, where the distinction between vocation and avocation was not emphasized or even clearly delineated. Only as a concession to the need of the day was it represented also as a professional training school.

The teaching of secular subjects was equally alien to the European yeshiva system of education. In principle, secular subjects were excluded from the curriculum, as was formal rabbinic training. The announcement that "a teacher will give instruction in the language of the land," again in view of later developments, could not have been more than a concession to the progress of the immigrants in the process of Americanization. The inclusion of the clause about secular education undoubtedly came, in part, out of the desire to keep the students from attending public schools by giving them a comparable or at least a passable education in that field. This arrangement brought their religious and secular education under one roof and made it possible for religious students to be spared the effects that a non-Jewish environment might have upon them.

Time was to demonstrate, however, that the two peripherally considered curricula, secular studies and preparation for the rabbinate, were to emerge as the most exciting and far-reaching contribution of RIETS to American Jewish life. By making provision for the study of secular subjects, the founders had laid the groundwork for the philosophy of synthesis in education that was brought to its highest expression under the administration of RIETS' great president, Dr. Bernard Revel.

The ideas of a rabbinical curriculum and English instruction were further related. The rabbinical student had to be equipped with secular knowledge in order to be adequate to perform his duties in America. What were considered by the founders of RIETS to be the least important aspects of the school later became the most important. The deficiency of the founders' vision in this respect was shared by the directors for at least a decade, creating the strange anomaly whereby the major requirements of the students were least satisfied. The requirements of the American rabbi were more quickly discernible to the student, who was pressed by professional needs, than to the directors of the school, who were further removed from the immediate problem and who adopted the more academic stand of study of the Torah for its own sake. In this respect, the students were closer to the grass-roots needs of the community.

It took some time, however, for this conflict inherent in the structure of RIETS to come to a head. In the early days of RIETS, material problems were more urgent. The question of finding a location for the new school was paramount. According to one account, the first meeting place of RIETS was at 1 Canal Street.[15] This location was also the meeting place of Yeshivat Etz Chaim, the elementary yeshiva organized a decade earlier, and some arrangement for common occupancy was presumably made by the new school. For a short period of time it is reported, the schools met side by side under the same roof. Another source, however locates the first meeting place of RIETS at 81 Henry Street.[16] It is impossible to determine whether any of these accounts are correct. In the newspaper announcement of January 15, 1897, it was indicated that RIETS was founded at the Mariampol Synagogue at 44 East Broadway by Rabbi Yehuda David Bernstein.[17] Oral tradition has it, however, that this "founding" did not mark the actual first meeting of the student body, but rather the official corporate organization of the school. A nucleus of young male students who had completed their studies at Etz Chaim had already been gathering in an informal study group with Rabbi Matlin.

Rabbi Matlin's own son, Akiva, had been entered at Etz Chaim in about 1892, when the family came to New York. In 1895 or 1896, Akiva was about sixteen and had absorbed as much as could be offered to him at the elementary school. His father, pious and anxious to see his son continue his religious studies, assembled several lads of the same age and taught them personally in his own apartment on the top floor of 172 Clinton Street. In addition to Akiva Matlin, were Hillel Rogoff and Aaron Abramowitz.[18] The news of this advanced class spread, and soon the group grew to about twelve students. Rabbi Matlin could not accommodate them in his home any longer and began to seek larger quarters. The father of one of the students who was a member of the Mariampol Synagogue persuaded his congregation to house the incipient yeshiva.[19]

When news of the death of Rabbi Isaac Elchanan Spektor of Kovno, reached the United States, the Orthodox Jewish community was shocked, and bereaved. Rabbi Isaac Elchanan was an undisputed master in the field of rabbinic lore.[20] His mind roamed the broad areas of Jewish achievement, taking giant steps in the Torah, the Talmud, the Codes, the thoughts and heritage of the rabbis of Israel through the ages. His life was characterized by personal sanctity, reverence, and humility. Rabbis from all parts of the world turned to him for legal decisions and advice. Acknowledged as the spiritual head of European Jewry, his picture hung on the wall of almost every Jewish home in Russia. At his death thousands of his disciples were left without a master. People all over the world who had been close to Rabbi Isaac Elchanan or who had been under his influence sought means to perpetuate his memory and the values of his life. Rabbi Matlin, who was himself ordained by Rabbi Isaac Elchanan, Rabbi Bernstein, who was born close to Kovno, and many of the founders and friends of RIETS who were of Lithuanian birth decided to create a memorial to the scholar and teacher in the best tradition of the Talmud by endowing a place of study in his name.[21] It was in the hope that Rabbi Isaac Elchanan's spirit would pervade and bless the new institution that the study group of young scholars was formally organized into a school to bear his name.

In 1897 the City of New York condemned a large area of tenement blocks surrounding the foot of Canal Street. This section was then to be developed into a new park area, Seward Park. If RIETS had actually been located at 1 Canal Street, this would have been a major factor accounting for its relocation to the Mariampol Synagogue.[22] The foot of Canal Street where number 1 was located in those days was situated in an overcrowded and rowdy neighborhood.[23] One block in that sector was known as "Kerosene Row," so called because a fire is said to have occurred there at least once every three days. Consequently, no insurance company would grant protection to the dwellers in that block. Another of the smaller streets was known as "Thieves' Alley," because it served as a clandestine meeting center, headquarters, and hiding place for shoplifters, pickpockets and burglars. Another block was called "Goldfeder's Haven," because of an apartment house owned by one Goldfeder, who was notorious for the many dispossession notices he issued to hapless tenants. The street in front of Goldfeder's apartment house was constantly cluttered with the odd sticks of furniture, bric-a-brac, and other possessions of the sorry tenants who could not meet the modest rental requirements.[24] It was from this colorful location at 1 Canal Street that Etz Chaim was forced to move. If RIETS had indeed been quartered with Etz Chaim, then when the latter transferred to 165 Henry Street, between Pike and Market streets, one may assume that RIETS made its move too, possibly with one or two short pauses, to the Mariampol Synagogue.[25]

The Mariampol Synagogue occupied the second and third floors of the building at 44 East Broadway[26] over a clothing store owned by A. Rosenthal. It was a flimsy building, later gutted by a fire that blazed up from an unguarded memorial candle. The space used by the congregation had originally served as the offices and printing establishment of *Die Jüdische Gazetten* and the *Jüdisches Tageblatt* as early as 1884.[27] It was subsequently converted to use as a synagogue, and in these quarters RIETS was formally organized.

Unfortunately, the record does not indicate how long RIETS was located at the Mariampol Synagogue, but it must have been only a brief stay. Following that period, there was a pause at the Congregation Poalei Zedek Anshei Olia at 126 Forsyth Street on the corner of Delancey Street. By June, 1900 the school had moved to Congregation Ohab Sholom, a synagogue favored by *shoḥatim*. This synagogue was located above Maier Freeman's butcher shop on the first floor of a building at 34 Ludlow Street, near the corner of Hester Street.[28]

At the Turn of the Century

RIETS was four years old: there were eighteen students in attendance. The *Jüdische Gazetten* described them thus: "Some are geniuses, all above average and very bright, and their teacher [Rabbi Nahum Dan Baron] was recognized as a giant in the Torah."[29] This high regard for the new Seminary, however, was shared only by the small circle of its immediate friends. The over-all Jewish community had not yet become acquainted with it. Mr. H. Bramson,[30] president of RIETS in 1900, felt it necessary to explain that the absence of popular support was not due to the inferior quality of the school but to the poor cooperation of the Yiddish press. "Unfortunately," he wrote, "very few Jews are acquainted with this institution and very few support it . . . the reason is not lack of interest but that the Yiddish papers give it little attention."[31]

His complaint was well founded. Both Sarasohn papers, *Die Jüdische Gazetten* and the *Jüdisches Tageblatt,* as well as Masliansky's *Die Jüdische Welt,* consistently gave the Jewish Theological Seminary of America front-page and editorial coverage and spoke of it as the stronghold of Torah in America. While granting the weakness of the rabbis ordained by the Seminary in the field of Talmud, the *Tageblatt* pointed out that the Jewish Theological Seminary was becoming a "Pumbedita" of the twentieth century,[32] and might yet produce *geonim* (geniuses).[33] (Pumbedita was the site of a great Talmudic academy, and Gaon was the title given to the head of the Academy.) When the Jewish Theological Seminary was reorganized under the leadership of Dr. Solomon Schechter, the *Tageblatt* proclaimed that "the old Torah has been victorious, pure Jewish teaching has triumphed."[34] As for Schechter, the *Tageblatt* called him a *Gadol* (literally a "giant" or great Talmudic scholar) and hailed him as the *Rosh ha-Yeshiva* (title given to the head of a traditional European rabbinical school) of the Jewish Theological Seminary.[35] The paper looked to him as a leader of traditional Judaism and wrote that "He must captain the army of Judaism and lead it forward. . . . Orthodoxy should certainly welcome a man who is of themselves."[36] In 1904, the Jewish Theological Seminary arranged a mass meeting at the Educational Alliance to encourage support for its program on the East Side. Again the *Tageblatt* expressed its affinity for the Seminary by urging its readers to attend this meeting in order "to become acquainted with this Yeshiva" because now "orthodox rabbis are coming forth from the Jewish Theological Seminary."[37] Rev. Zvi Hirsch Masliansky, the famous people's orator of the day, was featured prominently as one of the speakers at the rally.[38]

RIETS was never favored with such treatment although it certainly deserved the support of the people that it was created to serve. It was indeed strange that Kasriel Sarasohn, who, it was said, was himself an ordained rabbi, a great supporter of the Machzikei

Talmud Torah and a founder, should relegate the news and needs of RIETS to the most insignificant areas of his newspapers. Perhaps the magic names of Joseph Blumenthal, eulogized by the *Gazetten* at his death as "one of Orthodox Judaism's greatest representatives,"[39] Cyrus Adler, Louis Marshall, Jacob Schiff, and Leonard Lewisohn, who were the prime movers behind the Jewish Theological Seminary, cast an irresistible spell over him. The religious attitudes and affiliations of these people alone should have convinced him and Masliansky[40] that they could never father a truly Orthodox institution.

One mitigating word might be said for these publishers. They were aware, as few immigrants were, that the need of the time was for an approach to Judaism which did not deny the place and validity of secular knowledge. RIETS had an ultra right-wing orientation at this time. The course of study was also still unsettled. The editorial page of the *Tageblatt,* in one of its rare references to RIETS, addressed itself to the directors with the plea that they conduct the school "in accordance with the spirit of the place and the time: otherwise, they will create a Pumbedita, in New York."[41] It was quite unfair to chide RIETS for becoming a Pumbedita when the *Tageblatt* itself had used the very same term only a year earlier as a desirable goal in connection with the reorganization of the Jewish Theological Seminary. Nevertheless, it was with some measure of justice that the editorial writer said:

> ... the days have gone when it was a virtue for a rabbi to be alien to all other cultures. We are now living in a time and land which demand that our rabbis should know Torah and "derech eretz" (secular knowledge); perhaps in the words of the Midrash, derech eretz should even precede Torah. . . . It is the duty of the leaders [of RIETS] to bring more enlightenment into this institution and not go against the spirit of the times.[42]

To counter this attitude, Mr. Bramson wrote that rabbis ordained by the Hebrew Union College and by the Jewish Theological Seminary

> ... are not the kind that Judaism is accustomed to. They are not rabbis who are scholars . . . versed in Talmud and Codes. . . . The future of true Judaism in America is in RIETS. From here will

emerge rabbis who will cure us of reform on the one hand, and
unsuitable reverends on the other.[43]

Mr. Bramson's appeal for support was couched in simple logic. He
pointed out that Jews in New York had been creating hospitals,
synagogues, and other kinds of philanthropic institutions. However,
they had neglected the need for the most important factor of Jewish
security in America, the training of Orthodox rabbis. He continued:

> The imported rabbis, are not successful . . . and they certainly
> will not be with our children and grandchildren. The purpose of
> this institution [RIETS] is to rear in America great Jewish scholars
> who will study as did the scholars of the past. And they are to
> utilize as well the knowledge of the native language.[44]

Because of the absence of suitable newspaper publicity and the
school's great financial needs, the founders decided to send forth a
meshulah, a collector or solicitor of funds, "to create interest in the
School, to collect funds, to distribute collection boxes and enroll
members."[45]

RIETS's sojourn at 34 Ludlow Street was of short duration. By May
of 1901 the following year, it was already at the Congregation Sons
of Israel, otherwise known as the Kalvarier Synagogue at 13-15 Pike
Street.[46] The school met in the synagogue's Ladies' Gallery, not a
very imposing location, but probably an improvement over the previously occupied facilities.

The Kalvarier Synagogue enjoyed a fine reputation in the city as a
center of Jewish education. It was generally known as the Pike
Street Synagogue, and was considered the wealthiest Orthodox
Jewish congregation on the East Side. It housed not only RIETS,
but several hundred younger children who had been organized into
a Hebrew School through the efforts of the Orthodox Federation,
and under the leadership of Mr. Albert Lucas, its secretary. The
synagogue was described accordingly:

> Down in Pike Street there is a building with a dingy-looking
> Gothic brownstone front—it would be pretentious to speak of it
> as a facade. It has an entrance on either side, and between are
> stores. The entrance leads to one of the oldest synagogues of the

city, the Kalvarier, and a flight of stairs above the Synagogue leads
to a gallery, the front of which, facing the street, has on the oppo-
site side a line of windows, turning about on pivots, which give a
view of the Synagogue below.

When RIETS came to the Kalvarier Synagogue in 1901, there were
about 20 students in the school, according to one source. According
to an official announcement of RIETS, there were 45. The following year there were more than 50 students according to one source,
and 70 according to another.[47]

Each new student increased the budget of the school and exerted
greater pressure upon the directors to raise the necessary finances.
In a public advertisement, they estimated the expenses of the school
to be about $180 per week.[48] In order to raise this amount, they
followed the course set by Mr. Bramson, who sent out the first
collector on behalf of RIETS in 1900. In the early fall of 1901,
RIETS asked synagogues on the East Side to set aside ten or fifteen
minutes before the Torah reading on the Sabbaths for an appeal for
the yeshiva. They offered the services of Rabbi Avraham Eliezer
Alperstein, a dynamic Yiddish speaker, to address these assem-
blages.[49]

In November, Rabbi Joseph Litwin was engaged to travel into
"the country" for the purpose of raising funds. "The country" included the East, some Northern states as far west as Detroit, and
parts of Canada, including Montreal. During the next month, Rabbi
Duber Shapiro was added to the fund-raising staff. His district included Ohio, Illinois, the Western states and the Southern states.
Both these collectors sent in their proceeds every week.[50]

The technique of a collector upon arriving in a city was to seek
the sponsorship of the local rabbi.[51] This certification would help
in soliciting funds. Sometimes, the rabbi, himself, would introduce
the collector to interested people. On other occasions, the collector
would be introduced to the congregation as a whole during the
Sabbath service. The collector would then deliver a sermon with
the hope that he would create enough of a favorable impression
in the community to stimulate contributions.[52]

The students played their part, too, in soliciting funds by creating favorable interest in RIETS. They accepted warmly all invitations to address synagogues or other groups. Rabbi Moses Minaker is mentioned several times as having delivered brilliant sermons at Mariampol Synagogue,[53] where he was acclaimed for his erudition and scholarship. He was considered a rare person even among European-educated rabbis.[54] Rabbi Moshe Robinson, who also spoke at the Mariampol Synagogue,[55] wrote a fine article on Torah scholarship in the leading Torah monthly of the day.[56] Rabbi Moshe Zizkind is recorded to have addressed a woman's group on the occasion of a *Siyyum ha-Torah,* a ceremony which marks the completion of the actual writing of a Torah Scroll by a scribe and the dedication of the scroll.[57] Rabbi Ezekiel Rabad, another outstanding student, travelled as far west as Denver, Colorado, to speak before the Jewish community, earning a gratifying response and glowing comments about RIETS.[58] During the Sukkot holiday of 1905, Rabbi Nachman Zvi Ebin, also a student, was a guest rabbi in Pittsburgh. The congregation was so impressed with his scholarship and bearing that they pointed out in an advertisement that "whatever congregation will engage him as Rabbi will be fortunate."[59] Similar compliments were heaped upon Rabbi David Rachmillewitz,[60] who spent the holiday with Rabbi Bernard L. Levinthal of Philadelphia.[61] Rabbi Baruch Shapiro impressed the members of the Beth Hamidrash Hagadol at 46 Moore Street in Brooklyn,[62] as did Rabbi Elchanan Zvi (Henry) Guterman, who addressed the Mariampol Synagogue on a Shebu'ot afternoon.[63] In each case, these students reflected glory on RIETS.

Despite the organized effort to improve the income of RIETS, the directors still remained desperate. Only three weeks after Rabbi Shapiro was sent on his Western circuit, another collector was pressed into service. Like Rabbi Alperstein, the new addition, Rabbi Reuven Leibowitz, was to canvass local synagogues and speak to congregations on behalf of RIETS.[64]

In 1901, Moshe Hurewitz succeeded Mr. Bramson as president of RIETS,[65] and Baruch Pinchas Liberman became the new treasurer. Mr. Liberman had long been active in yeshiva affairs, having served as a vice-president of Yeshivat Etz Chaim as early as 1892.[66] Together with David Abramowitz, the secretary, the officers launched an energetic drive to strengthen the financial resources of the school. Of the original founders, Rabbi Yehuda David Bernstein, Rabbi Moses Mayer Matlin, Moses H. Bernstein, Samuel Silberstein, and Mendel Zuckerman remained as directors, in addition to the past president, H. Bramson. New additions were Messrs. Samuel Yitzchak Andron, David Brener, Abba Cohen, Zalman Cohen, Abraham Leib Dubowsky,[67] Eliezer Zev Eppner, Elias Ratkowsky,[68] Samuel Yitzchak Shpransky, Joseph Stern, Jacob Quint,[69] and Rabbi Yechiel Shapiro.[70]

The new directors endorsed the program of the collectors and speakers and continued to urge their friends to contribute to the collection boxes that were circulated through the streets and fixed in various homes.[71] That year the collection boxes produced $3,196.50, almost half of the entire budget and slightly less than the total expenditure required for the maintenance of the students.[72] The engagement of travelling solicitors had also proved profitable. In the period of less than a year that Rabbi Litwin was associated with RIETS, he brought in a net total of $1,140, and in a six-month period, Rabbi Shapiro brought in $286.[73]

At the end of their fiscal year, August 1902, the Auditing Committee—composed of Aaron Leib Dubowsky, Samuel I. Andron, Eliezer Z. Eppner, Treasurer Liberman and Secretary Abramowitz—reported a total expenditure for the year 1901-1902 to the extent of $6,242.01. The intensive efforts to meet this budget, however, proved to be successful, for the total income for the corresponding period had been $6,258.70 leaving a balance of $16.69. Together with the balance of $193.74 at the end of fiscal year 1901, the surplus of the institution in September, 1902, was $210.43.[74]

Expansion and Growth

The school not only required more money, but more space as well. The large student enrollment was very crowded in the Ladies' Gallery of the Kalvarier Synagogue. As the numbers increased, the age differential of the students widened until it was necessary to separate the older from the younger students.[75] (In the summer of 1902 an advertisement in the *Tageblatt* called for a "good Rosh Yeshiva" to teach the "middle class" of RIETS. The teacher was to be "well versed in Talmud and Codes."[76] Only a real need for another teacher would have permitted extending the budget at this difficult time.[77]) The need for expanded physical facilities emphasized the importance of a school building that would be devoted to the sole use of the institution. In addition to actual schoolrooms, office space was demanded, too. When it was announced in 1903[78] that the Kalvarier Synagogue was planning to raze its structure on Pike Street and rebuild it as a modern, beautiful synagogue, the directors of RIETS were confronted with finding another temporary location or, once and for all, acquiring a permanent home for the school.

Agitation for permanent quarters had already begun before the announcement that the Pike Street Synagogue was to be demolished. The movement received further impetus during the incumbency of a distinguished president, Dr. Philip Hillel Klein.[79] Following persecutions in his native Hungary, Dr. Klein came to the United States in 1891 to assume the ministry of the First Hungarian Congregation, Ohab Zedek. Dr. Klein was a lifetime friend and colleague of Chief Rabbi Jacob Joseph, and when the Chief Rabbi died, Dr. Klein was universally recognized as his unchallenged, though unofficial, successor.

The new president brought to RIETS a broader understanding of its function than the directors had hitherto possessed. Dr. Klein was himself the product of a blending of sacred and secular studies. Reared in strict traditionalism in the home of his father, who was a rabbi and the scion of a rabbinic family and having studied at the feet of the great master Dr. Israel Hildesheimer, Dr. Klein was also a master of secular knowledge and culture. He had been trained in Vienna and at the University of Berlin, where he earned his doctorate and served as a member of the faculty for a short time. Deeply involved in all leading Jewish activities of his day, he was esteemed by rabbis and laymen alike. His leadership qualities and modesty were such that he was frequently called "the Moses of Hungary." As

a staunch defender of traditional Judaism, he accepted with alacrity
the opportunity to lead RIETS. A later president of RIETS, eulogiz-
ing Dr. Klein, wrote:

> In him were harmoniously united the rockribbed strength of con-
> viction, the devotion to the point of sacrifice to the cause of the
> Torah and his people, a heart filled to overflowing with love for
> all, the tolerance that comes of the depth of understanding and
> the modesty and moderation of the truly great man . . . a true
> shepherd, a devoted guardian and leader of his people . . . a lover
> and seeker of peace, a lover of the people who brought them
> nearer to the Torah.[80]

This was the man who in August, 1902, was elected president of
RIETS.[81]

With the vigor that characterized his participation in countless
other organizations, Dr. Klein began his administration with a plan
calling for the immediate launching of a building fund to insure the
purchase of new quarters.[82] The step was necessary, for by the end of
that year, there were already between 65 and 70 students[83] supported
by RIETS, and an expense of more than $200 per week.[84] This
represented an anticipated budget of about $10,000 per year, half
again as much as the previous year's expenditures. The meager surplus of $210.43 in September, 1902, was only a hesitant step towards
meeting the additional income required and was even less meaningful in terms of a capital expansion fund. A special directors' meeting
was called on February 10, 1903, to consider the project. Among the
guests was Harry Fischel, a well-known philanthropist and communal worker. It was pointed out that applications of many potential students were received daily, but that action on them was held
up because of lack of space. Messrs. Fischel, Louis Kramer, Baruch
P. Liberman, Yechiel D. Shapiro, Moshe Hurewitz and Samuel
Yitzchak Shpransky were appointed to a special committee to explore new sites and work out a plan for fund raising. In order to
encourage large gifts, Dr. Klein suggested that the first ten major
donors have their names engraved in gold lettering on a plaque in
the new building. It was also announced that an anonymous, pious
woman of the "Ladies' Branch of the Supporters of RIETS" had

made a $1,000 contribution[85] to the fund.[86] Later it was revealed that this woman was Mrs. Yora Leah Manheim.[87]

The building fund drive was launched almost simultaneously with the announcement of plans for razing the Kalvarier Synagogue. It continued well into 1905, even after the new building had been acquired. To help raise money, a men's auxiliary of the institution was founded[88] under the presidency of Aaron Leib Dubowsky, one of the directors of RIETS, and a Ladies' Branch was reactivated[89] under a Mrs. Shil, daughter of Meyer London,[90] the matzo manufacturer. The organizations were known as *Tomchei Yeshivat Rabbi Isaac Elchanan,* the Supporters of RIETS, as differentiated from the parent body, which was called *Chebra Machzikei Yeshivat Rabbi Isaac Elchanan.*[91] Mrs. Manheim's gift was probably made through the Ladies' Branch,[92] although it was officially credited to have come as a result of Liberman's efforts.[93]

The beginning of 1904 marked a feverish period of activity for the ladies' group. Constant appeals were made to interested ladies to join the organization.[94] In January they announced the collection of a total of $1,127, of which $1,000 was Mrs. Manheim's, and the rest came from more than thirty-five other contributors.[95] The Mesdames Abelov, Dolgas, Frank, Mendelsohn, Shapiro, Steinberg, Sternberg and Weinstein served on a committee that sponsored a door-to-door project to raise money for the building fund.[96] The "uptown" Jews, who until now had been unresponsive and unsympathetic, were appealed to and invited to help in the "holy" work.[97] The women also made contributions of expensive sets of the Talmud and other volumes, necessary for the students in their study and reference work.[98]

The men, too, raised money regularly. It was reported that $618.50 was collected from 22 people.[99] No donation was too small to be acceptable as was evidenced by the $1.10 contribution, collected at the circumcision of a son of Moshe Weberman.[100] Harry Fischel gave a $100 gift to the building fund through the efforts of Yechiel D. Shapiro.[101] Baruch P. Liberman contributed $100 in honor of his grandson's *bar mitzvah* and collected $75 more from other members of his family.[102] A $500 gift by the widow Rebecca Epstein, on the occasion of the *Yahrzeit* of her husband, Shimon, was also re-

corded,[103] as was an $80 contribution pledged at a *bar mitzvah* cele-
bration for the son of Zvi Weinstein.[104] A special effort was also
made to enlist the Synagogues in a drawing for a pair of diamond
earrings,[105] and another collector named Mr. Kunkis was temporarily
engaged.[106]

RIETS was not merely a local institution confining its services to
the New York City area alone. On the contrary, the directors felt
that it was serving all of American Jewry by maintaining a center
from which Jewish scholarship would flow to the entire community.
By raising the level of Jewish knowledge in one place, they reasoned,
the level all over the United States would be raised. This contention
was bolstered by the fact that the rabbinical school would directly
affect all parts of the country to which the rabbis would be sent to
follow their calling. Further, the pogroms in Russia were breaking
out with increased violence, and new scholars were arriving every day
to seek shelter from oppression. The directors felt that these men
should not only find a haven at RIETS, but should be accepted and
supported by all of American Jewry as bona fide students to be
trained for the rabbinate. At the end of 1904, they made an open
statement to American Jews emphasizing the urgency of admitting
these young men and reaffirming that "the Yeshiva is not only for
New York City but for all the country—please help."[107]

The collectors had been dispatched on the theory that all Jews
were responsible for the support of RIETS. However, they could
not cover all the territory that was potentially sympathetic to the
school. Rabbi Israel Rosenberg of Bayonne and Rabbi Jacob Gutman
of Jersey City, two well-known rabbis, revealed their devotion to
RIETS during this difficult time. In order to supplement the work
of the regular collectors, they volunteered to leave their congregations and travel to different cities to urge assistance for the new
building.[108] Together they raised $200 in Pittsburgh.[109] In Cincin-
nati, Rabbi Rosenberg, assisted by Bernard Manischewitz and Rabbi
Alexander Lipshitz of that city, raised $180.[110] Even after the new
building was purchased, Rabbi Rosenberg continued to be at the
service of the directors, who were again faced with an empty treas-
ury when the first payment on the mortgage had to be made. So

Rabbi Rosenberg once more set out to visit different communities. In Montreal with the assistance of the local rabbi, Zvi Hirsch Cohen[111] and several laymen, he collected $146, of which $25 was a gift from the Butchers' Association. He also brought in $303 from various unspecified communities.[112] Rabbi Rosenberg, who had been with his congregation for only two years, was so respected by them that even after all his absences he was re-elected for a three-year term at a larger salary.[113]

During this second round of effort on behalf of RIETS, Rabbi Gutman, who had first travelled with Rabbi Rosenberg, was instrumental in receiving a $150 gift from Eliezer and Yenta Oppenheim of Jersey City.[114] The regular collectors, Rabbis Litwin and Shapiro, who also increased their efforts, won a public statement of thanks from the directors.[115] The directors were so impressed with the success of the solicitors that they announced that a plan to enlist more members was to be implemented by engaging another field man.[116]

Another type of effort to raise funds in this period must be mentioned. Early in 1905[117] a series of advertisements carried a joint appeal by RIETS and the Rabbi Jacob Joseph School for old and used clothes, which were to be sold and the proceeds of which were to be shared by the two institutions. The Rabbi Jacob Joseph School was an elementary, all-day school, reorganized in 1902[118] to bear the name of the late Chief Rabbi. A donation office was opened at 70 Pike Street[119] where the old clothes were collected. Authorized collectors with specially identified sacks canvassed the tenement area for contributions, too. Constant warnings appeared in the press cautioning against unauthorized solicitors. A little later, cognizance was taken of the uptown "sympathizers" of the schools, and a branch depot was opened for them at 170 East 105th Street.[120]

While sustained and intensive fund raising was in progress, the Kalvarier Synagogue was torn down. A permanent site had not yet been found for RIETS, and the old quarters at the Kalvarier Synagogue were no longer available. For the interim period RIETS was transferred in early 1903 to temporary quarters at the Yagustava Synagogue,[121] 32 Rutgers Street, near the corner of Madison Street. Its rabbi,[122] Rabbi Avraham Eliezer Alperstein, an occasional lecturer at RIETS[123] as well as one of its newly elected directors,[124] probably assisted in the arrangements which culminated in the transfer of the school.

In January, 1904, after a year at the Yagustava Synagogue and almost seven years to the day after the first public pronouncement of RIETS was made, the purchase of a building was announced.[125] The building, which was located at 156 Henry Street,[126] a short distance east of the location of Yeshivat Etz Chaim, cost $28,500. There are no records showing how much was raised toward the building fund from its inception to its acquisition. It appears probable that the directors did not even have sufficient funds for a down-payment. Since the title had to be taken within a month,[127] no sooner were the plans for the purchase revealed than an impassioned appeal ". . . to come in masses and make your contribution" was issued.[128] The final details of the closing and the agonizing search for the necessary funds have not been recorded, but it is known that title was taken to the new premises subject to two mortgages totaling $17,000. The $11,500 that was paid in cash must have drained the last available monies from the building fund. Later in the summer of that year, formal occupancy of the building was taken.[129]

"Best Yeshiva in the Land"

While the directors were involved in fund raising and the other activities attendant on moving into the new building, RIETS received support from a most influential and articulate source, the Agudat ha-Rabbanim, the Union of Orthodox Rabbis of the United States and Canada. Formed in 1902 in order to deal with the vital religious problems of the immigrant community, the organization was composed of respected and leading Orthodox rabbis who represented the traditional rabbinic authority in the New World. Through their congregations, the rabbis also spoke for many hundreds of thousands of Jews in the United States. Until the organization of the Agudat ha-Rabbanim, RIETS had enjoyed no commendation or support from any public source. The newspapers were still cold and unfriendly, and the school remained a semiprivate institution, valiantly maintained by the faith of a few. It was, therefore, a momentous occasion when shortly after its organization, the Agudat ha-Rabbanim publicly announced its endorsement of the program of RIETS.[130] At last, there was a recognition that had been wanting from the very beginnings of the seminary.

At their Philadelphia convention in 1903, the Agudat ha-Rabbanim adopted a motion by Rabbi Yehuda David Bernstein, a member of its Yeshiva Committee,[131] to the effect that RIETS should be recognized as the only yeshiva of higher learning in the United States.[132] It implemented this motion with the recommendation that all the members of the Agudat ha-Rabbanim should help raise funds for the school[133] and help the collectors who came to their cities.[134] At its Springfield conference of 1905, the exclusive recognition of RIETS as "the best [yeshiva] in the land" was again reiterated.[135]

The final recommendation of the Philadelphia convention in reference to RIETS reflected its understanding of the immediate needs of the institution. The convention urged the acquisition of a new building as soon as possible in order to accommodate the many students and the waiting list of applicants.[136] The call coincided with the urging of Dr. Philip Hillel Klein and added the full weight of the organized American Orthodox Jewish religious leadership to the drive.[137] Later, the Agudat ha-Rabbanim dramatized its support of RIETS by adopting a resolution not to recognize the Jewish Theological Seminary as an Orthodox institution, its many claims to the contrary notwithstanding.[138] Rabbi Bernard L. Levinthal of Philadelphia, who was associated with RIETS as a member of its ordination board until his death in 1952, was instrumental in causing this proclamation to be issued.[139] In 1907, the Agudat ha-Rabbanim further implemented its exclusive support of RIETS by calling upon the Yiddish newspapers to refrain from referring to graduates of the Jewish Theological Seminary by the title "Rav" (Orthodox rabbi). They urged the press to call them "Reverend or Doctor or even Professor, in order that the public should know the difference between a 'rav' and a rabbi."[140] They further stated "that such [rabbis] are not authorized to render decisions in questions of Jewish law, officiate at divorce proceedings, etc."[141]

The recognition of RIETS encouraged the directors to hope that at last the school was to receive the whole-hearted support of an organized and respected body needed to establish the institution on a firm footing. Indeed, it proved a most influential aid to the building drive and later development. Now the directors who had built the school with great patience and devotion from a difficult beginning, could look to the future with sanguine expectation.[142]

Following the occupancy of the new building in the late summer of 1904,[143] an official dedication was held on Sunday evening, November 6, 1904, and on Monday, Tuesday, and Wednesday evenings of that week.[144] Large crowds of well-wishers filled the rooms and heard inspiring speeches by prominent guests and students of the school.[145]

The excitement of those days moved the directors to issue a public message, saying, in part:

Approximately 3,000 years ago all of Israel rejoiced that they were privileged to bring the Torah into the Temple instead of carrying it from temporary shelter to temporary shelter, from Tabernacle to Tabernacle.

How great is our pride now, that we in America are privileged to bring our Yeshiva and its 100 great scholars into our own dwelling at 156 Henry Street. For until now, we were guests at one Synagogue or another.

Every Jewish heart must be entranced by the sound of the ancient melody of the Holy Talmud, like the melodies of the old Yeshivas in Europe, that is heard when passing the Yeshiva."[146]

Unfortunately, the public pride that resulted from this new sanctuary of Torah and the endorsement of the Agudat ha-Rabbanim did not bear a corresponding salutary effect on the school's income. Since the budget had risen to about $50 a day in addition to the cost of maintenance of the new building,[147] it was necessary to send another collector into the cities outside of New York. Rabbi Yehuda David Bernstein, who was one of the founders of RIETS, a director through the years, representative to the Agudat ha-Rabbanim, and now a vice-president of RIETS, undertook this responsibility.[148] He journeyed through New York, Connecticut, Pennsylvania, and Massachusetts. [149] The new building also brought on hitherto unexperienced mortgage trouble. The mortgage was to be the source of an oft-repeated lament in the years to come. In 1905, for the first time, the directors employed what was to become the grim chorus of RIETS' cry: "The time is approaching when we have to make our mortgage payment and we have no money."[150] Two years later the Agudat ha-Rabbanim was forced to make a desperate call for aid:

> We must openly state that those who offered their time and money for the Yeshiva are already tired of carrying the heavy load on their weak backs. There is a debt of over $7,000 due on the house and the creditors demand their money. It has reached a point where the building may be sold at auction. In addition, there is the cost of maintaining the students. . . . Unless support will be forthcoming, the directors will be forced to give up their noble work and the Yeshiva will be closed.[151]

Although the financial problems of RIETS were a major cause of concern for decades to come, the occupancy of the new house brought a sense of great fulfillment to the dedicated directors and friends of RIETS[152] and marked the rooting and establishment of the Yeshiva on a solid foundation.

Thus, in 1907, after eight years of existence and after an equal number of stops at various synagogue buildings, RIETS was re-established as a neighbor to Yeshivat Etz Chaim, the school whose hospitality and roof it shared at the time of its origin. RIETS was to remain at this location until 1915 when its ties with Yeshivat Etz Chaim were to be even more strongly cemented, not only by geographical proximity, but by actual union and merger.

CHAPTER 5. RIETS' FIRST DECADE OF SERVICE: 1897–1907

The new home of the Rabbi Isaac Elchanan Theological Seminary at 156 Henry Street was not a prepossessing one. It was hardly different in appearance or structure from the two-story brownstone houses that flanked it on either side. Like the other buildings, it had a narrow staircase leading to the basement and an entrance hall leading to the main floor and the floors above. Henry Street was at this time a quiet and aristocratic thoroughfare through which the busy excitement of the lower East Side occasionally erupted. The rear of the building, however, opened up on a panorama of drab backyards, myriad clotheslines, and tired-looking articles of apparel hung out to dry. The ordinary appearance of the front of the building was distinguished only by a faded sign bearing Hebrew characters that read: "*Yeshivat Rabbeinu Yitzchak Elchanan*" and an inscription in English saying, "Jewish Seminary."[1]

A contemporary, describing the new location of RIETS in a dispatch to a European publication, observed that the building was not initially designed for use as a school and came to the obvious and facetious conclusion that from the appearance of the building, RIETS "was apparently not supported by millionaires."[2] Unimposing as the house was, it nevertheless was the first home owned by RIETS and was to be its headquarters for about ten years.

Growth of the Student Body

The history of the early wanderings of RIETS brings to light the rate of growth of its student body. It is this growth and the consequent requirement for expanded facilities that probably was a major factor in the need for the school to move from one location to another.

The number of students at RIETS in 1897 was variously placed at "several lads,"[3] 10,[4] and 20.[5] In 1900, there were eighteen students.[6] At the Kalvarier Synagogue in 1901, there were from 20 to 45 students,[7] among them Aaron Abramowitz, Benjamin Friedman, Eli Friedman, Harry Handler, Sampson Lederhendler, Ephraim Lisitzky, Akiva Matlin (son of Rabbi Moses Matlin), Dov Ber Minoker,[8] Moshe Robinson,[9] Hillel Rogoff, Joseph Naphtali Rosenberg, a student named Ruchlin, Leib Solovay, and Moshe Ziskind.[10]

At the Yagustava Synagogue in 1903, the number increased to about 65 or 70 students.[11] Among them were Rabbi Benjamin Fleisher, Rabbi Henry Guterman, and Saul Schenker. By 1905, when RIETS was finally located at 156 Henry Street, there were at least 35-40 students in an upper grade and about 60 in two lower classes, totaling about 100 students.[12] In 1906, there were 63 students in the upper division and a similar number of younger students.[13] In the following years, the school was developed to include a total of four classes[14] and approximately 125 students in 1908.[15]

The relationship between the age groups was an interesting one. For a long time, the younger students were not completely recognized as an integral part of RIETS. They met on a different floor and probably were more "Americanized." The older students rightly considered themselves mature and pioneers in a new venture. They looked upon the knicker-clad youngsters as appendages to the school. Indeed, the differences in age, in background and even in origin, created an almost natural division between the groups.

The expansion of the school into several classes was the first sign of the readiness to serve the Jewish community on more than one level. Until RIETS arrived in its own building at 156 Henry Street, the entire school was composed of one class.[16] This arrangement was undoubtedly due to the limitation of space and inadequate facilities of the previous locations. The dearth of financial resources to permit expansion as well as the type and ages of the students were additional determinants of the division of classes.

In the first years of its existence the students were East European immigrants between the ages of eighteen and thirty.[17] Theirs was a sad lot in the New World. Many of them were entirely alone, without the comfort of relatives or friends. Even those who had relatives in the United States shared with their fellow students the constraints of poverty, the lack of a trade and the difficulties of adjustment. Some had already been ordained as rabbis or certified as *shohatim* in Europe, while others had been on the threshold of meeting such qualifications. All had had intensive Talmudic training in the countries of their origin and were scholars by temperament and inclination. The majority were of superior intellectual qualities and were later to make a mark on the American community despite their language handicaps. Of the dozen or so students that were known to have been in attendance at RIETS in 1901, Eli Friedman, Benjamin Friedman, Moshe Robinson, and Leib Solovay became physicians; Akiva Matlin attended the Medical School at the University of Tennessee but never completed his training;[18] Ephraim Lisitzky became one of the best known and beloved teachers and men of Hebrew letters in the United States; and Sampson Lederhendler became a successful journalist and contributor to the English press.[19] Of the others, Aaron Abramowitz and Harry Handler became Hebrew teachers, and Joseph Naphtali Rosenberg[20] continued in the rabbinate. This incidence of achievement was undoubtedly equalled by other students whose subsequent records are not known to us.

The scholars who found their way to RIETS faced the problem of choosing a path in this uncharted land which they now inhabited. They needed a tranquil spot which would be a stepping stone as well as a resting place and that would serve as a bridge between their European yeshiva experience and the American environment. They were pressured by the need for decision. Should they turn to the sweatshops and be swallowed up in the anonymity of the toilers whose value was measured not by the intensity of their souls or the creativity of their minds, but by the extent to which they would allow their bodies and hopes to be enslaved by machines? In the highly expressive colloquialism of the sweatshop, the employee was known not as a man, not as an artisan, not as a craftsman—not even as a laborer—but as a "hand." And what was to happen to the hearts of the young students and the love for scholarship they possessed?

If they were indeed destined to enter the market place, the halls of science, or any occupation other than the rabbinate, they had the right to hope that the choice would at least be made after a pause for consideration and evaluation. This bridge they found in RIETS. The hospitality of the school offered them the opportunity to choose without the exigency of an immediate, perhaps costly, decision. Those who wanted to continue their studies were able to do so in an environment of Torah and scholarship similar to that of its European counterpart. Those who later decided to find a different calling were able to make a slow, and safe adjustment.

Most of this group, destitute when admitted to the school, found a further incentive to attend RIETS. Admission not only relieved them of finding a place in which to become rooted, but also of the financial pressures of food, shelter and clothes. Fully realizing their elementary problem of subsistence, the directors offered from the outset free tuition and food to all students.[21] They soon added a stipend of from $1.50 to $3.50 per week—not a munificent scholarship, but enough to provide the barest necessities. A student who received a $2.75 weekly grant recalls his budgetary arrangement in 1901: "We paid $.75 weekly for lodging and $.25 daily for food. The remaining $.25 was for all the other needs of the week, mostly for medicine to supplement the lack of proper nourishment."[22] Later, students were receiving as much as $4 per week.

The scholarship, a great boon to the students, may have equalled the weekly salaries of unskilled and some sweatshop workers, and certainly was not much less than what they might have earned in such capacities had they left RIETS.[23] The granting of stipends, however, was a mixed blessing and carried responsibilities as well. The directors were sincere in making the grants, but they felt that the subsidized students were totally obligated to the school and should spend all of their time at the school in study. This created a severe limitation on students who were spending some of their time and some of their meager allotment, as well, at the preparatory schools that flourished on the East Side. In time, the attitude of the directors touched off an explosive critical incident in the history of RIETS.

Since the school's decision to be devoted only to higher education eliminated the inclusion of native students, immigrants formed the entire student body of the early days of RIETS. Young men emerging from the teens who had been brought up in the United States lost the opportunity to rise to the scholarly achievements of their contemporaries who were arriving daily from Europe, and only because they lacked a proper religious education. But as RIETS passed its first years of existence, its impact was felt. The New York community and many other areas were very impressed by the student representatives from RIETS whom they met.[24] The school had grown to include students from several parts of the country. At least one case is recorded of a student who was accepted from as far away as Rochester.[25] Furthermore, younger students from the ages of thirteen and fourteen, who were arriving from Europe, began to apply for admission. Boys reared in America and in some cases native-born were also seeking admission. These were graduates of the elementary school Yeshivat Etz Chaim, which was well ordered with graduated classes and a good organization. Because of the enlarged facilities at 156 Henry Street that permitted the absorption of this new age group, by 1905 the younger groups became part of RIETS. One source tells us that by 1908 most of the students at RIETS were native Americans.[26] The larger number of the native-born must have been among these younger students.

Budgetary Juggling and the "Penny Collectors"

The financing of RIETS always meant budgetary juggling. Indeed it had to be, in order to maintain the justifiable boast that "there is no equal to this institution in thrift of expenses."[27] Almost all personnel connected with RIETS worked for little or no salary including the teaching and maintenance staffs and the collectors of funds.[28] The officers were concerned only with the students' welfare. David Abramowitz, one of the founders of RIETS, was the secretary of the organization from its inception and received a weekly salary of $5.[29] The term "secretary" was as elastic in its application to Mr. Abramowitz as the finances had to be for RIETS. He was more than just a secretary. In effect, he served the institution as executive director, manager, controller, bookkeeper, registrar, dean of men, liaison to the ladies' group, as well as in many other capacities.

At 156 Henry Street, Mr. Abramowitz occupied an office in the basement of the building, which he shared with the caretaker. When a student applied for admission to the school, he was first interviewed by Mr. Abramowitz, who noted his vital statistics. The student was then turned over to a teacher for assignment to a class. Mr. Abramowitz, as the fountainhead of all subsidies, would decide on the student's stipend. Then, on specific days of the week, this tall imposing figure, with a big black beard would pass among the students and dole out their allotted pittance, which was sometimes all in pennies.

Mr. Abramowitz was over-all director of the fund raising, but the collection-box project was directly under the supervision of a Mr. Singer, who would send out twenty to thirty collectors at a time to canvass different areas of the city. Their duty was to install boxes in different homes and public meeting places like synagogues and to move through the streets soliciting direct contributions. At regular intervals the proceeds were brought to the office of Mr. Abramowitz, where, under his and Singer's watchful eyes, the pennies—they were mostly pennies—were counted into two piles. One pile went to the collectors as salary, the other pile remained for RIETS. It is estimated that more than $100 was netted weekly, which represented a large part, if not the largest, of RIETS' regular income.[30]

The first known teacher of English subjects at RIETS, Dr. David Harry Barash, recalls an interesting occurrence in the office of Mr. Abramowitz. Dr. Barash, while still a youngster, was engaged to teach in July, 1904 at a salary of $6 per week. During the six weeks he taught, he received no salary. He was told that this was an oversight, probably because the study of English was not considered too important and, more likely, because there was no money available for salaries. Young Barash needed his salary, and when he confronted Mr. Abramowitz in his office with this request, a collector had just brought in his box. The secretary opened the box, spilled the pennies in a mound on the table, and said, "Here is a collection box full of pennies. Take as much as there is."

The penny collection was not the most dignified fund-raising method. The students were embarrassed to know that pennies were collected in the streets of the East Side for their support. Frequently, they themselves were accosted and entreated to contribute towards the needs of the "poor yeshiva students." When RIETS was at its East Broadway location in the 1920's, the penny-box collectors would still buttonhole students lunching at Nimitz's Restaurant. One wag, it is reported, would advise the students to "give liberally because you will get it back on Friday anyway."[31]

Mr. Singer, who was also supported through these collections, often bemoaned the destiny which brought him to such a fate. He had seven daughters, who indirectly were similarly dependent on this form of revenue. As the collection boxes were opened and emptied, Singer would aways make some unhappy reference to his having been "blessed," like Jethro, with seven daughters, who had to be provided for and married off. On a particularly poor collection day he would always end with the statement, "I came to this country in the same year as Jacob Schiff and look what God gave him—and look what He gave me, seven daughters and a pile of pennies."[32]

Although the collection system was undignified, it did demonstrate that the simple working Jew of the East Side accepted the Yeshiva with all his heart and was willing to support a charity box placed in his home. When an occasional larger contribution was made, it was recorded on a bronze tablet affixed to the walls of the Henry Street building. Among these were a $1,000 gift from Jacob Schiff and a $500 gift from Mr. and Mrs. Joseph Spectorsky.[33]

System of Instruction

The history of the early days of RIETS requires some description of the actual system of instruction in the school. As has been pointed out, the older students probably represented the only class until the school was quartered in Henry Street. Having received intensive rabbinic training in Europe, they were too far advanced for any schoolroom activity; they were, in fact, such superb students, representing the cream of the immigrant intellectuals, that it was "difficult to find their equal in all the diaspora."[34] Their's was not only an intellectual pursuit, but also a discipline in preparation for the rabbinic career, a way of life and a labor of love. In an informal manner the students of the first class sat at tables or stood at lecterns for hours in complete absorption, divorced from the world around them, intensely concerned with unfolding and understanding the intricacies of the Talmudic Law.

While the class had no specific instructor, there were several rabbis who in turn served as *Rosh Yeshiva,* or headmaster. The function of the Rosh Yeshiva was to deliver regular lectures in Halakhah and to synthesize and delineate the passages on Jewish Law appearing in the various sections of the Talmud. The first Rosh Yeshiva was Rabbi Avraham Eliezer Alperstein,[35] who at that time was the spiritual leader of the Christie Street Synagogue. He was a *Gadol,* a penetrating scholar and a former rabbi in the city of Vilna.[36] He was succeeded by Rabbi Yerachmiel Isserson, who was rabbi of the Congregation Kol Yisroel Anshei Polen on Forsyth Street.[37] Later Rabbi Solomon N. Kotler, who had been brought to New York by Rabbi Jacob Joseph as a *dayyan,* served as Rosh Yeshiva.[38] There were also visits from rabbis who delivered lectures on a nonscheduled basis. Among them were Rabbi Moses Mayer Matlin, one of the founders of RIETS,[39] Rabbi Israel Kaplan[40] and Rabbi Chaim Yaakov Vidrevitz, known as the "Muscover Rav" (Moscow Rabbi).[41]

There was only one[42] rabbi who was employed by RIETS on a permanent basis, and his position was that of *mashgiah,* or classroom supervisor.[43] Rabbi Baron came to RIETS in 1898,[44] soon after it was founded. His function was to be available to answer difficult questions the students might raise in connection with their studies and to consult with them on all other pressing matters. But Rabbi Baron was more than a "supervisor." He was a friend as well as a teacher who created the spirit and atmosphere of scholarship that the school required. He inspired the students with a love for Torah, and they almost venerated him as disciples do a master.

Reb Nahum Dan, as he was affectionately called, was typical of many of the immigrants of his time. He came to the United States from Slutsk, Lithuania without his family, either because he hoped to establish himself firmly before bringing them or because he was contemplating only a temporary stay. In either case, Reb Nahum Dan, like many others of his stature, was in a strange land with only a sister who lived on Norfolk Street and with whom he boarded. His personal dislocation must have sharpened his sympathy, perhaps even his paternal instincts toward the struggling young men who, like himself, were seeking to adjust to the United States. Reb Nahum Dan was not a handsome person. He was short, shrunken, bent, pale and ascetic, with a stringy, blondish red beard. He looked far older than his forty-five or so years and his emaciated body was racked by a painful tubercular cough, but as one of his students described him: "His internal beauty outshone his externality. He was a lover of Torah, a profound scholar, and his students were as dear to him as the apple of his eye. He attracted the students with his love, but did not dominate them."[45] He was altogether a rare and wonderful spirit, who followed each young man with sharp, wise eyes. He made sure that his students had enough food to eat, became settled as soon as possible, made a good match and generally began to feel at home in their new environment. Rabbi Dan used to arrange for them to receive clothes and shoes for the holidays too. He furnished them with cards which were redeemable at Moshe Hurewitz's shoe store at 15 Hester Street and at Yechezkael Schlang's clothing store on East Broadway. During the time the school was at the Mariampol Synagogue, he also arranged for many of them to be fed by the sexton of the synagogue.

Unlike the directors of RIETS, Reb Nahum Dan was possessed by an overwhelming ambition to make RIETS a world-renowned academy of Jewish learning. He felt that if RIETS was to become a center of influencee in American life, it had to clothe its rabbinical curriculum in contemporary attire by giving status to secular studies. The heavy pressure for secular education had been felt in the school as early as 1900, but because of the directors' firm resistance to the idea, no action had been taken.

In total sympathy with the students' demand for secular studies, Reb Nahum Dan boldly defied the directors by granting one student permission to attend high school and then college. The student, Hillel Rogoff,[46] was the outstanding pupil of the day with a love for all forms of study. He viewed secular knowledge as a necessary complement to his Jewish learning. Unfortunately for Reb Nahum Dan, Rogoff soon found greater attraction in his secular studies and slowly drifted from his Orthodox convictions. In the East Side he became known as a "Socialist," which for the Orthodox Jew was synonymous with all evil. Gradually emerging as a significant force in the labor movement, Rogoff was later to become editor of the influential *Jewish Daily Forward*.

Reb Nahum Dan was never to live down his great "mistake." In later years, when the students were to press again for secular training, the directors had a ready-made response: "Look what happened to Rogoff." His intervention on behalf of Rogoff, as well as his daily generosity of spirit, made Reb Nahum Dan a nearly legendary figure to a decade of students at RIETS. The Agudat ha-Rabbanim, too, which was conservative in its praise, honored him by adopting a Convention resolution commending his ten years of "tireless service" to RIETS and his "devotion" to the students.[47] Rabbi Nahum Dan left RIETS in 1908[48] and returned to his native Slutsk, only to die of tuberculosis shortly thereafter.

The first organized classes on a level lower than the older group began at the Henry Street building. There is speculation that Rabbi Nahum Dan may have taught at least one lower class as early as 1901.[49] By 1906, there were two junior classes of twenty-five to thirty students each. They met on the first floor and accommodated students from the ages of thirteen or fourteen to eighteen. The more advanced of the classes was taught by Rabbi Israel Moshe Shapiro of the Olia Synagogue.[50] The lower class was taught by Rabbi Moshe Sobol of Congregation Tifereth Jerusalem.[51] When Rabbi Shapiro fell ill in 1907,[52] his place was taken by Rabbi David Rackman,[53] a RIETS student who had already been ordained in Europe. Rabbi Rackman, who remained until 1909, was succeeded by Rabbi Davidson, another of the ordained students of RIETS. Rabbi Benjamin

Aronowitz, who was to remain with RIETS until his death in 1945, then joined the faculty as Rabbi Davidson's successor.[54]

These classes followed a more formal course of study of Talmud and Commentaries than the senior class. They studied with great intensity the tractates of the Babylonian Talmud usually assigned to formal classroom work: *Baba Kama, Baba Metzia, Baba Batra, Gittin, Kidushin* and *Ketubot,* with at least the basic Commentaries of *Rashi* and *Tosafot.* The lectures and study period for the Hebrew studies lasted until 7:00 P.M., and there were occasional visits and tests by Rabbi Moses Sebulun Margolies of Congregation Kehillath Jeshurun, Rabbi Israel Rosenberg of Bayonne, New Jersey, and other dignitaries. Some afternoon hours were supposed to be devoted to secular studies, but because this program was not implemented, many students turned to other sources in order to satisfy their intellectual curiosity about their new culture.

Question of Secular Studies

The question of secular studies, as has been indicated, was one of the major issues in the evolution of the yeshiva. Indeed, it was one of the major cultural concerns of the entire immigrant community. In 1905 the percentage of Jewish young men in the high schools and in the City College was so large that the latter was "humorously named Jews' College."[55] The *Tageblatt* reported that in 1906, 90 per cent of the graduates of the City College were Jews[56] and that in 1908 three-quarters of the enrollment was Jewish.[57] The Executive Committee of B'nai B'rith, at the time composed almost entirely of German or native-born Jews, was told by its president that "It was indeed inspiring to see how the children of the immigrants, while they work, eat and sleep on the lower East Side, march every morning to what is called the uptown section of the city, to drink there from the fountain of knowledge, and, in the evening carry to what is called in the Ghetto, American ideas and ideals."[58]

Unable to attend the high schools or colleges because of their studies, the students at RIETS, who wanted to enrich their cultural background, slipped away for clandestine visits to the preparatory schools. Unlike the "prep" schools of today, the East Side preparatory schools of the early 1900's were the secular counterpart of the *ḥedarim*. They often consisted of one or two teachers, frequently just graduated from the immigrant class, who taught the rudiments of mathematics, reading, history and grammar. The schools and their instructors were unlicensed and followed only a sketchy syllabus. Yet the needs of the immigrant community were so great that the schools did a flourishing business in the late afternoon and evening when workers were released from their day labors. They catered to those who were too reticent to attend the large classes of the public night schools and to those who thought they could make quicker progress with private instruction received from teachers of their own kind. Many students who were able to get enough out of these schools to pass the State Regents' examinations could qualify for admission to City College or New York University.

The students of RIETS who were chided for attending the preparatory schools were indirectly driven there by an unfulfilled promise of the administration. The original announcement of the formation of RIETS carried the statement that a teacher was to be provided who could give instruction in the "language of the land." Despite frequent newspaper accounts about the number of English teachers on the staff, this pledge was never quite fulfilled.[59] Although the students' demand for English instruction was made on reasonable grounds, the directors felt that they were taking advantage of the school. The directors were firmly committed to a policy of "Torah for its own sake" without the dilution of secular subjects. They considered the ability to speak passable English a praiseworthy achievement and sufficient enough to convert a European rabbi into an adequate and satisfactory American rabbi. This divergence of opinion between students and administration was a serious one which caused the students' confidence in the directors gradually to erode and finally to disappear.

In July, 1904 when student demands for English reached a high point of pressure, one of the directors asked David Harry Barash, a sixteen-year-old high school student, to teach English at the

Yeshiva. Barash was considered a "good boy" because he came of a pious family and was himself a Sabbath observer. His father was a tobacconist whose shop on Henry Street was patronized by rabbis and laymen connected with RIETS. Another young man, a Mr. Jaffe, was asked to be his associate. Together they were entrusted with the duty of instructing the students in English and the secular subjects. The mandate to the teachers was broad and unspecified. Since there were no suggestions as to curriculum, methods, or administration of the new department, the teachers, both younger than many of their students, proceeded to organize their own curriculum. Realizing that their students were too old to start reading English with the usual "cat," "dog," "house" reading primer, Barash bought Montgomery's *Elementary History,* which was used in the early elementary school grades of the public school system. Written in story form, *Elementary History* served both as a reader and as a history text. Another public school grammar text by Reed and Kellogg was also used. It followed the usual textbook methods of teaching grammar by diagramming, parsing and the other techniques of the day. A text in arithmetic which began with a study of fractions was also used.

Young Barash's students, many newly arrived in the country, were bright and receptive even though they had never attended secular school before. Their English was a polyglot of accents influenced by their different national origins. Yet they struggled through the intricacies of grammar and the complexities of fractions with great devotion and with apparent consecration. Their interest in the secular studies was compelling. Many of them even came on Friday afternoons, when no formal courses were being offered, to study with the teachers, who were happy to give them additional instruction. The daily hours of English instruction were from 3:00 to 5:00 P.M., after which the boys recited their afternoon prayers and continued their religious (Hebrew) studies into the night. The age groups of the classes were varied with students attending the classes voluntarily. Some students of the Hebrew classes attended the English classes. Others did not. The only compulsion was the attraction of the subject matter. There were about eighteen students in each of the two

English classes, but the facts are not clear, and there may have been more. Harry Barash's students were most likely recruited from the younger grades. The older students did not consider this form of elementary education as suitable for them or as serving their needs.

If indeed this was the first formal instruction in English which was given at RIETS, then an auspicious beginning had been made. About six weeks after the first classes had begun, one of the directors suggested that since the High Holy Days were near, English instruction should be temporarily suspended until the first of October. The suggestion was accepted by the directors, and unfortunately, the English curriculum was never reinstated following the High Holy Days of 1904. Neither Mr. Barash nor Mr. Jaffe was reemployed, and English teaching was not resumed for some time.[60] In short, the history of Mr. Barash's and Mr. Jaffe's short tenure is indicative of the directors' attitude towards English in those days.[61]

Such fragmentary and elementary English instruction could obviously not satisfy the needs of a rabbinical student who would have to teach and preach to an American generation bewildered by changing cultural patterns and lacking direction. The directors' insistent desire that students receiving stipends should spend full time at the school created a feeling of discontent among many. They considered the directors unyielding and perhaps without vision, and for this reason many of the students left the school. Some, as we have seen, slipped off surreptitiously to study at preparatory schools or to receive private tutoring while still others studied English from translations of the Bible or studied secular books without guidance. Some became so proficient that they took the State Regents' examinations without formal education and after passing the examinations, entered the College of the City of New York and other colleges.

The students' dissatisfaction and the obduracy of the directors brought about continuous agitation in the school and highlighted the confusion of aims in the curriculum. From the turn of the century, there had been several controversies between students and directors on this subject, but the students were given no satisfaction. The resulting crisis can be defined in simple terms. Most of the directors, with the exception of several rabbis, were ordinary businessmen fired with a zeal for learning. They knew nothing of pedagogy, of the techniques of education, or even of the professional requirements of the modern rabbi. They had little need themselves for the services of rabbis as moral guides or religious teachers, and they had no idea to what extent or in what capacity the new generation would find use for rabbis. Their prime motive in supporting RIETS was to create a center for the study of Torah, like the ones that they knew in Europe, whether it led students to the rabbinate or not. The application of Torah as a basis for a rabbinical career was for the directors purely incidental, at best secondary. RIETS was to be a rabbinical school only in an ancillary capacity. As a result, the questions that rose specifically from the students' school experience dealing with the professional rabbinate were given little weight by the directors. At one time they even circulated a notice which strictly prohibited students from attending preparatory schools or receiving secular instruction.[62]

In this respect, they followed the historic pattern of the European yeshivot after which the beginnings of RIETS were modeled. The European yeshivot did not consider themselves professional schools, but rather academies for the pursuit of pure study. They did not ordain any student, for ordination was the professional climax of an academic career. If and when a student had spent a sufficient number of years in study and had perfected himself in the Talmud, Codes and Commentaries and then wanted to accept a call to the pulpit of a congregation, he would travel to the home of a prominent rabbi for examination. There he might present recommendations from the head of the yeshiva or from his teachers and possibly other credentials. Following his acceptance as a worthy candidate, the examiner would expose him to a long intensive oral examination that ranged over the wide field of Talmudic scholarship. Upon passing this exhaustive test, which lasted for days and sometimes weeks, the candidate then received *semicha,* ordination, at the hands of this rabbi, an event completely unrelated to the yeshiva which he attended.

This was the policy that RIETS adopted too. Recognizing no terminal point to the study of Torah and Talmud, the school offered no final examinations in the ordinary sense. However, in order to make provisions for ordination when the need arose, as in the case of a student called to assume the pulpit of a synagogue, RIETS entered into an agreement with the Agudat ha-Rabbanim whereby the latter was to become its ordaining body. By the terms of this arrangement reached in 1904, the Agudat ha-Rabbanim agreed to create a Semicha Board to examine qualified students of RIETS, subject to the standards and requirements of the rabbinical group.[63] Since so many of the early students at RIETS already possessed European ordination, it was not until the Sukkot Holidays of 1906 that the first Semicha Board was actually established. It was composed of three outstanding scholars of the day, Rabbis Philip Hillel Klein, Moses Sebulun Margolies and Samuel Z. Wien. Rabbi Bernard Levinthal was added to represent the Agudat ha-Rabbanim.[64] The members of the new board were known as reservoirs of Torah and Jewish Law. They had studied, served their apprenticeship and practiced in Europe, and had enviable reputations in the United States. Had they sat together as an examining committee, they would have been one of the most erudite, most august bodies in America. But even in the examination they clung to the European pattern. Candidates were tested separately by each of the examiners and received individual *semichas* from each of the members of the board, which certified to the worth and reliability of the candidate as a rabbi. Each *semicha* which was issued on the personal letterhead of the examiner, made no reference to the other examiners and was purely a private expression of ordination. Because the board had three members, each candidate found himself with three *semichas* at the end of his grueling examination period. The *semichas* bore an official reference to RIETS but expressed no formal opinion of its board or faculty about the candidate.

A fortnight or so after the Board was brought into being, the first students of RIETS, and perhaps the first young men to be ordained on American soil in full keeping with Orthodox tradition, were passed by the examiners.[65] They were Henry Guterman, Samuel Miller and a third unnamed student.[66] The first formal traditional ordination in the United States received almost no comment in the

press, but was commemorated by RIETS with an impressive celebration at the spacious new Kalvarier Synagogue a month after the
tests were given during Hanukkah of 1906.[67]

The responsibility towards ordination at RIETS was, therefore,
less than what a true professional school should have assumed. In
the many years of the school's early existence, little more was done
than "to assist in educating and preparing students . . . for the Hebrew
Orthodox Ministry as indicated in the Certificate of Incorporation. The promise that the "language of the land" and collateral
subjects would be taught, as found in the first announcement of
RIETS, did not become an actual fact until 1915 when a High
School Department was formed. Thus, the two major promises that
validated the establishment of the school were still unfulfilled a
decade after its organization.

Student Restiveness

The students showed greater perspicacity than the directors in their
evaluation of American life and the part that they might play in it.
They realized that they were witnessing and participating in an
unusual period of social adjustment and in a dramatic struggle for
cultural and religious self-preservation. They knew that the reproduc-
tion of the European yeshiva without adjustments to American needs
could not thrive even in the sheltered environment of the East Side.
Their restiveness became more than an uneasy stirring. It ultimately
became the leaven that helped convert the courses of instruction at
RIETS into a synthesis of ancient and contemporary cultures.

One interesting result of this persistent controversy indicated the
temper of the students and the extremes to which they were prepared
to go. This took place in 1907 when three students, Rabbis Nachman
Ebin, David Rackman and a Rabbi Wolf made an appointment with
Dr. Solomon Schechter, president of the Jewish Theological Seminary of America, for the purpose of exploring a transfer to that
institution if they were given the English instruction they wanted so
badly. The Jewish Theological Seminary offered no courses in Eng-

lish instruction and had a rule requiring that students should possess a college degree before they could be qualified for ordination. The members of the delegation could easily qualify for the ordination that was offered at the Jewish Theological Seminary on the basis of their Talmudic background if the college-degree requirement could be waived. It was to discuss this possibility and to arrange for a substitute course of English instruction that the interview with Dr. Schechter was sought. The students' motives in even projecting a transfer to the Jewish Theological Seminary are not quite clear. With the death of Dr. Sabato Morais and in the interregnum period before the arrival of Dr. Schechter as its president, the Jewish Theological Seminary had begun to drift from its Orthodox moorings. Dr. Schechter's position was clear and unequivocal in supporting and even urging departure from Orthodoxy, and under his direction the gap between the Jewish Theological Seminary and tradition was further widened. It is not conceivable that East European students, steeped in Orthodoxy and traditional Judaism and of the caliber of the three men involved, considered reorienting their allegiance. Perhaps the requested interview was in the nature of an exploratory excursion to find out just how the matter of English instruction was handled at the Jewish Theological Seminary, or perhaps it was an elaborate ruse designed to impress the desperation of the students upon the directors of RIETS. In any case, Dr. Schechter received the three young men graciously.

When the young men discussed their problem with Dr. Schechter, Jacob H. Schiff, who was one of the Jewish Theological Seminary's most generous benefactors, a descendant of a line of rabbis, tolerant of Orthodoxy and most interested in Jewish education, was consulted as well. The negotiations did not come to a successful conclusion, but one tangible result did emerge. Through his meeting with the three students, Jacob Schiff became interested in the Yeshiva. He paid a visit to RIETS and was impressed with the program to the extent of leaving a $1,000 contribution, which became an annual gift. Harry Fischel, who was a director of RIETS at this time[68] and active in the Yeshivat Etz Chaim, and who was to be a devoted benefactor of RIETS for the rest of his life, was the intermediary between Schiff and RIETS and helped solicit the contribution.

The visit to Dr. Schechter was not made on behalf of the entire student body and may even have been entirely clandestine, but it was nonetheless representative of student opinion. The students continued to complain publicly about the need of proper courses in secular subjects, and public opinion was slowly veering in their favor. A sympathetic writer of that day, speaking of RIETS, echoed student sentiment, saying: "The foundation is already laid . . . the students are good . . . all that is needed [at RIETS] is a secular school as good as its religious school. . . ."[69] Many of the students felt completely inadequate to assume the task of rabbinical leadership and could only look wistfully upon the possibility of a rabbinical career. Despite the arduous efforts of the directors, very few actually accepted the call to fill rabbinical posts. Instead, they struck out into other fields—medicine, law, Hebrew teaching, and business. The average tenure of a student at RIETS between 1897 and 1905 was from half a year to two years. One former student, who later became a successful businessman, spent exactly four hours—a morning session —at RIETS in 1902 and sensing the obdurate position of the directors, went out for lunch and never returned.[70]

Despite this long-drawn-out struggle over secular education, RIETS made great headway during the first decade of its existence. The valiant efforts of the handful of directors had been successful in several fundamental respects. After the school had occupied at least half a dozen different locations, they had finally put an end to its migrations and found a permanent location at 156 Henry Street. The lethargy of the East Side Jewish community had been penetrated, although not completely overcome, and RIETS was being recognized and supported as the central academy of higher Jewish studies of the Orthodox Jewish community. Through this accomplishment of the directors, a turning point in the maturation of the East European community in New York was reached. The first major Orthodox Jewish educational institution, independent of the assistance of the established American Jewish community had now been created. Through the years the student body had been growing steadily, and in 1908 there were about 125 students evenly divided between the older and the younger groups.[71]

RIETS was yet to be wracked by a great student strike and a complete reorganization in 1908, but as the year 1907 drew to a close, the first period of RIETS' existence marked a number of important accomplishments.

CHAPTER 6. THE BIG STRIKE IN RIETS

The year 1908 was a difficult one for the East European community in New York. The depression of 1907 had left an almost crippling effect on the immigrants. The recession had started in 1906 and settled like a blight upon the newcomers. The marginal earners—the peddlers, the unskilled workers, the odd-job men—and even the better established little businessmen were sorely hit. The severe limitations in their finances wrought unendurable hardships on their daily lives. As their earning power was reduced, their spending for the necessities of the home, for food, clothes, and utilities dwindled.

When the economic curve began its rise toward self-adjustment, the immigrants were still floundering. Being at the lowest rung of the financial ladder, they were the first to feel the blows of disaster and conversely the last to experience relief. From 1906 to 1908 the immigrants' lot ranged between destitution for many and serious dislocation for almost all. Only the well-established and the comfortable were able to continue without self-denial.

As a result of the depression and the years of its backwash, family budgets were pared to the minimum. Expenditures other than those for barest necessities were almost completely eliminated. Owing to inescapable economies, donations, contributions, membership fees, and other charitable spending were the first to be curtailed, and almost entirely eliminated. The reductions in philanthropic expenditures were reflected in the condition of many synagogues and *hevrot* impoverished beyond succor. Many resorted to advertising for more prosperous, or equally stricken, synagogues to merge with them on the theory that there was more hope for support in a united and enlarged membership. Other synagogues which were unsuccessful in availing themselves of this or that technique of survival saw their buildings fall as casualties to the auctioneer's hammer.[1] Even as they strove to extricate themselves from their financial predicaments, these synagogues were forced to close their doors and disappear from the American scene.

The *Tageblatt* devoted a great deal of space to this "crisis in the synagogue"[2] pointing out that "the richer Jews who built the synagogues have moved from the East Side" and as for those who remained, their "religious spirit is high but the finances are low."[3] Among the unfortunate congregations affected was the Mariampol Synagogue, which had been the spiritual source of the Machzikei Talmud Torah, the Yeshivat Etz Chaim, and RIETS. In December, 1908, succumbing to the paralyzing effects of a migrating membership and dwindling finances, its building was offered for sale in order to avoid foreclosure.[4] The *Tageblatt* announced a similar crisis in the Machzikei Talmud Torah. In an editorial the paper reported that "the first Talmud Torah in New York may have to close some of its classes."[5]

RIETS, like other immigrant institutions, did not escape the shattering impact of the depression. The purchase of its own building had made RIETS even more vulnerable to fluctuations in the financial conditions of its supporters. Ownership of the building added overnight the heavy burden of a mortgage commitment as well as maintenance responsibility. Neither of these items had appeared in earlier budgets of RIETS, and they did not produce any direct compensating income in return for their expenditure.

Signs of RIETS's faltering began to manifest themselves as soon as the Henry Street building was occupied. In November, 1904, RIETS openly called for "help."[6] A year later, a new cause for worry developed as the mortgage payment fell due,[7] and by 1907 the debt owed on the building was $7,000; there was an imminent threat that the building would be sold at auction and the doors of the Yeshiva closed forever.[8]

The Explosion

Against this painful background of economic worries and a Board of Directors "already tired of carrying the heavy load on their weak backs,"[9] a great student strike exploded that rocked RIETS to its very depths. Under the pressure of a heated student body and aroused

public opinion, RIETS underwent the beginnings of a reorganization, which in another decade took form in the pattern of Dr.
Bernard Revel's long-sought synthesis of religious and secular education. No one really knows how the strike began or what caused it.
Its eruption, however, had been foreordained in the bitter struggle
over secular education that had been raging within the institution
from the turn of the century. There was no letup in this *Kulturkampf*
and, from time to time, there were minor altercations involving the
students and directors.

In January, 1906, the smoldering unrest had come to one of the
rancorous climaxes that characterized the period. At that time the
directors circularized a document calling upon the advanced students
to forswear all secular education and to promise devotion to their
Talmudic studies exclusively. The penalty for violation of this pledge
would be forfeiture of all stipends and support. The students were
naturally incensed by this highhanded threat, but they were even
more shocked by what they termed the fanaticism of the directors
and their blindness to the needs of the students. The matter came to
an ugly head when stipends for the entire upper division were
suspended because a number of students either had not signed the
required pledge or had been apprehended violating its conditions.
The students, who found no receptive ear among the directors, felt
they had no alternative other than to place their case before the
public. Consequently, the following statement was issued to both the
Jüdisches Tageblatt and the *Jüdische Gazetten,* which were undoubtedly most happy to publish it.[10] The uninhibited statement, despite
its bitter tone, gives a very vivid picture of the students' position:

> We the students of RIETS have for a long time hidden our wounds
> in order that no desecration should take place. But since it has
> come to this final step we must publicize the following statement.

> It is known that there is a yeshiva in New York known as Yeshivat
> Rabbeinu Yitzchak Elchanan. . . . The Yeshiva was founded in
> order to produce great rabbinic scholars who would be acceptable
> to the people and know the language of the land. Unfortunately,
> however, the Yeshiva does not fulfill its purpose. It is true that
> we have scholars who are brilliant Torah students who are suit-

able to lead Orthodox synagogues, but we possess no secular education. When a young man comes to the Yeshiva, he is assured that he will be given the best teachers, but after the young man is there for several months he realizes that he lacks the opportunity to improve himself, and he begins to seek ways to leave the Yeshiva. The Yeshiva has already had the best of young men who were suitable to fill pulpits, but they were lost. They drifted with the stream because the Yeshiva did not give them the opportunity to study the English language. A young man will not and cannot accept a position when he is ignorant and cannot even speak the language of the land.

We bore all this as long as we did not have to engage in battle with fanatics. . . . Most of us found ways of acquiring our necessary studies in the preparatory schools. But these fanatics, who make up the Board of Directors and [Officers] . . . issued a decree against all secular studies. They demanded that we sign a document binding us to a strict discipline, and failing that discipline, subjecting us to the penalty of losing our support. They were as good as their word. They have already refused us our stipends for two weeks.

The directors are divided into two groups. One is strictly Orthodox and will permit no study other than Talmud and Codes, and the other, the more liberal, thinks that an elementary school education is good enough. Therefore, since we have no other recourse, we must turn to the people who support this institution and place these questions before them:
1. Should benighted people be directors of such an institution?
2. Should the Yeshiva provide more than an elementary school education?
3. Should the young men who are great Talmudic scholars be swallowed up in the stream and lost to our Torah?[11]

No one could deny the validity of the position adopted by the students, who were patient and long suffering as they awaited liberation from what they considered a scholarly serfdom. As might be expected, the Yiddish press championed their cause. In a foreword to the published statement, both the *Tageblatt* and the *Gazetten* went to the very root of RIETS's *raison d'être* as a justification for the inclusion of secular subjects. If RIETS were not to be the fountainhead of both Jewish and worldly knowledge, then what indeed was its purpose? The editorial writers formulated their support for the student body in the following analysis:

> Three types of rabbis are being prepared in America. The students at Cincinnati are one type. The second type are the students at the New York [Jewish Theological] Seminary and the third type are the students of RIETS.

> What was the contribution of RIETS? We needed a Yeshiva where our good students, our excellent young men, those who come here with the scholarship and the qualities of the old generation and the old world, could become Americanized, cultured and developed in order that they might become rabbis possessing both important qualifications: Jewish scholarship and secular knowledge. . . . This need created RIETS. RIETS is necessary only if it prepares for us old country scholars with American attainments.[12]

The issue of secular education was the major one upon which the entire student position was based. However, the lackadaisical, unbusinesslike character of the directors was a contributing factor to the deterioration of student-administration relations.

Following the presentation of their grievances, a series of demands signed by "all the Students of the Yeshiva" was issued which evidenced clear and constructive thinking:

> We demand that there should be a systematized curriculum. The proper things should be taught at the right time.

> [We demand] the opportunities to study Hebrew, Jewish culture and Jewish history.

> There should be a curriculum in the native language and general knowledge.

> There should be instruction in the art of public speaking.

> Our material needs should be so taken care of that we should not have a "to do" every time that we need something.

> And the last and most important thing is that such a Board of Directors of fine religious Jews be elected that we will be able to hold in esteem and respect.

> We pray all Jews to whom the Torah and Judaism is dear to come to our help.[13]

The "Trouble in the Yeshiva"[14] provided excellent copy for the Yiddish press, which was enjoying a field day at the expense of the "only ultra-orthodox rabbinical school in the country." The *Tageblatt* found this a heaven-sent opportunity to make biting remarks about the faculty, officers and directors, whom they openly reviled.[15] Carrying the students' demands to their ultimate conclusions, the *Tageblatt's* English columnist, the "Observer," wrote:

> The only hope for the Yeshiva is a thorough clearing out of the present officers of every state and condition and the election of liberal, modern, religious Jews at the head thereof . . . The studies must follow a definite, well planned program, giving sufficient attention alike to the Hebrew and English subjects. Numerous other improvements must follow. Then there may yet be a chance of the Yeshiva to become to this age what the ancient Babylonian Yeshivot of Sura and Nehardea were to their times.[16]

The administration was probably not as uncompromising as the *Tageblatt* made it out to be, nor even quite as unheeding as the students had pictured it. Nevertheless, the battle had already been joined and made public. Furthermore, the students had already moved from Henry Street to a neighboring synagogue where they pursued their studies.[17] There was nothing for the directors to do but reach a speedy agreement or face the dissolution of the Yeshiva.

An Unreal Peace

The accusations and grievances had found their way into print on January 18 and 26. A week later, on February 4, an urgent meeting of the directors was held, followed by another session on February 12. We have no inkling as to what transpired, but it is known that out of the deliberations emerged a new slate of officers and directors. Since the election of officers had always been held in August, these meetings must have been exciting and heated, probably culminating in wholesale resignations.

The new president was Rabbi Moses Sebulun Margolies, who in the same year had come from Boston to assume the pulpit of Congregation Kehillath Jeshurun. Dr. Klein was elected to the position of honorary president. Rabbi Israel Rosenberg of Bayonne, New Jersey, became first vice-president, with Harry Altschul of Jersey City and Rabbi Yehuda David Bernstein as second and third vice-presidents. Jonathan Shepp was the new treasurer, and David Abramowitz continued as secretary.[18]

The major change in the administration was in the presidency and in the treasuryship, while the Board of Directors was almost entirely composed of the previous Board. Nevertheless, the prompt action of the Board in holding new elections was a tacit admission of the need for some remedial action, if not a complete acquiescence.

Rabbi Margolies was known to be a man of great tact, patience, and gentleness and was held in high esteem for his cool and even temper. These qualities fitted him admirably for the difficult position which he was called upon to assume. Under his leadership, the students were pacified and returned to RIETS as the tense situation was temporarily relieved. However, the basic issues were not adjusted, and a restless truce ensued in which both sides marked time uneasily against the day of final resolution. The directors still considered the students an undisciplined and fractious group agitated by a handful of "liberals," while the students remained unaltered in their estimate of the directors as "benighted" tyrants dedicated to an inflexible European Judaism.

The *Tageblatt*'s "Observer" predicted the inevitable, saying that the strike

> has been temporarily postponed but . . . is liable to be resumed next week or the week after [since] strained relations between the Talmudical students and . . . the faculty are chronic in this establishment . . .[19]

Had the financial position of RIETS been more secure, the unreal peace might have been extended and the reorganization staved off for several years. However, as the financial pressures increased and budgetary problems became almost unbearable, the internal pressure created by the students finally caused the break.

Early in 1908, it was apparent that RIETS was being financially

crushed to the ground. A considerable portion of its heavy budget
was allocated to the weekly student stipends. The older students in
the rabbinical division had been receiving up to $4 weekly for sub-
sistence. Since there were about sixty students in this category, the
stipend cost ranged from $200 to $250 each week, a little more than
half of the budget of the school.[20] The directors, who were desperately casting about for some relief from their financial difficulties,
seized upon this large item as a logical area for economy. It is un-
thinkable that the directors should have scrutinized the students'
support account with a view to extorting a picayune revenge for the
humiliation to which they had been exposed in 1906. More likely
they were motivated by the honest desire to conserve their finances,
and perhaps at the same time, weed out the students they considered
undesirable. Nevertheless, their decision was very difficult to justify.
Early in May it was announced that fifteen young men would be
dropped from the stipend rolls, in the interests of economy.[21] The
students claimed that by design this number corresponded to the
outspoken and aggressive students whom the directors had long ago
singled out as leaders in the movement against the administration
and for secular education. Since no student could continue at RIETS
without the assistance of stipends, the order had the effect of remov-
ing the major opponents of the administration from the scene and
at the same time putting the directors in the righteous position of
solving their financial problem. As in 1906, the students were
scandalized by this highhanded move to exact cooperation and con-
formity among the scholars by means of financial discrimination
against the dissenters.

To counter the plan of the directors, all the students offered to
accept a reduction in their stipends, which would produce the desired saving without excluding even one student from the school's
support. This the directors refused, and they closed the school forth-
with. Simultaneously with the action of the directors, the students
declared a strike, saying they would not return to RIETS unless
the inequities were removed and their curriculum requests granted.
In the absence of any other contemporary record, we must again
resort to a press report for a description of the facts.

A "strike" and a "lockout" are now going on at RIETS. The administration says that the crisis and the students are responsible but the students state that this is not true. . . . According to Mr. Chaim Robinson, Vice President of the Yeshiva, the income of the School is too little to cover the needs of all the students who are receiving $3.50 or $4.00 a week plus clothes. The Yeshiva owes $7,000 but even exclusive of the debts, the weekly income does not meet the expenses.

"The directors have held a meeting," says Mr. Robinson, "and decided to decrease the expenses by excluding fifteen young men [from receiving support]." The students are united, however, and insist that either all remain or none shall study. The directors are, therefore, resolved to close the Yeshiva for some time until they will be stronger financially. Then they will accept all those who will send in their applications. The students of the Yeshiva, however, tell an altogether different story. They say that the excuse of the financial crisis is only a subterfuge. They say that they are prepared to accept a proportionate reduction in their stipends so that no individual students will have to be dropped. Furthermore, they say that during this time new students had been admitted.

The young men say: "It is the old story of the battle against worldly knowledge that the directors have been waging against us. We want the Yeshiva to be a real educational institution for American rabbis but they look upon it as a charity institution to provide us with food that we might study Torah for them. We demand a systematic teaching of Jewish and general knowledge, a better administration and, consequently, that the Board of Directors should be reorganized. We want to produce rabbis who will be a source of pride for Jewry in America."[22]

Having given what purported to be a factual account of the strike, the Sarasohn papers also gave what was considered to be the philosophy behind the battle. In the editorial comments appended to the students' published grievance of 1906, the newspaper had emphasized the difference between RIETS and the Jewish Theological Seminary of America. In doing so it stressed the potential capacity of the former to produce great Talmudic scholars who would also be equipped with necessary secular knowledge. In analyzing the strike of 1908, the newspapers followed the same line.

Putting aside the Cincinnati reform factory [*sic!*], there remains the competition between Schechter's rabbinical school and RIETS. Schechter's Seminary, according to the intent of the founders and supporters of RIETS is Jewish but not religious. And here we come to the conflict of the Yeshiva students and the leaders of RIETS. "We want," claim the students, "to know Talmud and Codes better than the students of Schechter's Seminary. We want to know all the material that the rabbis of Russia do. But we want to have as much secular education as the students of Schechter's Seminary. We cannot be satisfied with the bit of English that the Administration permits us to study."

And the Administration thinks this way: "A rabbi is neither obligated to study nor requires too much secular knowledge. Too much secular learning conflicts with Judaism. . . . It is quite sufficient for a rabbi to be able to talk English and be able to answer . . . in English . . ."

The institution that wants to compete with the rabbinical school of Prof. Schechter cannot win by giving its students *less* training. . . . The Yeshiva may be Jewish, religious, orthodox, but that does not imply that the students must be backwards. . . . Being backward is not an essential of Judaism. It is also not necessary that a rabbinical school should not have a clear program of studies. . . . Judaism has no fear of the light of culture. The defenders of Judaism were never ignorant. Maimonides and his philosophical knowledge, Judah Halevi and his philosophy and medicine, the Vilna Gaon and his science and mathematics—these were the representatives of Judaism. Open the windows, give more light to those whom you wish to place at the head of American Jewry.

Those who are behind the times can never stand at the head of a movement. They will never be leaders![23]

These impassioned lines painted the picture of the strife in all blacks and whites with no intermediate shading. For the *Tageblatt* and the *Gazetten,* the directors were of a malevolent cast and the students of a purely idealistic mold. The editorial writers for these papers could only conclude that "The Battle of the Students in RIETS" was a battle for principle, "for Torah and Haskalah."[24] In contrast, by implication, the directors were for Torah as against Haskalah (worldly knowledge).

The *Jewish Morning Journal,* generally more restrained in its treatment of RIETS than the Sarasohn papers, hurled an editorial bombshell into the fray by challenging the veracity of the directors' claim that RIETS was undergoing a financial crisis. On the contrary, the *Jewish Morning Journal* claimed, RIETS had collected $20,000 during the year, "as much as had been collected in the best years."[25] What was taking place was a "lockout, not a strike."[26]

The newspaper did not, however, clearly explain the reason for the alleged duplicity, except that it might be an excuse for eliminating the unwanted students. Disregarding any specific reference to the question of secular training, the *Jewish Morning Journal* suggested that the directors had failed in their duty to prepare European scholars for the American rabbinate, for which "noble purpose" the Yeshiva was founded; that they were expelling the advanced students and retaining the younger ones who had not even begun to master Jewish scholarship and were reducing RIETS to an elementary school.[27] If the directors did not improve their attitude, said the paper, "new troubles could be expected in a few weeks or in a few months."[28]

Among the newspapers, *Ha-Yehudi* adopted the most reasonable attitude. It admitted that all was not as it should be at RIETS, but refused to accept the Sarasohn papers' pat simplification. Implying that the problems of RIETS were basically financial, its correspondent sided with the directors, stating, "Alas, a goodly gem is hung around the neck of the Jewish community of New York and it does not know how to take care of it."[29]

On the matter of general education, however, *Ha-Yehudi* saw no great divergence between the students and the directors. Even Rabbi Margolies, it reported,[30] was for Haskalah and not against secular education. The central issue was not over whether or not to include secular training in the curriculum, but how much should be included and where should the emphasis lie. It would be sufficient, ventured *Ha-Yehudi,* for a rabbi to have the equivalent training of four classes of the European *gymnasia,* which was roughly equivalent to a similar number of high school classes and a knowledge of English. Certainly, *Ha-Yehudi* concluded, a rabbi "does not have to know Homer and Virgil."[31]

If, indeed, this was a battle between the Jewish Theological Seminary and RIETS as the *Tageblatt* and *Gazetten* implied, then, averred *Ha-Yehudi,* RIETS should fight the Jewish Theological Seminary not with proficiency in secular subjects, but on its own grounds with Torah.[32]

In the space of a few short days, the quarrel between the students and the administration of RIETS had been transferred from the relative insignificance and obscurity of a local struggle to one of wider importance. It received national and international coverage in the Yiddish, Hebrew and Anglo-Jewish press as well as some prominence in the English press, which often completely confused the issues, places and people involved.[33]

This time the students did not surrender as easily as they had in 1906. The strike was well thought-out, and the discipline among the students was rigid. No sooner was the strike declared than a prepared plan was immediately put into effect. The first news of the strike had appeared on May 5. Only three days later on Friday, May 8, the newspapers announced that a number of students would speak on the subject of the strike in various prominent synagogues the following morning during the Sabbath services. Their purpose was "to explain their trouble with the directors of the Yeshiva."[34] Rabbis Ben Zion Perl, Chaim Moseson, Moses Nathanson, Baruch Metz, Eliezer Mehler and Abraham Hirmes were to carry this assignment.[35] The fact that they were permitted to use congregational pulpits for this purpose was indicative of the public's tacit support of the students. Rev. Zvi Hirsch Masliansky also delivered an address on the same day in the Educational Alliance calling upon the worshippers to support the students.[36]

Newspapers received a heavy flow of letters from both the public and members of RIETS favoring the students' position.[37] An Albany rabbi, who wrote to justify the students' request, stated that the Yeshiva "must not be a lodging place for the great scholars of Russia, but an educational institution." There is precedent for such an institution, he opined, "in the Yeshiva of Rabbi Yitzchak Yaacov Reines where in 6 years of study a student covers 13 or 14 Tractates of Talmud, Codes, as well as seven classes of gymnasia."[38]

Most of the mail upholding the students discussed the popular issue of curriculum reform. The significant demand for overhauling the administration was less widely discussed or understood. A revealing letter on this latter subject, which supported the students' accusation was sent to the *Tageblatt* by Rabbi Moshe Shimon Sivitz of Pittsburgh, one of the directors of RIETS. He wrote:

> As one of the directors, I will now say publicly what we have hitherto discussed only in private. The Yeshiva needs an important man with comprehension, a man of great understanding, who will be able to impress the young men of the Yeshiva and be able to address the world on behalf of the Yeshiva. We have a suitable man in this country for the position. He is Rabbi B. L. Levinthal of Philadelphia. If this great rabbi will accept—then we can be assured that the Yeshiva will be placed on the level of spiritual and material heights to which it is entitled . . .[39]

Rabbi Sivitz' letter substantiated the students' charge that there was no effective or respected leadership in the administration and left the impression that had there been less floundering as to aims and purposes, the strike, as well as the intransigence on both sides, might have been averted. It further implied that the directors themselves were unhappy at having been maneuvered into this galling and untenable position.

The position of the directors was made more uncomfortable by the final strategy of the students. In another public statement, the students completely severed their relationship with the administration, refused to negotiate with them and turned to the public as the final arbiters. This announcement repeated all the previous charges and also introduced a crushing denunciation of the administration. The statement reads in part:

> The students of RIETS plead that the rabbis and Jewish scholars should create a program for the Yeshiva.

> The students have issued the following statement: "The Yeshiva in its present condition has no program which makes clear what its program is—what to teach and how to teach. The directors who have no program to follow, change their minds every moment and hinder the development of the students.

> "We have, therefore, broken off all negotiations with the present directors and demand: That leading rabbis and prominent Jewish scholars should be chosen who will work out a program to make

it possible for the Yeshiva to produce rabbis who will be equally distinguished in general knowledge and Jewish science as Jewry of this country demands . . ."[40]

Redefinition of Purposes

As a result of the wide publicity, the dispute had become public property. Many outstanding laymen of the East Side, not directly identified with the administration of RIETS, were shocked by the outburst on Henry Street. Acting quickly to resolve the problem, twenty prominent Orthodox men under the chairmanship of Leon Kamaiky, one of the proprietors of the *Tageblatt,* met exactly one week after news of the strike appeared in the press. Several unnamed students of RIETS were present, too, in order to defend their position.

The meeting was convened at the Hebrew Immigrant Aid Society building on East Broadway at 4:00 P.M. on Tuesday, May 12 and continued into the evening. At 7:00 P.M. the meeting was electrified by a call from Nathan Lamport, the president of RIETS, inviting the discussants to attend a meeting of directors and "uptown" friends of RIETS that night at Congregation Kehillath Jeshurun, Rabbi Moses S. Margolies' synagogue. Acceding to the request of Mr. Lamport, the East Broadway meeting repaired to 85th Street where deliberations were resumed at 9:00 P.M. and lasted well past midnight.[41]

The night session was chaired by Rabbi Margolies, who two years previously during a similar emergency had been cast in the same role of great compromiser. A. Z. Lewin-Epstein of the Carmel Wine Company, who had been secretary of the afternoon meeting, continued in the same capacity during the later gathering. The meeting, now composed of lay leaders and communal workers of "uptown" and "downtown," as well as members of the Board of Directors and officers of RIETS, concerned itself with the demands of the students and the financial needs of the school which had indirectly precipitated the upheaval. It is not known whether the student representatives were also present at the late meeting. Nevertheless, the deliberations seemed to produce a completely reasonable and satisfactory decision. The report of the agreement appeared on the front pages of the *Tageblatt* and the *Jewish Morning Journal* under the headlines "New Order in Yeshiva, Dispute Settled" and "RIETS Becomes University for Rabbis." This was the first time that RIETS had occupied such an important position in either of these newspapers.[42]

The major result of the meeting was a redefinition of the purposes of RIETS. It was decided that the Yeshiva was to become "an institution of Torah and *ḥakhma,* secular knowledge,"[43] which would produce Orthodox rabbis "according to the spirit of the times."[44] In order to implement these purposes, it was decided to develop a complete college curriculum.[45] The hope was expressed that English courses, so far as possible, should be taught in the Henry Street building so that the students would be spared the need to attend outside preparatory schools or colleges. Rabbis Margolies and Rosenberg and Messrs. Samuel Wilner, Nathan Lamport and A. Z. Lewin-Epstein were appointed to recommend a suitable president of the faculty.[46] Another committee of ten was appointed to work out a curriculum, establish admission standards, conditions for ordination and other related student needs. Five members of this committee were to be concerned with Hebrew studies, the other five with secular studies.[47]

Apparently the question of the presence of younger children at RIETS that had agitated the *Jewish Morning Journal* in its earlier criticism was again raised at this meeting; for at the meeting, it was recommended to turn over the training of these younger students to Yeshivat Etz Chaim. Harry Fischel, a director of RIETS and also vice-president of the elementary yeshiva, speaking on behalf of Etz Chaim, said that the school was ready to accept the youngsters and provide their Hebrew and English studies.[48]

The matter of finances also held a weightly position on the agenda. It was reported that the Seminary's income had been drastically curtailed since the past winter. About $6,000 was usually contributed by large donors in the $50 to $700 category. But this basic amount, as well as income from other sources, had been greatly reduced. A committee of ten was therefore appointed to draw up a budget to cover the new operation, reduce expenditures, and increase the income.[49]

On the morning following the long day of sessions and decisions, the new Finance Committee met to examine the books of RIETS. Their investigation confirmed the truth that money was needed badly. More than $7,000 was required for outstanding debts and mortgage payments. The students, too, had not received their stipends for sometime. Apparently the *Jewish Morning Journal's* accusation that the director were exaggerating their financial difficulties was unfounded. On realizing the condition, several of the committee immediately made personal contributions to tide the school over. Nathan Lamport gave $300; Joseph Spectorsky, $250; Leon Kamaiky, $100; and Sam Zaretsky, $20.[50]

While the directors and interested laymen had each called a meeting to deal with the happenings at RIETS, the Agudat ha-Rabbanim had convened its Yeshiva Committee. The call was issued by Rabbi Israel Rosenberg, chairman of the committee, and Rabbi Samuel Z. Wien for May 14. Rabbi Bernard L. Levinthal of Philadelphia, the apparent successor to the presidency of RIETS, was among the thirty-one rabbis of the Agudat ha-Rabbanim who answered Rabbi Rosenberg's call. The Yeshiva Committee recommended that the students should receive all their back stipends[51] and permission to attend outside schools until secular studies were established at RIETS. It was also decided to call another meeting of representatives from all New York synagogues in order to enlist their support for RIETS.[52]

From Rabbi Sivitz' straw-in-the-wind letter and from Rabbi Levinthal's special trip to attend Rabbi Rosenberg's meeting, it was apparent that the Philadelphia rabbi was being groomed to take over the helm of RIETS. A position of leadership at RIETS at any time was far from a sinecure. The mortality in office was high, the barbs sharp, the pressure merciless, and the credit nil. At this moment the requirements called for a statesman, visionary, pacifier, scholar, and above all, a devoted servant. Rabbi Levinthal[53] was all of these and was respected by the students as well. In addition, he was one of the major figures in the Agudat ha-Rabbanim, which meant that if he were to identify himself completely with RIETS, he could continue to hold firm the support of that rabbinic body. All the qualities that fitted him for leadership singled him out as the lone suitable personality acceptable to the rabbis, the students, and the community alike.

Rabbi Levinthal was strongly urged to step into the breach and save the already torn and greatly weakened yeshiva. Despite his hesitancy and the fact that his responsibilities in Philadelphia were great, Rabbi Levinthal yielded to the importunities of the directors. On Monday night, June 22, 1908, he was unanimously elected to a newly created position, president of the faculty. The office was an expanded version of the Rosh Yeshiva of early RIETS days. Now, however, the school and staff were much larger and the older students were of such mature and advanced scholarship that the directors felt that the head of the academic functions of the school should have a more fitting and imposing title.[54]

Rabbi Levinthal accepted the position without salary[55] and with the condition that he would be allowed to commute from Philadelphia, spending half of the week in New York until after the High Holy Days.[56] After the Holy Days, Rabbi Levinthal planned to settle in New York. The news of Rabbi Levinthal's impending removal from Philadelphia created an intense reaction in the city that loved him. Protest meetings were planned and fervid personal pleas were directed toward Rabbi Levinthal.[57] Unable to resist his people's wishes, the new president was obliged to amend his qualified acceptance. He asked that his term of office be temporary and that he be permitted to step down after reorganization and stability were effected.

The new president of the faculty was greeted with great happiness by the directors, who imagined that he would play the same role as Dr. Schechter did at the Jewish Theological Seminary.[58] They were "full of hopes that through the work of Rabbi Levinthal it would be possible to maintain the Yeshiva on the principles of the reorganization and keep it on a firm footing, so that it will no longer be in constant danger of being closed down."[59]

They reaffirmed the decision "to produce devout and observant rabbis who are equipped with knowledge in the spirit of the times."

It was emphasized that both religious and secular studies would be directly under Rabbi Levinthal's supervision, and that he would commute regularly from Philadelphia to supervise them.[60]

Taken altogether, the results of Rabbi Margolies' and Rabbi Rosenberg's meetings actually fulfilled all the conditions of the students, even to the extent of yielding to the unpublicized demand to pay back stipends lost during the strike and in the period immediately prior to it. This concession, made in the most acute financial straits, was equivalent to complete capitulation. No impressions of sulky surrender accompanied the remarks of rabbis and laymen who participated in the meetings. An intelligent sense of recognition of the inevitable seemed to pervade the remarks of the directors and other participants in the discussion, who looked forward to stablization of the institution and a happy new understanding with the students. The students, too, had reason to be satisfied. Not only were they given everything they had asked for, but they also now had a man in a position of authority who was the embodiment of their ideals and above all a sincere friend.

Even the *Tageblatt,* although voicing some reservation, was

> ... satisfied with the result of the meeting which gave the Yeshiva a progressive plan.... We are happy that ... the leaders of RIETS have at last understood that America is not the place for a Yeshiva dedicated exclusively to study [of the Torah ... but] that the Yeshiva is a rabbinical school ... will work out a program according to which it will produce cultured, progressive and truly Jewish rabbis for the Jews of America, then it will receive the support of the Jews of America....[61]

This satisfaction was obviously premature, for the human factors— the directors' unilateral acts and the students' corresponding disrespect for the administration—remained unaltered. These, in addition to the problem of finances, were to manifest themselves in the ensuing months.

CHAPTER 7.   THE AFTERMATH OF THE STRIKE

At the end of July, the Agudat ha-Rabbanim held its annual convention in Paterson, New Jersey and heard a report by Rabbi Levinthal on the reorganization of RIETS and a stirring appeal for support.[1] More than one hundred rabbis listened to the impassioned plea for assistance.[2]

As in the past, they responded to the call by deciding to send out rabbis to enlist financial aid for RIETS.[3] One dozen members volunteered their services in an effort to ameliorate the persistent problem of funds.[4] The rabbis also reaffirmed RIETS' unique position as "the only [institution] in the country which can spread the rays of Torah"[5] and assured all that "it was now being reorganized as an institution for Torah and secular knowledge" because "Torah and secular knowledge go hand in hand."[6] The directors placed great hopes in the efforts of the Agudat ha-Rabbanim. They appealed to their "brethren in this country" to "please accept the visits of members of the Agudat ha-Rabbanim" because "the struggle due to shortage of funds in the Yeshiva is indescribable. Unless we receive speedy help, the Yeshiva will, God forbid, go under."[7]

More Catastrophies

Unfortunately neither the hopes of the directors nor the efforts of Rabbi Levinthal and the Agudat ha-Rabbanim were of great avail. Perhaps the rabbis did not even have the opportunity to go forth on their mission, for on Friday, August 21, less than a month after the Convention of the rabbis, it was again announced that RIETS had closed its doors.[8] The directors explained:

> We have done all that was possible to keep RIETS open. No effort was too great for us. . . . During this time, however, we incurred

a $7,000 debt which we cannot cover. . . . We have, therefore, decided to close the Yeshiva . . . until our supporters will furnish us with the means to reopen. . . .[9]

After its initial thrust at the directors in May, the *Morning Journal* reversed its position completely on the subject of the finances of RIETS. It commiserated now with the directors and championed their defense in anticipation of the attacks that would follow on the heels of the new catastrophe. "Those who used to characterize . . . the difficulties of RIETS as 'strikes,'" it editorialized, "will probably now view the closing of the institution as a 'lockout.' However, it should rather be called a 'bankruptcy.'"[10]

The *Jewish Morning Journal* was correct in its anticipation of a bitter attack on the directors. The *Tageblatt,* in its report of the closing, was in character. "RIETS is closed again," it stated, "supposedly because of lack of funds," but "we hear that the parting between the administration and the students was not a friendly one."[11] The newspaper editorialized that "The school will have no permanence unless peace between the students and directors is established."[12]

The *Tageblatt* seemed to detect something comic in the predictable pattern that was developing in the student-administration crises at RIETS. There was an almost invariable repetition of what appeared to be standard procedure for these occurrences. First there was a directors' claim followed by a student denial or vice versa. Then came a directors' meeting followed by the announcement of a solution and the appointment of committees. It was all so obvious, thought the *Tageblatt,* that unless some improvements were instituted, reopening the Yeshiva would only mean that "the public will again have the opportunity to hear of new strikes and new quarrels in RIETS. . . ."[13] Finally, it concluded, "If the Yeshiva is to be reopened for quarrels and strikes—it would be much better that it never be opened."[14]

The directors and rabbis were, however, greatly interested in the survival of RIETS, and they strove to find a solution. Once more, as earlier in the year, they acted with great speed. On Monday night, August 31, they held a meeting in the Henry Street building and unanimously decided to reopen the school. The directors now followed a well-trod path. A finance committee was immediately appointed to re-examine the financial needs of the Yeshiva and make appropriate suggestions for fund raising. Members of the committee were Messrs. Chaim Dolinsky, Chaim Robinson, Jonathan Shepp, Jacob Leib Andron, Aaron Leib Dubowsky and Rabbi Abraham Marin. The inevitable curriculum committee for sacred and secular studies included Rabbis Moses S. Margolies, Bernard L. Levinthal, Abraham A. Yudelowitch, B. Cohen, Abraham Marin and Isaac W. Wendrofsky, who acted as secretary of the group. A press committee was also appointed. It consisted of Rabbis Yehuda D. Bernstein, Isaac W. Wendrofsky, editor of the "Letters to the Editor" department of the *Tageblatt* and Harry Altschul. While functions of this committee were not specified, its apparent duty was to create better public relations.[15]

What might have appeared comic to the *Tageblatt* was sad indeed to the directors. In announcing the results of this meeting, they appended a special plea to the women asking them "not to cease giving the pennies which they were accustomed to put in the collection boxes . . . for these pennies help educate rabbis. . . ."[16] The plea demonstrated the great financial pressure under which the directors were bowed. The most important issue facing RIETS had to be solved by the pennies of the collection boxes.

The month of September was filled with frenzied activity. The directors held almost weekly meetings to deal with all the complex factors of reopening the school. On September 4, the directors, acting with all dispatch, announced that RIETS was open again[17] and "accepting applications" from students. For the first time, too, they set a definite date for the beginning of secular studies, which "would be instituted immediately after the Sukkoth holidays."[18] Within a fortnight, too, they had called for the election of a new board,[19] and the following month in the presence of a large number of members election for new officers took place.[20] In accordance with his wish, Rabbi Levinthal had been allowed to retire, and Samuel Wilner, who was considered to be a man "who knows the temper of the times"[21] became the new president. Harry Fischel, Nathan

Lamport, and Baruch Pinchas Liberman were the new vice-presidents.[22]

Before the elections, however, one important decision had been taken. The criticism that had been levied against the administration, prompted the directors to call for the resignation and replacement of the entire "old staff." This was done in order "to satisfy all and that there be no misunderstandings." An imposing array of fifteen rabbis and school officials signed the announcement[23] calling for the resignations. Broad as the directive to replace the old staff appeared to be, it could have referred to only two major figures on the "staff" that were of any significance. One was David Abramowitz, the secretary, and the other, Rabbi Nahum Dan Baron, the *mashgiaḥ*. Since Abramowitz remained with the school despite the "resignation" of the entire "staff," the order seemed to be directed exclusively against the beloved and devoted Rabbi Nahum Dan. This would explain the long list of signatures. Although the official reason for his departure and subsequent return to his native Slutsk in Russia was "ill health," Rabbi Nahum Dan's dismissal can be attributed to one fact. Rabbi Nahum Dan had devoted his years at RIETS to the students and their welfare, and he had strongly supported their interest in secular knowledge as in the early case of Hillel Rogoff. In all probability he had sided with the students in their struggle against the directors. Someone must have wanted his removal very badly, and in gaining his resignation, the directors permitted the only man who was universally loved, admired and respected by a decade of students to leave the portals of RIETS.[24]

The election meeting evaluated the position of RIETS.[25] The outgoing president, Nathan Lamport, reported the sad financial status of RIETS and stressed the need for greater income. The blackest part of the picture, however, was reported by Chaim Robinson, the vice-president, who had figured in the May strike. He gave an account of the "recent trouble" and revealed that the enrollment at RIETS had dwindled to a mere forty students, less than a third of the number originally enrolled.[26]

It is difficult to assay the true feeling of the directors. In its last issue of the fateful year 1908, the *Gazetten* grudgingly editorialized that:

The leaders of the Yeshiva assure . . . that if they had the financial means they would institute the modern system that is required. The question now is not of principle but of means.

Since the new officers of the Yeshiva are actively at work, it is to be expected that as more funds will become available there will be a better system.[27]

The directors, however, did not reveal such a complete commitment to the new direction. Feeling constrained to make an official explanation of the events that had so disrupted RIETS, they issued a statement declaring "the true reason for closing the Yeshiva." They declared:

The main reason . . . was the [insufficiency] of money. The bad times of last year reached us too and we did not have our necessary $400 per week. Secondly, there were some young men among the students whose conduct was not becoming and dissatisfied the directors. Because of these students we could not go on with our work properly. Therefore, the Yeshiva was closed and after two weeks, was reopened again. We took back the good students of the previous group, accepted satisfactory new students and the institution became again what it should be . . .[28]

Great significance must be attached to the decreased enrollment reported by Chaim Robinson, which showed that the students had no faith at all in the satisfactory outcome of their negotiations. Many of the older students who were well-advanced in rabbinical studies realized that the directors were not yet ready to reorient their opinions as to the goals of RIETS. These students knew that if they wanted to become rabbis in America, they could not afford to wait indefinitely for the establishment of a secular curriculum in RIETS. Furthermore, they were humiliated by the system which forced them to accept a stipend for simply sitting and studying.

Yeshiva le-Rabbanim

When RIETS was closed down in August for a second time, some students left to study at the Jewish Theological Seminary, while others began to plan for a new school which would make up for the deficiencies in RIETS. It would offer specific courses to prepare men who had already achieved the necessary Talmudic scholarship to be well-rounded American rabbis. These intentions were expressed in the name that was given to the proposed school: as differentiated from an undirected yeshiva, it was to be a Yeshiva le-Rabbanim, a Yeshiva to train rabbis, a rabbinical seminary.

The first meeting of the new school was held on Thursday night, August 27, 1908, at Congregation Adas B'nai Yisrael at 123 East Broadway.[29] Unfortunately, the newspapers do not record those present at the gathering; they merely note that several rabbis and prominent laymen were on hand. However, it later appeared that Rabbi Shlomo Elchanan Jaffe of the Beth Midrash Hagadol was at the head of the new movement.[30] It was decided at this initial meeting to found a yeshiva for rabbis, and a committee was appointed to seek a charter and prepare a curriculum.[31]

With the sarcasm that it reserved for the discussion of all yeshiva news, the *Tageblatt* reported that "There was not sufficient money to operate one Yeshiva—so a second is being opened." Further, it said that the second yeshiva would not be any better than the first:

> Seeing those who stand at its head [of the Yeshiva le-Rabbanim] we are convinced that it will not provide the students with more academic freedom than the first [RIETS]. The belief that Rabbi Jaffe is more liberal and more in favor of secular education than the leaders of RIETS—is pure madness.

The *Tageblatt* also evoked the moral issue, crying out: "And where is the decency in destroying an old institution when it is certain that no better one will be created."[32]

Despite the censure and vicious attack of the *Tageblatt,* the work to build the Yeshiva le-Rabbanim continued apace. On September 20 another mass meeting was held in the Fifth Street Synagogue in Jersey City. Again "prominent rabbis" from New York and "Yeshiva students" addressed the gathering.[33] The Eldridge Street Synagogue at 12-14 Eldridge Street was the scene of the next meeting, held on the evening after Rosh Hashanah. In addition to various yeshiva students, Rabbis Shlomo Elchanan Jaffe, Shochor, Lazarov, Rosen, Dr.

Rabinowitz and Rev. Zvi Hirsch Masliansky were scheduled to speak.[34] During the intermediate days of Sukkot, a meeting was held at the Olia Synagogue on Forsyth Street.[35] The Yagustava Synagogue on Rutgers Street, one of the early homes of RIETS, was another meeting place of the sponsors of the new Yeshiva. Again Rabbis Jaffe, Shochor and Lazerov were the speakers. In addition Rabbis Broida and Zaks were on the program.[36]

It is interesting to note that in the period of four years Rev. Zvi Hirsch Masliansky had spoken in the interests of the Jewish Theological Seminary of America, served on its Board in 1904, delivered an address on behalf of the striking students of RIETS in May, 1908, and was now speaking in behalf of the new seminary. Rabbi Jaffe, on the other hand, had been on the Yeshiva Committee of the Agudat ha-Rabbanim and was now urging a splinter group to separate from RIETS. The motives of these two men are not clear. They may have been truly devoted to the idea of secular education, although the *Tageblatt's* comments on Rabbi Jaffe would seem to exclude this appraisal. On the other hand, Rabbi Jaffe was the stormy petrel on the rabbinic scene, known as an impetuous nonconformist who rushed in without fear when his mind was made up.

Presumably organized, the Yeshiva le-Rabbanim proceeded to seek funds. On October 20 and on various dates through November, the committee advertised for city and "country" collectors,[37] who were asked to apply at 213 East Broadway, which was probably the head-quarters of the school.[38] In mid-November, Naphtali Kaplan, the secretary, announced that Rabbis Kaufman, Dickstein and Rosen were designated to travel on behalf of the new seminary.[39] At the end of December, the organizers engaged Yitzchok Chaim Skliar,[40] and in February of the new year, Mate Newman and Rabbi Yerachmiel Cohen volunteered to travel, too.[41]

There seems to be no record at all of the officers, teachers, or students of the Yeshiva le-Rabbanim. For that matter, no one knows where any sessions were held, or even if there were any.[42] Nor is there any idea of the size of the budget or curriculum. The *Jüdische Gazetten* decided to revise the previous position of the Sarasohn papers on the subject of the Yeshiva for rabbis since it was desirous of saying "something good about the program of the Yeshiva le-Rabbanim." It proclaimed:

> The purpose of the new Yeshiva according to the program is to produce rabbis who are well grounded in Torah and secular subjects. . . . In this program are included Jewish history, Jewish philosophy and a full-course university curriculum.[43]

Beyond this statement in the Yiddish press no further news of the Yeshiva le-Rabbanim appears. The new protest school, which met with momentary enthusiasm and limited newspaper and public support, was too large an undertaking to subsist on the limited interest it was able to evoke. Although the ill-fated venture was short-lived, it existed long enough to help confuse the loyal adherents of RIETS, bedevil its directors and lure a number of its finest students, who never again returned to Henry Street.

The final sardonic comment on the year of attrition was made by the *Gazetten,* which wrote:

> The battle between RIETS and the striking students has ended in the best possible manner. The Yeshiva has remained [under] the previous administration and [with] mostly new students who study for the sake of study itself; and the other Yeshiva students have opened a new rabbinical seminary—whence will go forth rabbis possessing an American education.[44]

To all appearances, the great strike had been a successful catharsis of an old feud, and the subsequent reconciliation should have been a firm springboard from which to launch RIETS into an era of good will and achievement. However, both the procedure of the directors' meetings and their conclusions left some bitter disappointments. At only one of the meetings were any student representatives present. They had no part in the final determination of their case. The results were handed to them without an opportunity to suggest modifications or even to voice agreement. In short, they had not yet been granted official recognition by the directors. This lack of recognition may have been due to the directors' desire to put their own house in order privately before receiving the students, or the absence of communication channels following the students' announced break with the administration. The students' arrogant behavior in calling the strike and their determined handling of public relations as well as their general conduct during that time may have convinced some directors that it would be dangerous to give official recognition to such a highly charged and volatile element.

The final decisions of the administration and its friends were also wanting in other respects. While a great stride forward was made in according sanction to secular studies and granting students temporary permission to attend outside supplementary schools pending the establishment of a satisfactory program at RIETS, there was no promise as to how long it would take to develop a program. In addition, the financial instability of the institution was in no ways improved by the establishment of a new committee which merely carried on the efforts of the previous administrations. All that had been introduced was a change of name rather than a change of methods and approach. Nevertheless, RIETS was definitely on the road to a synthesis even though all the stumbling blocks had not yet disappeared.

CHAPTER 8. THE DREAM OF A GRAND MERGER

At the final session of the first convention of the Agudat ha-Rabbanim in 1902, a resolution had been adopted ending with the hope "that if possible, Yeshiva Etz Chaim and RIETS should be united."[1] RIETS was almost six years old then and already exhibiting a precocious aptitude for financial instability. The rabbis felt that a merger between the younger, more volatile school and the sedate Etz Chaim would benefit both. RIETS would gain a measure of financial security and a permanent home, while Etz Chaim would acquire a more mature level of students and scholars and the status of a European academy.

Although the hope of the Agudat ha-Rabbanim was referred to a convention committee for action, it was not immediately fulfilled. RIETS continued to produce Talmudic scholars and great financial deficits with equal ease and regularity, while Etz Chaim maintained the steady, unspectacular pace of the predictable. There was an air of informality about RIETS that would have been exciting or charming had it been confined to the spirit of the students and the environs of the study hall. When, however, this casualness seemed to be more reflected in the activities of the directors, the matter became tragic.

The Agudat ha-Rabbanim may have viewed the merger possibility from an idealistic point of view by considering not only increased mutual benefits for the two principals, but also prospects for greater joint service to the community. In fact, however, the merger did not come about as a planned constructive effort. It came for RIETS—after a decade of arduous attempts to maintain a separate identity—out of need and pressure and of final capitulation to difficult days and unsympathetic times. The turning point for RIETS came between 1907 and 1908 when the depression and the student strike revealed the economic and curricular weaknesses of the Seminary.

The strike was a particularly damaging blow, for financial emergencies could be explained away as universal ailments, but academic revolutions implied wrongs and neglects that should have been corrected.

Educational and Practical Shortcomings

The favorable reaction of the press and of most of the rabbinate and the East Side to the students' demands for secular education pointed the direction that RIETS would have to take in order to justify its claims to the Jewish community. The "settlement" of the strike, which failed to go to the root of the matter, only relieved the pressure of complaints by treating nothing more than the symptom of the weakness.

In contrast, the Jewish Theological Seminary encouraged college training for its students and claimed that it required its rabbinical students to possess a college degree before ordination. Therefore, it did not find it necessary to offer secular courses under its own sponsorship. RIETS, however, was not as selective in the make-up of its student body. The hesitant concessions the directors had made to secular education during the difficult years were too tardy, too limited, and much too elementary to be satisfactory.

As a result a host of young men transferred from RIETS to the Jewish Theological Seminary, or to the short-lived Yeshiva le-Rabbanim, while many others simply left RIETS in despair. And many students were to continue to transfer to the Jewish Theological Seminary even after the strike.[2] In 1912, the student body stood at about 75,[3] in 1913 it was down to 55,[4] less than half the roster in 1908.

The alarming decrease in enrollment precipitated a full-scale hearing before the twelfth annual convention of the Agudat ha-Rabbanim. A stalwart friend of RIETS, Rabbi Moses S. Margolies, was forced to criticize the unrealistic curriculum of the Yeshiva as the cause of the student defection. The younger rabbis, who were alumni of RIETS, added a new charge to that of Rabbi Margolies by accusing the administration of "mismanagement," a veiled term that had frequently cropped up during the strikes. The upshot of the session was a resolution introduced by Rabbi Bernard L. Levinthal of Philadephia, which strongly condemned the Jewish Theological Seminary and its adjunct, the United Synagogue of America as non-Orthodox.[5] At the same time, it supported Rabbi Margolies' important suggestion for the Agudat ha-Rabbanim to organize a new yeshiva which would present a satisfactory secular education, not in conflict with traditional Judaism.[6] Neither of these recommendations was acted on directly, both being referred to committees for study,[7] but the suggestion to create a new yeshiva with adequate secular education was testimony that even the rabbinate was convinced of the need to formulate such a curriculum.

The glaring omission of secular studies in the curriculum was matched by an equally important neglect of the field of Jewish scholarship other than Talmud. RIETS was lax in providing instruction in theology, Jewish history, philosophy, literature, Hebrew grammar and related subjects. The need for secular training was more pressing, but the absence of a satisfactory grounding in all the cognate fields of Jewish knowledge and science was more shocking.

For the incipient rabbi remaining at RIETS, there was still another problem. The school had not organized any placement service to locate pulpits for the graduates upon completion of their studies. The directors depended on members of the Agudat ha-Rabbanim to relay news of vacant pulpits to the school or personally to recommend graduates to congregations. Occasional announcements in the press offering the service of students and graduates to congregations during the holidays represented the major effort made by the directors to place their rabbis.[8] These educational and practical shortcomings of RIETS emphasized the nonprofessional attitude of the school and were the factors that discouraged many from continuing and others from enrolling in RIETS.

In addition, the directors after 1908 were as unsuccessful in producing needed funds as their predecessors. RIETS had no philanthropists of the status of Jacob H. Schiff, Adolph Lewisohn, Felix Warburg, or Daniel Guggenheim, as did the Jewish Theological Seminary, to ease the financial pressures. Samuel Wilner, who had taken the helm of RIETS at the end of 1908 after the school had twice been closed for lack of funds, had managed by financial legerdemain to keep the school on an even keel. In May, 1909, a five-year mortgage for $20,000 was granted, and in December another for $1,200 was assumed[9] primarily to satisfy the original mortgages of $17,000 dating back to the purchase of the building and to pay other accrued debts. However, in the following year, as the interest payment on the mortgage fell due, RIETS was again without funds. An advertisement for aid stated:

> it is impossible to carry on . . . not only is our income insufficient to cover our weekly expenses, but now we must meet a $1,200 mortgage payment . . . and we have no means whereby to raise it . . .[10]

The burden of the $20,000 mortgage was a crushing load on the backs of the directors. Not only were they unable to meet this obligation, but even the $300 weekly budget could not be covered. In 1914, as the mortgage fell due, RIETS was again threatened with the grim prospect of foreclosure and loss of the building.[11] In marked contrast to the desperate condition of RIETS came the announcement from the Jewish Theological Seminary of America that its annual budget of $45,000, at least triple that of RIETS, was covered by $28,000 from its $600,000 endowment fund, $7,000 from collections and sundry contributions and the remaining $10,000 by "friends" of the Seminary.[12]

David Cohen, who succeeded Wilner as president of RIETS in 1910, inherited a $6,000 debt.[13] Although the directors strove valiantly to reduce it,[14] it was never completely shaken off. When personal resources proved insufficient to cope with daily expenditures, the directors' only alternative was to appeal for more help. Again and again they turned to the public for contributions, specifically for the "mortgage fund." But they had very little success.[15]

The constant shortages unquestionably hampered expanding the Talmud faculty and may have contributed as much to the absence of an adequate secular faculty as did the directors' shortsightedness and fear of the New World culture. The nagging, constant need for money must have shortened their tempers and added to their dis-comfiture. David Abramowitz, the Secretary of RIETS and its execu-tive officer, was probably the target for a share of the blame. Whether he was criticized for his work or simply exhausted by the super-human task, we do not know, but in 1910, Abramowitz curtly an-nounced, "I have resigned my position as Secretary of RIETS. From this day on, I have no further connection with the Yeshiva."[16] He had been with RIETS since its formation in 1897 and was one of its founders.

The board meeting at which this resignation must have been con-sidered reported no reference to Abramowitz's resignation. In a unanimous action, Chaim Robinson, a one-time vice-president and active director of RIETS, was elected to replace Abramowitz[17] with the new title of Superintendent.[18] The next year, however, without explanation, the directors announced that Abramowitz had been re-appointed to the recently created post of Superintendent.[19] Nothing else is known about the temporary retirement of Abramowitz and the momentary flurry of excitement that must have struck the directors.

One Great Center of Torah Leadership

That the difficult days at the beginning of the second decade of the century passed without too much friction despite great difficulties must have been owing to the leadership of David Cohen, the new president of RIETS. It was Cohen who now brought the hope of union between RIETS and the Yeshiva Etz Chaim to the discussion stage. Carrying it a step further, he included the Rabbi Jacob Joseph School, which was still in its infancy, in the plan for one great center of Torah scholarship. In addition, he initiated an important effort to transfer the location of the projected new institution to the "uptown" section of New York where it would find more social acceptance and hence greater support among the wealthier Jews.

Cohen was in some respects, typical of the Jews who lived "up-town." Having come from Suwalk, Lithuania to the United States in 1868 at the age of fourteen, he began his business career as a peddler, traveling to distant parts of the country to build up a route. When the problems of Jewish observance in such an itinerant life became acute, he turned to other occupations that kept him in the city where Jewish life was easier. In rapid succession he turned from tinware to the manufacture of clothes and then to real estate where he became the president of the firm of Gold and Cohen on lower Broadway. However, unlike many other immigrants who "arrived," Cohen continued his Jewish studies in his free time and became a scholar. As he became more successful, he devoted more time to communal needs. When David Cohen was named president of RIETS, he was already known as a founder of the Eldridge Street Synagogue, the Uptown Talmud Torah, Beth Israel and Lebanon Hospitals, the Bronx Machzikei Talmud Torah and the Hebrew Teachers' Institute, as well as a supporter of many charitable institutions and synagogues and a member of the Advisory Board of the New York Kehillah (the overall Jewish community organization of the City of New York, founded in 1908).[20]

Cohen was the kind of president that RIETS needed. He had experience in philanthropies and wide acquaintance among the wealthier Jews who could help the foundering institution. An energetic and forceful man, Cohen possessed a love for Torah and reverence for Jewish learning complemented by a healthy appreciation of secular accomplishment. The new president also commanded the respect of his board and the membership at large.[21] Under his regime, the directors' meetings were well-attended and well-directed. Even the general membership began to attend, frequently swelling the directors' gatherings to forty and fifty in number. After Cohen had been in office for only a month, the board reported that "RIETS was once again on its financial feet and moving in a new and healthy direction."[22]

As the spring of 1911 approached, Cohen's well-thought-out program for RIETS and for yeshiva education began to emerge. Much groundwork must have been done to prepare the projected plan. Undoubtedly, there were personal meetings among the officers of the three yeshivot and much behind-the-scenes activity. It appears that each of the two elementary yeshivot was dealt with independently of the other, for the first public notice of the discussions came in the form of newspaper reports that a meeting had taken place between representatives of the Rabbi Jacob Joseph School and RIETS for the purpose of effecting a merger. The conference was called at the home of Zalman Tennenbaum, treasurer of the Rabbi Jacob Joseph School. Samuel Y. Andron, the moving force behind that school, was the chairman of the meeting. Others present, in addition to the above named and David Cohen, were Shapiro, Chaim Dolinsky, Aaron Jacobs, Nathan Lamport, Samuel J. Abrams, Chaim Robinson, Abraham M. Levy, Raphael Joseph, Jonathan Scheff, Chaim Harris and Jacob L. Andron. After the proposal was debated and studied, the group decided to call another meeting of the special committees of both schools within the week to give the schools a further opportunity to study the blueprint and work out the details of the merger.[23]

Four days later, David Cohen convened his board to consider the plan. After presenting the plan of the proposed merger with the Rabbi Jacob Joseph School, Cohen added that he had reason to believe that Yeshivat Etz Chaim would join in the merger as well, thereby bringing all three yeshivot under one administration.

The ensuing deliberations revealed four major advantages of the Cohen proposal. The yeshivot overlapped in different areas of instruction, duplicating their educational services. Their competition for recognition and material assistance from the community substantially affected their individual incomes. Two obvious advantages could therefore be gained by eliminating the overlapping between the institutions' programs and consolidating the budgets. At the same time, there was a third advantage in that the pressure upon the directors would be diminished, giving them more time to concentrate on the vital educational problems of the schools. Lastly, Cohen reasoned, a united Yeshiva building could become the focal point for all manner of Jewish activity and a center of Orthodox Jewish strength and influence. Cohen's presentation was well reasoned and tenable, and his proposals seemed most desirable. The competition between the yeshivot for recognition and for financial support was fierce and often tinged with acrimony. Cohen reported that philanthropists had been so badgered by the different yeshivot and the many appeals that would-be supporters had ceased giving altogether. The plan for the merger was vigorously supported by the board. Chaim Dolinsky pointed out that many gifts had been pledged contingent on a successful merger that would otherwise never have been offered. Nathan Lamport, Rabbi Isaac W. Wendrofsky, Baruch Pinchas Liberman, Harry Altschul and Maier Freiman also spoke in favor of the plan. Rev. Adas and Chaim Robinson dissented but abstained from voting against the merger. At ballot time, the plan was successfully carried; only three members voted against it.[24]

While the directors at RIETS were arriving at a favorable decision, the directors of the Rabbi Jacob Joseph School also were meeting and ratifying the proposal. It was decided that each school would appoint a committee to complete the merger plans. Rabbis Yehuda David Bernstein and Isaac W. Wendrofsky, together with Nathan Lamport, Jonathan Scheff, H. Lass, Abraham Levy and Maier Freiman, made up RIETS' delegation.[25]

The tenor of the meetings and the practicality of the plan seemed to create a propitious climate for its satisfactory adoption. According to newspaper reports, both groups seemed ready to confirm the union. The negotiations were still underway when the *Jewish Morning Journal,* favoring the union, optimistically editorialized that "the union is imminent and soon to be consummated."[26]

The proud names of Rabbi Isaac Elchanan and Rabbi Jacob Joseph, however, were not destined to be united in a merger between the schools that commemorated their lives. For just as suddenly as the negotiations began, they were dropped and never heard of or referred to again. The plans to unite RIETS and the Rabbi Jacob Joseph School were probably aborted by fierce jealousies rooted in the competition to capture the same sympathetic ears and generous pockets.

The Rabbi Jacob Joseph School pursued a very aggressive public relations policy, laying claim to all the progress and achievements in yeshiva education, especially the distinction of having been the "first" school to follow a combined program of Hebrew and secular studies. When the Rabbi Jacob Joseph School launched its campaign for a new building, the *Tageblatt* stated that "ten years ago in America there was not a single institution where Hebrew and English studies were taught . . . [The Rabbi Jacob Joseph School] was the first Jewish-secular school in America."[27] Later the directors themselves made the claim that the Rabbi Jacob Joseph School was the "first Yeshiva in America, whose students receive a synthesized program"[28] and whose graduates were accepted in high schools and the City College.[29] Obviously, none of these claims were founded in fact, for both RIETS and the Yeshiva Etz Chaim had been established earlier. The latter had been organized a full fifteen years before the Rabbi Jacob Joseph School offered a course of elementary school secular subjects and was actually the prototype for what is the present day-school movement in America.

Further, the directors of RIETS were incensed by the attempts of the Rabbi Jacob Joseph School to appear its equal in Talmudic achievement. They felt that the elementary school had no right to imply that it was a full-scale yeshiva since it taught only younger children and offered no instruction leading to ordination. Their indignation was epitomized in the action of Chaim Robinson, who had originally urged against ratifying the merger proposal. Perhaps more impetuously than wisely, he traveled to Roxbury, Massachusetts, to present charges before a convention of the Agudat ha-Rabbanim that the Rabbi Jacob Joseph School was "only a Talmud Torah" in comparison to RIETS, and that it had no right to the title "Yeshiva" which was incorporated in its name. Consequently, Robinson demanded that the Rabbi Jacob Joseph School should be forced to yield the title. Rabbi Wendrofsky, a director in both schools, objected to the proposal on the grounds that the elementary school had already been using the title for over ten years and to deprive it of the designation would now harm the school greatly. As usual, in dealing with a controversial matter, the Agudat ha-Rabbanim took no direct action on the complaint but referred the subject to a committee.[30] Robinson's trip, however, made the position quite clear of at least one of the directors of RIETS on the subject of relations with the Rabbi Jacob Joseph School.

Concurrently with the merger proposal, David Cohen had put into motion his second plan, which was to move the yeshiva "uptown." Only a month after the RIETS had approved the preliminary details of the merger, in March 1911, the directors met again to report the purchase of two houses at 40 and 42 West 115th Street between Fifth and Lenox Avenues in Harlem. The buildings were to be razed, and an imposing school building was to be erected on the site.[31]

Harlem was then the fashionable Jewish neighborhood of the day. It boasted of new, modern tenements and modish brownstones that attested to the well-to-do condition of their inhabitants. The section was contiguous with Central Park and Mount Morris Park and had a stylish promenade area on Fifth and Seventh Avenues where rich and famous Jews strolled on the Sabbaths and Sundays. The area between 110th and 116th streets was dotted with synagogues. Dr. Klein's Ohab Zedek Synagogue, occupying a prominent position on 116th Street, was soon to be joined by the Senier Synagogue and the new Institutional Synagogue organized by Rabbi Herbert S. Goldstein, an emerging figure on the American-Jewish scene. Other East Side synagogues had also been relocated in this new, thriving Jewish environment. The Rabbi Israel Salanter Yeshiva was at 74 East 118th Street, the Yeshiva of Harlem, on 114th Street, between Fifth and Lenox Avenues; the Yeshiva Torat Chaim, at 105 East 103rd Street and the Jewish Theological Seminary, on 123rd Street. The proposed site on 115th Street was almost in the center of this newest and most influential Jewish population area, the proper location for a modern yeshiva. Cohen himself lived on West 113th Street, and he hoped that by bringing the Yeshiva "uptown" he would make it fashionable.

It is not clear whether the board of RIETS was already aware of the nullification of the merger plan with the Rabbi Jacob Joseph School, but within the week that the report of the purchase was revealed, the Board of Directors of the Rabbi Jacob Joseph School convened to consider similar plans for the construction of its own building.[32] After all the sanguine anticipation, hope for a merger between RIETS and the Rabbi Jacob Joseph School seemed to be destroyed forever.

Unfortunately for RIETS, for the chances of union and for the plans of the Harlem school, David Cohen died on April 18, 1911, at the age of 57, little more than half a year after he had assumed the presidency. The newspapers reported that Cohen had been sick for three weeks, probably while the purchase of the proposed new site was being discussed. Had he lived, there is no telling what progress might have been made. Instead, the directors of RIETS—and thousands of other Jews who attended his funeral—paid their respects to a dedicated servant of his people,[33] who was the prime mover in the enlightened effort for the development and modernization of the yeshiva movement.

CHAPTER 9. THE RABBINICAL COLLEGE
OF AMERICA

David Cohen's loss was deeply felt by RIETS. His administration, though short-lived, had been energetic and constructive. During his term the plans to combine the three oldest yeshivot on the East Side and to move "uptown" emerged as the most positive steps taken in the fifteen-year history of the Rabbi Isaac Elchanan Theological Seminary. Although the merger with the Rabbi Jacob Joseph School had not materialized, the principle of union which Cohen had sponsored remained as an inspiration for his successor. Negotiations with Yeshivat Etz Chaim continued uninterrupted under Harry Altschul, the next RIETS president[1] until 1912, the year the two yeshivot ratified the union in principle.[2] In 1915 with the name Rabbinical College of America, the new institution moved into its own quarters at 9-11 Montgomery Street under the presidency of one of the great scholars and personalities of the age, Dr. Bernard Revel.

The merger with Etz Chaim was the only part of Cohen's program successfully carried out. Unfortunately, in the course of arriving at an agreement, the directors of RIETS and Yeshivat Etz Chaim decided to dispose of the Harlem property and allow the new institution to remain "downtown."[3] Thus, the golden opportunity to move to a better location was abandoned for sixteen years. It was not until 1928 that RIETS finally moved to its present headquarters in Washington Heights. All the details of the merger were never fully revealed, but by its terms Yeshivat Etz Chaim was to become the high school or preparatory school, while RIETS was to be devoted to the more mature students who were preparing for ordination.[4] In this way a self-contained and integrated Jewish educational unit, ranging through the highest level of Talmudic scholarship, was established for the first time on American soil.

The merger came at an opportune moment for RIETS. The financial obligations had become staggering during the latter years. Not one cent had been paid towards reducing the $20,000 mortgage that was due in May 1914, and the water bill had not been paid since 1910. Debts were pyramiding with frightening rapidity and no relief was in sight. The final blow came when RIETS, unable to stave off the mortgager any longer, was served with a summons on August 30, 1915, after which action to foreclose was begun.[5] As a result of the union, RIETS acquired a more secure financial position based on the solvency of Yeshivat Etz Chaim. It is not clear where the new institution had originally intended to make its home, but when it became apparent that RIETS would not be able to meet its mortgage payment, the whole school moved west to the Etz Chaim building at 85 Henry Street.[6]

The housing arrangements which brought the two schools together under one roof were only temporary, because the Etz Chaim building was dilapidated and overcrowded even for its own students.[7] Earlier, a decision had been taken to build a new home for the combined schools, and Harry Fischel, who at times had been a director of both yeshivot, was selected chairman of the committee to seek a site and prepare plans. Fischel was an excellent choice. He had fulfilled a similar task for Yeshivat Etz Chaim in 1899 when its building at 1 Canal Street had been condemned by the city to make room for Seward Park. Through his efforts, the 85 Henry Street building was purchased while Fischel, himself, made the initial payment.[8]

By 1915, Mr. Fischel was already well-known as a philanthropist and devoted Jew. He was serving or had served as the treasurer of the Hebrew Sheltering and Immigrant Aid Society, a director and benefactor of the Hebrew Free Loan Society, a director and vice-president of Beth Israel Hospital, a member of the Advisory Board of the Montefiore Home, a founder of the American Jewish Committee, an organizer of the Hebrew Day Nursery, president of the Uptown Talmud Torah and the Machzikei Talmud Torah and treasurer of the Central Relief Committee.[9] Serving on the building committee with him were Nathan Roggen, who had been treasurer of Etz Chaim and Jonathan Scheff, who had been treasurer of RIETS.[10] After considerable effort, they bought two buildings at 9 and 11

Montgomery Street, between East Broadway and Henry Street, at a cost of $20,000.[11] These were to be razed almost entirely and a new building was to be erected on the site.

A New Epoch in Jewish Education

On Thursday, July 1, 1915, the cornerstone ceremonies for the new building took place,[12] and Harry Fischel was given the honor of setting the cornerstone. Jacob Hecht, the new president of the combined schools, Rabbis Moses S. Margolies, Avraham E. Alperstein, Philip Hillel Klein, Commissioner of Education, I. M. Levy and other prominent rabbis addressed the large audience.[13] Mr. Fischel in his remarks restated the purpose of the new Rabbinical College as it had been hammered out through the vicissitudes of the previous years:

> The new Rabbinical College, whose birth it is now our privilege to witness, holds forth as its object "Orthodox Judaism and Americanism," that is, its aim shall be to educate and produce Orthodox rabbis who will be able to deliver sermons in English, so that they may appeal to the hearts of the younger generation, and, at the same time, who will be thoroughly qualified to occupy positions with congregations demanding conformity with the strict requirements of Orthodox Judaism.

Following the ceremony of the cornerstone laying, an appeal for funds was made by Rabbi Herbert S. Goldstein and Rev. Zvi Masliansky in response to which more than $10,000 was subscribed.[14]

Harry Fischel's experience in this field expedited the work, and the building was soon completed. Only the two side walls butting the flanking buildings were retained. The rest of the building was a modern, new, fireproof structure. So well had Fischel planned that the entire construction cost, estimated at $25,000,[15] was reduced to a little more than $16,000.[16] In its final form, the facilities of the school, in addition to a dining room and kitchen in the basement[17] and "all the latest sanitary devices, including shower baths of the newest design,[18] were described in the *Rabbinical College of America Register* of 1917:

> The building is divided into:
> Ground floor which contains business offices, supply and reading rooms, and laboratory for the high school department.
> First floor which contains the office of the President of the Faculty, a teacher's room, and a synagogue.
> Second and third floors which contain the study rooms of the College.[19]

The dedication was celebrated by a week-long program of activities beginning Sunday, December 5, and culminating on Sunday, December 12, when Dr. Bernard Revel was formally inducted as president of the faculty.[20] Whether by accident or intent, the arrangements committee[21] scheduled the dedication ceremonies to coincide with the Festival of Hanukkah, which commemorated the rededication of the Temple in Maccabean days. During that week, prominent rabbis, laymen, and communal figures, who addressed the afternoon and evening audiences, compared the Rabbinical College to the Temple of old.[22] The *Jüdische Tageblatt* extolled it as "the highest [Torah] institution in the United States"[23] that "will bring to fruition the dream that a great number of Jews have had for years."[24] The enthusiasm of the press was infectious. The *New York Tribune,* generally uninterested in Jewish affairs, showed its ignorance, albeit its enthusiasm, by predicting that the dedication of the "Jewish Seminary . . . marks the end of the ancient 'cheder.' " This is how the reporter of the *Tribune* saw and evaluated the event:

> Young men with long forelocks and drooping shoulders mounted with quick, springy steps the stairs of eleven Montgomery Street yesterday. The forelocks were prescribed by Orthodox Jewish Law and the droop of the shoulders was due to a life occupied mainly with poring over their ancient tomes and yellowed print. They should have been sitting along narrow benches with skull caps perched on their heads and rocking to and fro as they intoned, in sing song fashion, passages from the Talmud. But these students who had come from Russia, Galicia and Roumania, were to be introduced to the Occident and its ways. New York has seen the last of the ancient "cheder" where Jewish youths studied the

Talmud through the watches of the night. . . . Old country methods of educating Jewish spiritual leaders were abolished yesterday. . . . Therefore, the East Side, which in many ways is trying to forget what it suffered abroad, celebrated.[25]

The directors, of course, never intended the Rabbinical College to replace the *heder*. The emphasis was in a different direction. Ephraim Caplan, a keen analyst of the Jewish-American scene of the day, foretold that the new Rabbinical College would "create a new epoch in American Jewish education" and saw in its formation the "most important event in the spiritual history of the Jews in the United States." He wrote that the new yeshiva would raise the standards of all the Talmud Torahs and the elementary yeshivot by providing an educational level towards which they could aim.[26] Instead of abruptly ending instruction at their present point, the elementary schools could create higher classes that would lead to admission to the Rabbinical College. In this way, American children rising through the ranks of these lower schools could be channeled into the College just as they would be directly from Yeshivat Etz Chaim. Caplan, indeed, underscored an important function of the College, not only as it applied to the school's own purpose of producing rabbis, but in the larger sense, as it pertained to all Jewish education. The effect the Rabbinical College might have on Jewish education could not be overrated because, in the final analysis, it meant leading American-born students through the levels of education to the highest of all, ordination. By 1915 several thousand students had already been taught at Yeshivat Etz Chaim and five hundred older students had been trained at RIETS.[27] Of these, only a handful were American-born, and of the thirty or so rabbis who had been ordained by RIETS,[28] none were natives. The world situation in 1915 did not offer much hope for greater immigration from Europe in the near future, and the continuity of the rabbinate in America depended on the successful encouragement and enlistment of native Americans in the rabbinical school. The directors, through long experience, had come to realize that in order to fulfill their obligations, the Rabbinical College could not be another European yeshiva on American soil; it had to be an American yeshiva serving all the needs—American

and Jewish. Harry Fischel articulated this thought during the dedication ceremonies. As he formally presented the key of the building
to Jacob Hecht, the president, he said: "Since the supply of students
which we could formerly expect from foreign countries has been cut
off, it is our duty to interest American young men in the study of
Rabbinical culture."[29]

By all standards, the dedication ceremonies were successful. The
school was finally launched, and $2,000 had been collected on the first
day of the week-long activities.[30] Ephraim Caplan again made a
shrewd comment about the affair when he pointed out that the
"uptown Jews had not participated nor contributed as they should
have" and that they "had given much more to Reform activities than
to Orthodox, despite the fact that they call themselves Orthodox."[31]
The *Jewish Morning Journal* was equally abashed that only the
"lower and middle classes" had shown interest in the new school.
The paper made a virtue out of it, however, by pointing out that the
Yeshiva was a democratic organization and close to the people,[32] but
the rationalization convinced no one, for the Yeshiva needed much
help and would need it for many years to come. Perhaps David
Cohen's proposal to move "uptown" would have been the wisest plan
after all and would have accelerated the Yeshiva's financial progress
by ten or fifteen years. As it was, Caplan could imply with great
justice that the "uptown" Jews looked down on the East Side Yeshiva
as not quite socially acceptable or desirable.

The Orthodox "uptown" immigrant Jews, independent as they
pretended to be of their Reform and native American brethren, had
not entirely escaped the determined devotion of the latter to the
policy of "Americanization." Ironically, men like Israel Friedlander,
who stood in the forefront of the movement for Jewish education,
could not realize the importance of the yeshiva movement. As one
of the exponents of the theory of "Americanization," he warned the
Jewish world that the Beth Hamidrash and yeshiva were doomed
from the beginning and although attempts at reproducing them
had been made, they had not yielded any tangible results.[33]

The *American Israelite,* a publication of the Reform movement,
carried on its relentless propaganda against the Yeshiva and did not
hesitate:

to pronounce the New York Yeshiva an anachronism for which the United States had neither the time nor the place and every dollar spent for its maintenance is that much wasted or worse. A legitimate use can be found for every dollar that the Jews of the United States can spare and there is none to waste for transplanting into American soil an institution of the medieval ghetto.[34]

In the sense that the Yeshiva emphasized maximum Jewish learning, it did epitomize sectarianism and, consequently, was often termed parochial. Precisely this quality which should have rallied Orthodox Jews to the support of the new Rabbinical College, paradoxically, made the school unpalatable to the "uptown" Jews.

The East Side Jews, on the other hand, who were unaware of or unaffected by the philosophical battle raging about them, continued doggedly to strengthen the foundations of the Rabbinical College. Although their efforts were only moderately satisfactory, they were successful enough to merit the judgment pronounced a year after the merger of RIETS and Yeshivat Etz Chaim:

> without any help from "higher ups," the large Jewish masses of the country have built up an institution which is to give life and content to American Judaism in the future.[35]

This passage was written in the first issue of the *American Jewish Chronicle,* only nine months after the dedication of the new college; already the driving force of Dr. Bernard Revel, which permeated the institution, was being felt.

Dr. Bernard Revel: Man of Vision

Dr. Revel was inducted into the new office three months after his thirtieth birthday and remained until his death, a quarter of a century later.[36] When he became president, Dr. Revel was still a clean-shaven young man of slight body and average height. His youth, his unbearded face, his secular degrees and a pronounced stammer would have been insurmountable obstacles to the average candidate for the head of an Orthodox rabbinical seminary.

But Dr. Revel was a gifted intellect with rare vision, boundless energy and dedication. Like the proverbial "cemented cistern which loseth not a drop," his memory was prodigious. As a child of only six he could repeat entire pages of the tractate *Baba Kamma*. At twelve, his father and teacher, Rabbi Nachum Schraga Revel, who was a close friend of Rabbi Isaac Elchanan, passed away. The young lad continued his studies at the Yeshiva of Telshe and privately with many great scholars. Before the death of his father, he had been brought to Rabbi Isaac Elchanan, who was the spiritual leader of his native Kovno. The great sage blessed him and foretold his brilliant future. In 1906 when Dr. Revel came to America from Lithuania, his mental powers and reputation as an *illui* (precocious or unusually brilliant student) were already well known.

Unlike the average young rabbi of that period, Dr. Revel refused to permit himself to be drawn into the quagmire of routine. With equal enthusiasm, he devoted himself to secular studies and *ḥakhmat Yisrael,* the Wissenschaft des Judentums (the Scientific Study of Judaism).

In 1906, he entered RIETS as a student for a brief period and shortly thereafter began his studies at New York University where he earned his M.A. degree. Revel continued his graduate work at the Dropsie College for Hebrew and Cognate Learning when it opened in Philadelphia. Here Revel was urged by Rabbi Bernard L. Levinthal, who befriended all young *talmidei ḥakhamim* (talmudic scholars) to pursue the studies that prepared him for leadership. The flexibility of Revel's mind and the diversity of his interests at that time are gleaned from a letter he wrote to a friend then at RIETS.

His daily regimen included studying "the philosophy of the early Hindus, Oriental languages, economics, the development of the American Constitution, and Roman, Anglo-Saxon and American law." He was also "writing articles for journals in Russian, engaged in responsa on halachic questions and working on an introduction to the Order of *Mo'ed* of the Jerusalem Talmud." In this letter, too, Dr. Revel answered a request for an article in the *Philadelphia Jewish Exponent* by saying that he did not know which one was asked for "since I write one almost every week."[37] Dr. Revel's goal at the time was to achieve his Ph.D. from Dropsie College, and in 1912 he received its first Ph.D.[38] His dissertation on Karaite Halakha was a tour de force in *ḥakhmat Yisrael* and Halakha. In it, Dr. Revel refuted the generally accepted thesis, set forth in the nineteenth century by the brilliant scholar Abraham Geiger, that the Karaite Halakha was a continuation of rabbinic Halakha.

Even in the company of such venerable rabbis as Bernard L. Levinthal, Moses S. Margolies, Philip Hillel Klein, Shlomo Jaffe, Samuel Z. Wien and Avraham E. Alperstein, who made up the inner circle of the Orthodox rabbinic elite, Dr. Revel shone. When they sought a president for the new Rabbinical College of America, Dr. Revel's name was submitted by Rabbi Levinthal and unanimously accepted.

Rabbi Moses S. Margolies, president of the Agudat ha-Rabbanim, expressed the evaluation of the "greatest rabbis of the land" when he wrote, "Dr. Revel is one of the Torah giants of our generation and perhaps the only one in general knowledge and science."[39] Shortly thereafter, the press carried an announcement of the appointment of the new president of the faculty. It was signed by Jacob Hecht, president; Maier Freiman, Nathan Lamport and Rabbi Moses S. Margolies, past presidents; and Rabbis Solomon E. Jaffe of New York, Gershon Lesser of Cincinnati and Bernard L. Levinthal of Philadelphia. Dr. Revel was to be in charge of the secular and religious departments of the college. He was also to give regular *shiurim* in advanced Talmudic subjects.[40]

Dr. Revel threw himself into his new duties with zeal. Sincerely concerned with the welfare and future of the Jews in America, he refused to accept the reality of the struggling institution. In 1908 he wrote a colleague at RIETS:

> Some times I envy you because you are in the midst of our people on Henry Street and it is easy for you to observe at first hand the life and nature of our brethren in New York which is destined to be the center of all Jewry, and to see what they are doing and what they need . . .[41]

He was convinced that RIETS had an important role to play in serving that need. Long before there was any possibility of his affiliation with RIETS, Dr. Revel expressed his feeling about the rabbinical seminary. There had been talk by the students at RIETS about creating a new institution. The purpose of the proposed school, possibly the same as that of the Yeshiva le-Rabbanim, was to provide a way station for young European-trained students and rabbis until they could become adjusted to the new environment. The emphasis was not to be on training new rabbis but on making a hostel for these young men. On this subject, Dr. Revel wrote to his friend:

> You are quite right in what you wrote about a new yeshiva from the point of view of need . . . but not from the point of view of the much-torn resources of our people. If we are not rich enough in wealth and people to build and support two schools, then the more important need—a House of Torah for the training of rabbis —must take precedence over the lesser need—a hostel for scholars who come from Russia and Poland until they become adjusted and marry.

> I am aware of the need in every city where there is a substantial Jewish population and the potential to establish yeshivot, for youngsters who will not make Torah their profession . . . but as great as this work may be, they will not solve the problem of an advanced academy for the training of rabbis . . .[42]

For Dr. Revel, an advanced academy for rabbis was a necessity, and that these rabbis should be grounded in secular studies and Jewish science was equally important. He saw no danger in a general education. In a newspaper interview published to coincide with the cornerstone ceremonies of the Rabbinical College, he said, "I see no conflict, no inconsistency between Americanism and Judaism."[43] Instead, he urged "harmony."[44] Like Samson Raphael Hirsch to whom he was compared,[45] he believed in the saying, "I bless emancipation, if Israel does not regard it as the [complete] goal."

Dr. Revel's primary interest was to meet the oldest students' demand for secular education. With a rapidity unknown in the early days of RIETS and with a daring none of the previous leaders had possessed, Dr. Revel brought together a faculty of great distinction to teach secular subjects and Jewish science in the upper division. With one exception, every member of that faculty possessed a doctoral degree. Dr. Nahum Slousch of the Sorbonne gave several courses in Jewish history and literature; Dr. Henry Pereira Mendes presided over homiletics; Dr. Bernard Drachman taught pedagogy, Dr. Moses Seidel specialized in Bible, and Dr. Solomon Theodore Hurwitz offered Hebrew, Biblical and Aramaic grammar. Judah David Eisenstein, a well-known literary figure and editor of the *Otzar Yisrael,* the Hebrew encyclopedia, taught Midrash. Dr. Revel himself taught a course in ethics and philosophy as well as Talmud and Codes. In the latter courses he was assisted by Rabbis Benjamin Aranowitz, Joseph D. Levine, and Samuel Gerstenfeld.[46]

Talmudical Academy and Teachers Institute

While Dr. Revel wheedled, cajoled, and pleaded with supporters of the college for more assistance and enlisted scholars for his higher faculty, he was also thinking of the preparatory division. Together with Dr. Solomon Hurwitz, a young idealist who was on the faculty of Columbia University as well, Dr. Revel fashioned the division into the first high school in America where secular subjects and religious subjects were taught under Jewish auspices. As a new school within the Rabbinical College it now bore the name of the Talmudical Academy.

The first class of the Talmudical Academy, which numbered thirty odd, met on Sunday, September 3, 1916. Dr. Hurwitz was the prinpal and taught English language and literature. Dr. Georges Bacarat taught foreign languages; Dr. Benjamin Horowitz, physics and chemistry; Rabbi David S. Stern, M.A., mathematics. Isaac Rosengarten, B.A., editor of the *Jewish Forum,* taught civics and history, and Dr. Israel Kliegler, later the chief health officer of Palestine and professor of bacteriology at the Hebrew University, taught biology.[47] Later, Drs. Shelley R. Safir, Reuben Steinbach, Max Winkler, Elihu Pain, Maxwell S. Heller, Max Lieberman, and Solomon Friedman were added to the faculty.[48] When Dr. Hurwitz died in January 1919, a victim of the influenza epidemic that ravaged New York City, Dr. Safir replaced him as principal.[49]

During the years between the inception of the school and the first graduation, the high school was successfully recognized by the Board of Regents as a junior and middle senior high school. Just prior to the date of the first graduation in June 1919, Dr. Revel received word from Albany that the Talmudical Academy had been recognized as a full-fledged high school and entitled to the same privileges as all the city high schools. At this first graduation, six students received their diplomas: Marcus Abramson, Abraham Weitz, Samuel Bernstein, Hyman Rosen, Joseph Lesser and Benjamin Axelman. One was awarded a state scholarship.[50]

Within a few years, Dr. Revel had shaped the beginnings of a truly great institution of learning out of a small, struggling yeshiva. Never satisfied, he continued to exact of his own body and soul in behalf of the Rabbinical College even more than he sought from others. In 1917, the school had a total enrollment of 170 students of whom 90 were in the elementary grades, 40 were in high school, and 50 were pursuing advanced studies for the rabbinate.[51]

While he was still a student in New York City, Dr. Revel had been introduced by Rabbi Moshe Shimon Sivitz of Pittsburgh to Miss Sarah Rabinowitz Travis, daughter of Mr. and Mrs. Isaac Rabinowitz Travis. The Travis family was well known and distinguished for its piety and philanthropy. Dr. Revel and Sarah Travis were married on June 24, 1909 and had two sons, Norman, born in 1912, and Hirschel, born in 1913. Before and for some time after Dr. Revel became president of the Rabbinical College in 1915, he maintained a relationship with his inlaws' business interest. For several years, from the latter part of 1913 through 1922, he spent a good deal of time in Tulsa where he joined his brother-in-law Solomon Travis in operating the family's Oklahoma Petroleum and Gasoline Company. From March 1922 until Dr. Revel's return to full-time duties at the Yeshiva, Rabbi Meyer Berlin served as president of the Board of Directors and Rabbi Israel Rosenberg, as acting *Rosh Yeshiva,* or head of the Talmud Department.

It was Rabbi Berlin who was responsible for the addition of a new division, the Teachers Institute, to the yeshiva program.[52] The Teachers Institute had been established by the Mizrachi Organization of America in 1917 as the first Hebrew teachers' training school in America.[53] Its primary purpose was to provide qualified teachers of

Rabbi Isaac Elchanan

Rabbi Doctor Bernard Revel

Rabbi Moses S. Margolies

Rabbi Doctor Philip Hillel Klein

Rabbi Solomon Polacheķ

Rabbi Benjamin Aranowitz

Rabbi Moses Soloveitchik
Rabbi Bernard L. Leventhal

The First Graduating Class of the Talmudical Academy (1919)

FACULTY: *seated, left to right:* S. Posin (chemistry), Dr. David Stern (mathematics), Dr. Shelley R. Saphire, Principal (biology), Dr. Reuben Steinbach (English), Morris Cohen (history). GRADUATES: *standing, left to right:* Marcus Abramson, Abraham Weitz, Samuel Bernstein, Hyman Rosen, Joseph Lesser, Benjamin Axelman.

The First Faculty of Yeshiva College

Standing, left to right: Prof. Abraham B. Hurwitz (physical education), Prof. George M. Falion (Latin), Dr. Solomon A. Rhodes (French), Dr. Gustav F. Schulz (public speaking), Dr Moses L. Isaacs (chemistry); *seated:* Dr. Jacob R. Silverman (physics), Dr. Isaac Husik (philosophy), Dr. Charles F. Horne (English), Dr. Bernard Revel, Dr. Shelley R. Saphire (biology), Dr. Nelson P. Mead (history), Dr. Bernard Drachman (German), Dr. Jekutheil Ginsburg (mathematics). *Not shown:* Benzion Rosenbloom (psychology) and Dr. Solomon Gandz (librarian).

The Ground-Breaking Ceremony for Yeshiva College
Left to right: Morris Asinoff, Samuel Kamlet, Meyer Vessel, Nathan Roggen, Louis Roggen, Fabian.

Bidding Farewell to the Rabbi Isaac Elchanan Theological Seminary (301 East Broadway)

FIRST ROW: *holding Torah scrolls, left to right:* Rabbi Joseph D. Levine, Rabbi Moses S. Margolies; *center, first row:* Dr. Bernard Revel, Harry Fischel; *holding Torah scrolls, to the right on lower two steps:* Rabbi Sholom Rackovsky, Rabbi Aaron D. Burack; SECOND ROW: *holding Torah scrolls, left to right:* Rabbi Benjamin Aranowitz, Rabbi Jehudah Weil, Rabbi Samuel Gerstenfeld, Rabbi Ephraim M. Steinberg, Rabbi Chaim Shunfenthal, Rabbi Moses Aaron Poleyeff.

The Early Faculty of the Teachers Institute (ca. 1929)

> *Seated, left to right:* Dr. Samuel K. Mirsky, Dr. Nathan Klotz, Dr. Yechiel Kaplan, Dr. Pinkhos Churgin (Principal), Mr. Abraham Soyer, Mr. Abraham N. Perlberg; *standing, left to right:* Jacob I. Hartstein (Secretary), Dr. Solomon Wind, Prof. Moses Gildin, Mr. Shabsai Turboff.

The First Graduation Class of Yeshiva College (1932)

> *Top row, from left to right:* Max Hoch, Harry A. Steinberg, Joseph Kaminetsky, Hugo Mantel, Max Hirschman, Julius Washer, Joe Lief, David Golovensky, Chaim Golden; *front row, left to right:* Eli Levine, Joshua Matz, Louis Izenstein, Louis Engelberg, Hyman Muss, Dr. Shelley R. Saphire (Dean), Dr. Bernard Revel (President), Israel Upbin, Alex W. Nissenbaum, Morris S. Penkower, Mendel H. Lewittes, Jacob I. Hartstein.

Dr. Samuel Belkin, second president of Yeshiva University

Israel's Prime Minister David Ben Gurion (center), Dr. Belkin (left), Rabbi Joseph B. Soloveitchik (right)

Mrs. Franklin D. Roosevelt receiving an honorary degree

Albert Einstein receiving an honorary degree

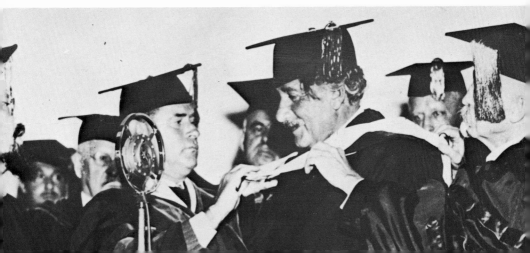

Vice President Richard M. Nixon receiving an honorary degree

Left to right: Chairman of the Board of Trusteees Max J. Etra, Chief Justice of the Supreme Court Earl Warren, Dr. Samuel Belkin, Senator Jacob K. Javits

Dr. Samuel Belkin with Israel's Prime Minister Levi Eshkol

Dr. Samuel Belkin and the Honorable Ar J. Goldberg

tor John F. Kennedy receiving the convocation award

Dr. Samuel Belkin and Vice President Lyndon B. Johnson

Dr. Samuel Belkin and Senator Robert F. Kennedy

Shmuel I. Agnon of Israel, Nobel Prize Laureate in Literature, receiving an honorary degree

Dr. Samuel Belkin with General Yitzhak Rabin, Israel's Ambassador to the United States

Justice Benjamin N. Cardozo receiving an honorary degree

Hebrew and religious subjects for the Jewish community of New York City and its environs and the American Jewry as a whole. We have already seen how inadequate were the provisions for Jewish religious education; teachers were unlicensed, uncertified and unprepared for their important duties. The "siddur peddler" was a prime illustration of the depths to which instruction in this field had sunk.

The lack of a training school for teachers of religious subjects was as serious a problem for the early Jewish immigrant community as the lack of a rabbinical seminary. In this instance, as in the case of the seminary, no established organization existed to create such a school. The Mizrachi Organization was a religious Zionist group formed in 1902 by Rabbi Yitzchak Yaacov Reines in Lida, Russia, to arouse the masses of Orthodox Jews to the support of a Jewish homeland, to represent them at the World Zionist Congresses and to defend the religious tradition in the developing Zionist philosophy. In 1909 an American division of the Mizrachi Organization was formed. Rabbi Meyer Berlin (Bar-Ilan), a distinguished Mizrachi leader in whose memory Bar-Ilan University in Israel was established by the Mizrachi Organization of America in 1955,[54] was president of the American Mizrachi in 1917. He assumed the duty of making American Jewry conscious of Zionism and reasoned that religious Zionism and a commitment to the Holy Land could best be stimulated through Jewish education, which would transmit the love of Hebrew, the holy tongue, the yearning of the prophets for the return of Zion, and the traditional relationship of the Jew to the land of Israel. Rabbi Berlin thus envisaged a teachers' training school which would qualify young men to staff the Talmud Torahs, elementary Jewish schools of education; by teaching Judaism and the Hebrew language effectively, they would become catalysts in the conversion of Jews to active, political Zionism.

With Rabbi Judah Leib Fishman (Maimon), who in 1948 was to be the first minister of religion of the State of Israel and who came from the Holy Land to help strengthen the work of Mizrachi in America; Rabbi Jacob Levinson, another influential Mizrachi leader, and Dr. Meyer Waxman, Rabbi Berlin established the Teachers Institute. In addition to being the first Jewish teachers' training school in the United States, it was also the first school of higher learning in this country to use Hebrew as the language of instruction. By so doing, it made Hebrew once again a viable, living language, and students of the Institute became proficient in its daily use.

Twelve students comprised the first class of the school at 86 Orchard Street on the lower East Side. It was a supplementary school for students of high school age who attended lectures at the Institute in the late afternoon and evening after their regular studies in the public high schools. The first principal of the school was Rabbi Jacob Levinson, who had just come from Chicago, and who was a leader in the younger group of the Mizrachi. In addition to Rabbi Levinson, Dr. Meyer Waxman and Dr. Yechiel Kaplan made up the faculty. The curriculum included the study of Hebrew language, Bible, prophets, Hebrew literature, Jewish history, Jewish laws, Talmud and pedagogy. Students were to spend two years in each of two classes and would receive their diplomas at the end of four years to coincide with their graduation from high school.

The Talmudical Academy and the Teachers Institute bore a natural relationship to each other. The former was a high school under religious Jewish auspices, the latter, a supplementary religious school for high school students. It was logical for the Talmudical Academy to seek the Teachers Institute students, who, because of their religious education, would integrate easily into its program. On the other hand, the Mizrachi Organization of America, while committed to religious education, was not an educational institution. Nor was it sufficiently endowed with funds to continue the sponsorship of a growing school. The two institutions could serve their common purpose best by joining their schools; consequently, in 1921, the Rabbi Isaac Elchanan Theological Seminary undertook to conduct the Teachers Institute in conjunction with the Mizrachi Organization of America.

There were now fifty students enrolled in the Teachers Institute, which was meeting in larger quarters at the Mizrachi building, 138 East Second Street. Dr. Solomon Zeitlin and Dr. Pinkhos Churgin, who were members of the faculty of the RIETS, joined the teaching staff of the Institute. Dr. Moses Seidel and Abraham N. Perlberg were also engaged to serve the increased student body. Rabbi Jacob Levinson resigned to take a rabbinical post in Brooklyn and Dr. Meyer Waxman succeeded him as principal.

Under the new arrangement, the students of the Teachers Institute transferred from the public high schools to the Talmudical Academy where they received their secular instruction in the afternoons. Their Institute program was still given at East Second Street, but was now taught in the mornings to correspond to the Talmudical Academy schedule. In 1922 RIETS took over the Institute completely[55] and relinquished the East Second Street location. Dr. Waxman, who in the interim had become secretary of the Mizrachi Organization, was unable to continue as principal because of his organizational duties, and Dr. Churgin became principal of the Teachers Institute. Dr. Yechiel Kaplan was named chairman of the faculty, and Norman B. Abrams, secretary. Later Dr. Churgin became dean of the Institute, a post he held until his retirement in 1955 to become the first president of Bar-Ilan University in Israel. He was succeeded by Dr. Hyman Grinstein, named director of the Teachers Institute.

In 1921, when RIETS joined the Mizrachi Organization in sponsoring the Teachers Institute, the building at 9-11 Montgomery Street, which had been dedicated with such pomp to the needs cf the Rabbinical College of America, had already been outgrown by the school. After little more than five years of occupancy, RIETS had to leave its home for a new location. This time the school took over an old age home called The Home of the Daughters of Jacob, at 301 East Broadway, the corner of Scammel Street.[56] The five-story building was taller and considerably larger than the building on Montgomery Street, but still was an "old dark house with twisted narrow steps and dimly lighted small rooms."[57] It was into this building with a "big mortgage"[58] that the Teachers Institute was absorbed as it became part of the Rabbi Isaac Elchanan Theological Seminary.

Despite its limitations, the building provided two great advantages over the Montgomery Street location. Because of its larger size, a dining room for the students was established in the basement and dormitory space for out-of-town students was created in the top story.[59] On the ground floor were the offices of Dr. Safir, the principal of the high school and of Samuel L. Sar, whose official title was secretary. But Sar was also office manager, in charge of fund-raising, responsible for the placement of the rabbis and Hebrew teachers, public relations man and adviser to the president. This was no mean responsibility, for the growing student body, the constantly rising budget, the administration of the number of divisions of the school, the distribution of regular weekly stipends ranging from $2 to $10 per week for each student,[60] directing the field representatives of the Yeshiva, who traveled to different cities to develop campaigns for funds,[61] as well as placing the scores of rabbis and teachers who graduated from the Yeshiva,[62] were enough to keep more than one man busy. With a calm and deliberate manner, Mr. Sar was always in control of the situation. In his mind he carried thousands of names and addresses of people he had never met but who had made a contribution to the Yeshiva; he never forgot a name, a face, an occupation, or a joke. He was a diplomat, a tactician and a skillful negotiator. An accomplished scholar in the Talmud, Bible, Jewish history and philosophy, Sar had studied in the Yeshiva of Telshe in Lithuania, was by training a lawyer and had been superintendent of a network of Talmud Torahs in Baltimore before he was brought to RIETS by Dr. Revel in 1919. For more than forty years he served the Rabbi Isaac Elchanan Theological Seminary. In later years he assumed the additional duties of professor of Bible in the Teachers Institute and in Yeshiva College, and dean of men of the College. But above all, Mr. Sar was the friend, confidant, and counselor of all the students. In 1962, he sustained a fatal heart attack as he presided over the ordination ceremonies in the Bet ha-Midrash of the Yeshiva. His last words, as he collapsed, were "and now I have the honor to present the President of Yeshiva University . . ."[63]

The rest of the ground floor was occupied by the Bet ha-Midrash, a combination synagogue and study hall where the senior members of the faculty delivered their *shiurim* to the students who were preparing for ordination. Here, too, the students prepared for and reviewed the lectures. The rooms on the upper floors were classrooms for the other students. The second floor of the building was given over to President Revel's office and to the library, which was presided over by Dr. Solomon Gandz. This library was enclosed in a small room and was only a token gesture toward the general reading and research needs of the students.[64] The heart of the reference library was found in the Bet ha-Midrash, where hundreds of copies of the Talmud, *Rishonim* and *Aḥronim* (earlier and later commentaries on the Talmud and Codes) were mulled over by the advanced students. In time, however, the second floor library was augmented by various important collections including 43,000 rare volumes purchased in 1926 from the estate of Rabbi Philip Hillel Klein, former president of the Rabbi Isaac Elchanan Theological Seminary, and presented to the school by David Ellis of Philadelphia.[65]

But the new building soon became overcrowded, too. Although the Elementary School Division, which had come with the absorption of Yeshivat Etz Chaim in 1915, was discontinued in 1924 (there being a number of elementary yeshivot in the city by that time), there was once again a pressing need for more school space. There were now almost 600 students in the various departments of the school,[66] of whom approximately 250 were enrolled in the Yeshiva Department, 200 in the high school and 100 in the Teachers Institute.[67] The Teachers Institute alone had doubled its enrollment in three years and added another sixty students in the spring term of 1925, while a number of applicants to the Seminary were turned away for lack of space.[68] There were fifteen classes in the school,[69] the faculty of the Yeshiva Department was now an even dozen,[70] and the budget had grown to between $150,000 and $250,000 per year,[71] an astronomical increase from the $10,000 budget of 1915.[72]

The Talmudical Academy was also growing apace and was admitting students from all parts of the country, including Seattle, Des Moines, Bridgeport, Houston, Scranton, Philadelphia, Cincinnati, Hartford, Jersey City, as well as from Ottawa and Windsor, in Ontario,[73] and even from Shanghai.[74] Greater numbers of students were also coming from Eastern Europe owing to an exemption in the restrictive Immigration Acts granted to the Rabbi Isaac Elchanan Theological Seminary.[75]

The increase in the student body reflected the growing acceptance of the Rabbi Isaac Elchanan Theological Seminary as an important Jewish educational center. RIETS had a high school, the Talmudical Academy, a Teachers Institute, and a Seminary Department. Most important, however, was that under Dr. Revel the school had a direction and a program which were in harmony with the needs of the times. The larger enrollment also proved that the Jewish immigrant community had accepted the principle of bicultural education under Jewish auspices. Under the stewardship of Dr. Revel, RIETS was soon to become a full-fledged college in more than name only, and later, a university. But more important, it was to emerge as the focal point of Orthodox Judaism for American Jewry. Indeed Dr. Revel, who had crammed the hours and days with heart-rending labor, a labor that took its toll of his great spirit, created for American Jewry one of its greatest service institutions.

CHAPTER 10. THE FOUNDING OF
YESHIVA COLLEGE

The need for new school quarters coincided with Dr. Revel's almost compulsive desire to create a collegiate division within the Yeshiva. When he assumed the presidency of the institution, it was known as the Rabbinical College of America, and although use of this name had long been discontinued, the word "college" echoed in his memory and absorbed his mind. While the idea of a Jewish college in itself was revolutionary, it was nevertheless a natural outgrowth of the Talmudical Academy which could provide a parallel school of general studies for the older students of the Seminary in the same way that the high school served the younger students of the Yeshiva Department and the Teachers Institute.

Dr. Revel envisioned the college as an instrument to retain the students of the Talmudical Academy, who upon graduation from high school, interrupted their religious training at the Yeshiva to attend day colleges. He saw the college, too, as a means of improving the intellectual resources of the rabbis who would go forth from RIETS. The college would also serve to attract young religious men, who were anxious to prepare themselves for vocations other than the rabbinate, which required a college education. Such young men, who attended colleges in all parts of the country, could not continue their religious education. A college like the one Dr. Revel had in mind would fulfill all the secular needs of the intellectual and ambitious student, but would also offer a parallel curriculum of religious studies. In advocating the importance and purpose of a college division within RIETS, Dr. Revel stated:

> The traditional concept of education and its aims are . . . the building of character and the harmonious development of man's intellectual, religious, moral and physical faculties. . . . The goal of education, according to Judaism, is the preparation of man for,

and his dedication to, his duties as a member of his family, country and Faith. The Yeshiva proposes to establish a College of Liberal Arts and Sciences . . . with the double purpose of educating both liberally and Jewishly a number of Jewish young men who have been already imbued with the spirit and the sanctity of Judaism and its teachings, so that these men may not be lost to us . . .

In existing colleges, Jewish students are led to efface their Jewishness. . . . Some of our idealistic and talented young men will find in a College of Liberal Arts and Sciences under Jewish auspices a congenial home, unhampered by real and psychological restrictions, which stifle the spirit; a home where they will be able to realize their energies and mental endowments for the enrichment of general and Jewish culture.

Jewish young men who wish to prepare themselves for the rabbinate, for Jewish social service, for teaching in religious schools, for Jewish scholarship or communal leadership are to be trained in an institution of higher learning of recognized rank, which is in keeping with the highest educational standards in this country. . . .

Secondly, Jewish young men who consider Jewish learning an indispensable part of the moral and mental equipment that they wish to attain through a college education are to have the advantage of such a combined education.[1]

A Collegiate Division: Opposition and Acceptance

The proposal for the college was condemned alike by the Jewish radical press and by those who opposed the teaching of secular subjects under Jewish religious auspices. Like the Rabbinical College a decade earlier, the new project was viewed as an unwarranted financial burden and as a misfortune for American Jews brought about by segregating them from the rest of the community. The *American Hebrew* which had termed the college a "preposterous proposition," further characterized it as "a movement towards a Jewish parochial school system, which has no place in our Commonwealth. Propaganda for such institutions is fraught with harmful possibilities."[2] The Reform *American Israelite* carried on its propaganda against the

Yeshiva in a relentless manner. In 1908, it had not hestitated "to pronounce the New York Yeshiva an anachronism."[3] When Dr. Revel announced the plans for the new college, the *American Israelite* was even more emphatic, recalling that "the *Israelite* from the very start considered the establishment of such a school as a misfortune for American Jewry."[4] The publication also predicted that the establishment of a college under Jewish auspices would "injure the Yeshiva rather than benefit it" since the other colleges would further limit the admission of Jews to their student bodies.[5] Louis Marshall, considered to be one of the outstanding Jews in America at the time, wrote a long letter in response to an invitation by the editor of the *American Israelite* on the subject of the proposed college. He objected to the creation of a school where rabbis would receive their college training

> in an institution in which secular studies are pursued in the same atmosphere in which the theological training is received. A wall of difference is created between those who are graduated in such an institution and the outside world, and those who are graduated under such conditions are apt to be one-sided and to be deprived of the most valuable part of college or university training, that of contact with men of varying opinions. . . . And I have no hesitation in saying that the establishment of a Jewish University, as had at times been mooted, would be most unfortunate.[6]

Similarly, in later years, he was even more critical of the Yeshiva, prophesying, "It is destined to failure and sure to do much harm to the best interests of the Jews in America."[7] The *American Israelite,* assessing "the activity now being displayed by the leaders of Orthodox Jewry," gave its verbal coup de grace to the entire movement by vouchsafing that "it is doomed before many years to dwindle into numerical insignificance."[8]

The radical Yiddish press as well joined with the Reform spokesmen in attacking the college. The *New Wahrheit,* in a villifying article, condemned the Rabbi Isaac Elchanan Theological Seminary for planning to raise funds for a new building when Jews were starving in Europe.[9] It presented its argument in an editorial under the sensational headline "Hunger Dead in Ukraine and Five Million

Dollar Yeshiva in New York."[10] At the same time the publication carried a horrible half-page cartoon depicting fat, thick-lipped decadent men and women feasting while large masses of people were being mowed down by Death wielding a scythe.[11] The seminary was described as being filthy[12] and "only a Talmud Torah."[13] Its faculty were pedestrian,[14] and its directors were "brainless philanthropists."[15]

Undaunted by these criticisms, Dr. Revel constantly exerted his influence upon his friends and adherents hoping to bring them over to his view and persuade them to undertake a new and broader approach to the program of RIETS. Steadfast patrons and supporters of the old Yeshivat Etz Chaim and RIETS—men like Nathan Lamport, Harry Fischel, Meyer Vessel, Samuel Levy, Judge Otto A. Rosalsky, Rabbi Moses S. Margolies, Nathan Roggen, Baruch Pinchas Liberman, Mendel Gottesman, Louis Gold, and Benjamin Winter— were captivated by Dr. Revel's persuasive reasoning and by his powerful personality. With the exception of Rabbi Margolies, these were all successful businessmen and long-established philanthropists whose support was both valuable and encouraging.[16] Wherever he went, whatever he wrote and wherever he spoke, Dr. Revel presented his idea of a college. Slowly the idea captured the imagination of the American Orthodox Jewish community and was hailed as marking the awakening of Orthodoxy in America.[17]

Earlier in Europe the Odessa Seminary, headed by Professor Chaim Tchernowitz, the rabbinical seminaries of Vilna and Kremenitz and even the Lida Yeshiva, which was founded by the famed Rabbi Yitzchak Yaacov Reines, had been criticized for the introduction of daily instruction of some secular subjects. By accepting the college, American Orthodox Jewry demonstrated the great strides it had made in its cultural growth and showed that it was far ahead of European and Palestinian Jewry.[18] The Yeshiva was hailed as full of initiative[19] and a pacemaker, and it was reported that the Berlin Yeshiva under Dr. Chaim Heller was being patterned after it and was "trying to do for Europe what the Rabbi Isaac Elchanan Theological Seminary is doing for America."[20] Dr. Revel, who had been considered a "dreamer,"[21] now represented the guiding force in the maturing of American Orthodoxy, which in turn, had found a new vigor and direction and was acquiring "a greater sense of dignity."[22] Dr. Revel's own educational background, his secular degrees, his voracious search for all forms of knowledge, were the perfect illustration of the kind of synthesis between religion and secular knowledge that he proposed to incorporate in his college.

The nonradical Yiddish press and the Anglo-Jewish press were more receptive than the radical press to the project. The *B'nai B'rith Magazine* observed about the College:

> There are those who will at once protest against such an institution. They will say that a Jewish college serves to build a ghetto wall about the Jewish student. . . . They may be answered thus: There are also colleges conducted by the Methodists . . . with purposes similar to those that animate the Yeshiva. Are the students of these institutions cut off from participation in the common life because they are being educated within their communions? Why are we Jews forever afraid of any expression of ourselves as Jews?[23]

While Dr. Revel was agitating for the development of a college, he was also negotiating with the University of the State of New York to amend the Charter of RIETS to allow RIETS to grant doctoral degrees. On March 27, 1924, permission was granted the Seminary to award the degrees of doctor of divinity and doctor of Hebrew literature.[24] This new privilege provided another occasion for ridicule on the part of the unfriendly press, in this case led by the *Jewish Daily Forward.*[25] The more moderate *Jewish Morning Journal,* however, pointed out that since the University of the State of New York had given recognition to the importance of RIETS secular educational program, the Jewish community should all the more lend its support,[26] especially since sixty to seventy per cent of the school's students were now native Americans in search of a complete secular education.[27]

The attitude of the University of the State of New York was a bellwether of the academic community. As soon as the plans for the college were publicized, messages of congratulations and encouragement began to pour into Dr. Revel's office. Leading college presidents sent messages of approval, among them Nicholas Murray

Butler of Columbia University, Sidney E. Mezes of the College of
the City of New York, Walter Dill Scott of Northwestern University,
William Lowe Bryant of the University of Indiana, Frank Aydelotte
of Swarthmore College, Henry McCracken of Vassar College, Ray
Lyman Wilbur of Leland Stanford University, Frank L. Speares of
Northeastern University, as well as Provost J. H. Penniman of the
University of Pennsylvania and Dr. Israel Schapiro, chief of the
Semitic and Oriental Division of the Library of Congress. Dr. Charles
Parker Cadman, president of the Federal Council of Churches of
Christ in America, also issued a congratulatory message.[28] Professor
Charles E. Torrey of Yale University summarized the position of
the academicians in affirming: "the Yeshiva . . . would be of tre-
mendous service to America and that all true American scholars
and institutions rejoiced at its birth."[29]

The New York Board of Rabbis, composed of Reform, Conservative and Orthodox rabbis, also endorsed the project.[30] The idea of
a secular college under yeshiva auspices was far removed from the
image and structure of the traditional East European seminary, but
it was accepted by the Orthodox rabbinate as well. The Agudat ha-
Rabbanim was most helpful to the Yeshiva, as it had been in earlier
days, and many of the leading members participated in raising funds
for it.[31] Undoubtedly, Dr. Revel and the other members of the
Praesidium of the Agudat ha-Rabbanim—Rabbi Moses S. Margolies,
Rabbi Israel Rosenberg, Rabbi Bernard L. Levinthal, and Rabbi
Eliezer Silver[32]—were instrumental in soliciting this aid, all, with
the exception of Rabbi Silver, had long been deeply involved in the
growth of the school.

The greatest assistance came from the Union of Orthodox Jewish
Congregations, which under the presidency of Rabbi Herbert S.
Goldstein,[33] guaranteed the necessary minimum annual income required by the Board of Regents of the University of the State of
New York for institutions conferring higher degrees.[34] Rabbi Goldstein, the son-in-law of Harry Fischel, was the spiritual leader of the
Institutional Synagogue in Harlem and a lecturer in homiletics at
the Yeshiva.[35] Characterized by the press as the "Jewish Billy Sunday"
for his religious zeal, he was an American-born rabbi dedicated to

serving the young people of the Jewish community. His interest in the Yeshiva was deep and abiding.

An Educational Complex

Early in 1924 Harris L. Selig, a driving and idealistic personality, was drafted by Dr. Revel to head a special fund-raising campaign to provide $5 million for the creation of a new educational complex. Dr. Revel and Selig, assisted by Samuel L. Sar, became the nucleus of the new effort. Samuel Levy, an attorney who later was elected borough president of Manhattan, was chairman of the executive committee of the campaign. Harry Fischel and A. E. Rothstein were the vice-chairmen, and David Berg and Joseph Durst were the treasurers. The general campaign committee was headed by Rabbi Moses S. Margolies and assisted by Albert Sokolsky and Meyer Vessel, father-in-law of Samuel Levy. The building committee was directed by Harry Fischel, chairman, and Jacob Levy, vice-chairman.[36]

A number of sites for the school were proposed. Among them were the Gould Estate in Lakewood, New Jersey; a large tract in the area of Boston Post Road, Pelham Parkway, Gunhill Road and Baychester Avenue in the Bronx (in the general area where Yeshiva University's Albert Einstein College of Medicine is now located) and the present site of the Columbia-Presbyterian Hospital and Medical Center, between 165th and 168th streets from Broadway to the Hudson River in Washington Heights. These were all rejected because they were either too far from New York City, too large, or too expensive. Finally, the building committee settled on a two-block area, known as the Barney Estate, lying west of Amsterdam Avenue between 186th and 188th Streets, in the Washington Heights section of upper Manhattan. This represented about fifty city building lots.[37] Later, additional property to round out the parcels on the west side of Amsterdam Avenue[38] and the Horton Estate on the east side of Amsterdam Avenue were acquired.[39] The total real estate value of the purchase was reported to be $1,274,960.[40]

Dr. Revel's aim of synthesizing the Talmudic and secular tradition so that "the Jewish studies will be on the same plane of importance and dignity as the classical and modern culture,"[41] was reflected in the plans for the academic center that was to be built on a campus overlooking the Harlem River. Adequate space and facilities for high school, college, seminary, library, and dormitory buildings were projected to provide study and classroom areas for 2,500 students and residence halls for 250. The preliminary drawings of the new complex showed a number of impressive buildings in the Byzantine style of architecture, grouped around fountains, sculptured lawns, and cloistered walkways. They also included plans for a sports stadium and athletic fields.[42]

The magnitude of this venture galvanized the campaign committee of the college into great effort. In June, 1924, it had been reported that the members of the building committee had made an excellent beginning in pledging among themselves the sum of $300,000.[43] The campaign committee then sponsored and paid for a dinner for two hundred large contributors at the Astor Hotel in December, 1924. It was addressed by Rabbi Moses S. Margolies, Samuel Levy, and Rabbi Herbert S. Goldstein; Judge Otto A. Rosalsky was the toastmaster, and Cantor Josef Rosenblatt sang.[44] During the proceedings, the guests were electrified when Nathan Lamport, in accepting the deed to the new property from Harry Fischel, announced a pledge of $100,000. They were moved to an even higher pitch of enthusiasm when Harry Fischel rose to match the Lamport pledge. Immediately, the celebrants began to double and treble their own gifts until $800,000 had been subscribed to the Building Fund,[45] "a record which has never been equalled in any other appeal for funds for a Jewish educational project in America."[46] In announcing his pledge, Nathan Lamport summed up the mood of dedication which had captured the builders of the Yeshiva: "The Yeshiva is my life and, if necessary, I will mortgage my life in order to make this $100,000 contribution towards the great institution of learning which is our hope and dream."[47] Before his death in 1928, Lamport had given a total of $200,000 to the Rabbi Isaac Elchanan Theological Seminary.[48]

In the spring of 1925, 1,200 men and women paid $1,000 each to attend another dinner in behalf of the college. Six of the assembled guests pledged a total of $127,000 in addition to the admission subscription. Many increased pledges that they had previously made, bringing the total amount pledged to $2 million, the highest sum ever raised at a dinner of its kind.[49] This led the *Jewish Day* to comment that "far from being dead or even ill, Orthodoxy is quite well and displaying amazing vitality and vigor."[50] The *Brooklyn Daily Eagle* wrote a perceptive editorial about the dinner:

> If anybody really doubts the idealism of the Jews of New York, let them contemplate a dinner at $1,000 a plate, at which 1,200 persons paid to enrich the fund for the Yeshiva of America, the new Jewish seminary and college. There's a thrill about relieving the starving anywhere, but what Nordic business man worries $1,000 worth about the preservation of learning.[51]

To this the *Tageblatt* added a footnote which gave a full evaluation of those who were committed to the Yeshiva:

> That is just the difference between the "superior" Nordic and the "inferior" Jew. The latter never forgets that Talmud Torah (the study of Torah) is greater than everything else and that "man does not live by bread alone."[52]

Concomitant with the solicitation of large gifts, a number of fundraising activities were started in different parts of the city and in neighboring cities. The members of the Women's Branch of the Union of Orthodox Jewish Congregations assumed the goal of a quarter of a million dollars to furnish and supply the dormitory,[53] and the rabbinic alumni of RIETS, headed by Rabbi Nachman H. Ebin, pledged $100,000 in honor of Dr. Revel.[54]

In January 1926, spurred by the impetus of this great outpouring of support, actual construction of the Main Building began.[55] To mark the occasion, a "Million Dollar Musical Festival" was held at Madison Square Garden under the chairmanship of Adolph Lewisohn. Twelve thousand people paid a total of $1 million to hear a concert featuring Jewish contributions to music. Ossip Gabrilowitch, conductor of the Detroit Symphony, arranged the music, and Alexander Smallens led an augmented New York Philharmonic Orchestra. Cantor Josef Rosenblatt appeared in an historical Hebrew opera, *King Solomon* by Peter Joseph Engels. Mendel Gottesman paid $50,000 for a reserved box for the festival.[56]

On Sunday, May 1, 1927, a year and a half after the construction was begun, a joyous cornerstone ceremony was held. No event was truly as great for the Orthodox Jews of New York. The trolley cars of the Third Avenue Railroad Company, which ran by the construction site on Amsterdam Avenue, were rerouted and the streets surrounding the area were cordoned off by the police for the celebration. Crowds began to gather early and soon filled the two-block-long grandstands that had been constructed for the occasion. When the 10,000 seats were filled, latecomers gathered for four blocks around while hundreds more hung from window sills, fire escapes and the roofs of surrounding apartment houses to catch glimpses of the dignitaries and participants in formal attire. Those who were close enough saw the jaunty mayor of New York City, James J. Walker; United States Senators Royal S. Copeland and Robert F. Wagner; Dr. John H. Finley, president of the University of the State of New York, a former editor of the *New York Times;* and representatives of twenty American universities and colleges.

Loud-speakers carried the voices of Dr. Revel, Judge Otto A. Rosalsky, Harry Fischel, Mayor Walker and other participants to crowds estimated between 10,000 and 50,000. Six men—Nathan Lamport, Harry Fischel, Adolph Lewisohn, Frederick Brown, Meyer Vessel, and Samuel Levy—stood ready to cement the cornerstone in place. In a dramatic moment, a *megillah,* which described the history and purpose of the school,[57] was deposited under the cornerstone. This scroll memorialized the pioneers who had worked for the establishment of the school: Rabbi Moses Mayer Matlin, Rabbi Yehuda David Bernstein, David Abramowitz and Baruch Pinchas Liberman. It also recalled Dr. Philip Hillel Klein, David Cohen, Moshe (Marks) Hurewitz and Nathan Roggen, "who acted as Presidents and Trustees of the Yeshiva," and the "Deans of the Yeshiva," Rabbi Moses Shapiro, Rabbi Moses Segal, Rabbi Nahum Dan Baron and Dr. Solomon Theodore Hurwitz, "the first superintendent of the high school."[58] Finally, a letter of greeting and congratulation from President Calvin Coolidge was read.[59]

In the winter of 1925, only a short time after the Yeshiva building campaign had been launched, a behind the scenes movement was initiated to explore the possibility of effecting a merger between the Jewish Theological Seminary of America and RIETS. The initial meetings were held between Judge Otto A. Rosalsky, Samuel Levy and Samuel C. Lamport, son of Nathan Lamport, on behalf of RIETS, and Dr. Cyrus Adler, president of the Jewish Theological Seminary and Louis Marshall. The negotiations continued into 1927, even while the construction of the new building was taking place. Among those who also participated in the discussions at different times for RIETS were: Rabbi Moses S. Margolies, Rabbi Bernard L. Levinthal, Abraham Levy, Mendel Gottesman, Harry Fischel, Nathan Lamport, David Berg, and, of course, Dr. Revel. Israel Unterberg, Sol M. Stroock, Professor Louis Ginzberg and a member of the Warburg family represented the Jewish Theological Seminary.

In retrospect, it is almost impossible to imagine what grounds the negotiators could have even considered as a common basis for the merger, and the proposal seemed doomed to failure from the outset. There had been continuous friction between RIETS and the Jewish Theological Seminary. One of the important figures in the discussions, Louis Marshall, had long been an outspoken critic of the Yeshiva. Yet the participants were men of good faith, motivated by constructive intentions, and the exigencies of the time must have temporarily soothed their respective reservations.

The direct cause for the merger plan was obviously financial, for at this time both institutions were in difficult financial straits. The Jewish Theological Seminary had only a short while earlier proclaimed its dire fiscal condition. Dr. Cyrus Adler had already appealed for funds "so that the institution be not compelled to close its doors."[60] At the same time, the Jewish Theological Seminary was considering a new building campaign with all its attendant problems. The Yeshiva, which was by now committed to undertake a huge construction program, felt an equal pressure.

For the laymen involved in the discussions, the doctrinal differences between Orthodox and Conservative Judaism as represented by RIETS and the Jewish Theological Seminary were vague and not clearly established. Certainly, the spokesmen for the Jewish Theological Seminary, who were themselves Reform in practice, were even less conversant with the growing chasm that separated the two schools. For them, both seminaries were "traditional," one being more "liberal," or conversely, one being more "fundamentalist" than the other. As philanthropists, ready to serve the needs of higher Jewish education, they considered a union between two "traditional" institutions, both of which were about to embark on a financial campaign and construction of new facilities, to have untold financial advantages. Another benefit of such a merger could be had if a theological entente was achieved at the rabbinic level. Thereby a split along sectarian lines in the traditional segment of the Jewish community could be avoided. The Yeshiva representatives were undoubtedly similarly motivated.

The specific issues raised and discussed at these meetings has not been revealed, but they apparently foundered on both practical and ideological grounds. It was pragmatically impossible to agree on the head of the proposed merged seminary. Neither Dr. Revel nor Dr. Cyrus Adler could be expected to yield to the other, and selecting a layman as president would hardly solve the internecine problems that would follow the demotion of the two heads. Further, Dr. Revel was unalterably opposed to the union in principle. He pointed out that the graduates of the Jewish Theological Seminary, with the acquiescence of their alma mater, ministered to congregations that tolerated the mixed seating of men and women during religious services, a deviation "from the standards of Orthodoxy." He also objected to the retention of Dr. Mordecai M. Kaplan, an articulately aggressive stray from Orthodoxy and an influential member of the Jewish Theological Seminary's faculty. Dr. Revel is said to have summarized the proposal in the statement, "You are offering us annihilation not amalgamation." Louis Marshall observed that the proposal failed because "the leaders of the Jeshiba [sic] were so ultra-Orthodox that they imposed conditions that we were unwilling to sanction."[61]

As a result of the negotiators' inability to find a common ground for agreement, the possible opportunity to maintain intact the non-Reform religious element of Jewry in the United States was lost. Dr. Revel and Dr. Adler returned each to his seminary, where, coincidentally, they had begun to serve in the same year, 1915, and which they continued to head with distinction again to the same year, 1940. Meanwhile their respective schools continued to move towards the construction of their own buildings.

Scholarly and Intellectual Growth

Even before the new Yeshiva building was completed, the Board of Regents of the University of the State of New York had amended the charter of RIETS to allow it to establish a college to be known as Yeshiva College with the right to confer the degrees of bachelor of arts and bachelor of science,[62] the first college of liberal arts and sciences in the world under Jewish auspices.

"Yeshiva College" was an amalgam of the names of the two great traditions of learning that were now to become part of the dual instruction program, the Yeshiva of olden days and the college of modern times. In the fall of 1928, thirty-five students enrolled in the first class of Yeshiva College. Since many supporters of the Yeshiva were members of the Jewish Center of New York, and its rabbi, Dr. Leo Jung, was himself one of the great friends of the College and later a member of the faculty, it was fitting that the first class should hold its sessions in the Jewish Center building at 131 West 86th Street.[63] After the new Yeshiva building was dedicated on Sunday, December 9, 1928,[64] the entire school was transferred to Washington Heights. Rabbi Shimon Shkop, the great sage and head of the Yeshiva of Grodno, Poland, made a special trip from Europe to participate in the dedication festivities.[65]

Meanwhile, the scholarly and intellectual growth of the Yeshiva had more than kept pace with its building program. When the Yeshiva had moved to East Broadway in 1921, Dr. Revel invited the renowned *illui,* Rabbi Solomon Polachek, to form the nucleus of an outstanding rabbinical instruction faculty. Born on December 4, 1871, Rabbi Polachek was raised in the village of Meitschet (Mulzad in Russian). After he had exhausted the learning available to him at a number of yeshivot at which he had studied, he was brought to the Yeshiva of Volozhin at age twelve. There he was examined first by the great Rabbi Naftali Zvi Yehuda Berlin (known as the "Neẓiv," an appelation created by the first initials of his name and meaning "Prince" in Hebrew) and later by his associate, Rabbi Chaim "Brisker" Soloveitchik. Rabbi Soloveitchik was so astounded by the youth's knowledge that he called him the *Meitscheter Illui,* the Talmudic genius from Meitschet. Thus began a long and endearing relationship between Rabbi Chaim Brisker, the master, and his young student. Rabbi Polachek had a phenomenal mind which thirsted for all forms of knowledge. When his long day of Talmudic study, stretching far into the night, was ended, he would read all secular books that came to his hands. In later years he lulled his children to sleep by reading them stories in Russian and German, languages that he mastered without a teacher, as he did mathematics. So wide was his reputation that at twenty-seven Rabbi Yitzchak Yaacov Reines asked him to become senior instructor at the yeshiva which he was starting in Lida, near Rabbi Polachek's birthplace in Russia. Rabbi Polachek remained at Lida for nine years until the death of Rabbi Reines in 1915. For six years he continued to head the yeshiva in the different cities it was forced to migrate to under the persecution of czarist and revolutionary forces until he received the call to the Yeshiva in New York City.

The Lida Yeshiva was the first East European Yeshiva to offer secular studies, and Rabbi Polachek himself was well acquainted with the Haskalah and conversant with the literature of a number of European countries. He was a modern man and well suited to his position at RIETS. Like Dr. Revel, he appreciated and defended the historical analyses of the Talmud which opened the door to even greater understanding of Jewish scholarship. His *shiurim* at the Yeshiva were given in the Bet ha-Midrash to the preordination students. On Thursdays, when his *shiurim* were open to the public, laymen of the city crowded the Bet ha-Midrash to listen, although many of them came to his student lectures as well.

There were other scholars of equal magnitude in Europe and Israel, but Rabbi Polachek was the first East European *gadol* to serve in a professorial capacity in the United States. His qualities and reputation were, therefore, shed upon the Yeshiva, and he helped set the precedent for other scholars of his rank to accept similar invitations in the future. In total, his presence in the Yeshiva reaffirmed the institution's position as the most important Orthodox institution of Jewish higher learning in America. Unfortunately, late in his fiftieth year he was infected by an abscessed tooth and died of osteomyelitis of the jaw on July 8, 1928. It was only seven years since that he had come to RIETS and half a year before the institution was to move into its new home, but the *Meitscheter Illui* did not live long enough to make the final migration with his newly adopted Yeshiva. Rabbi Polachek's funeral was held at the Yeshiva's old building on East Broadway where 15,000 students, colleagues and scholars, as well as laymen who had revered him, came to pay tribute. Dr. Revel, who had loved Rabbi Polachek with all his heart, delivered the eulogy and collapsed on the steps of the building as he bade "farewell to his friend, associate and teacher."[66]

Under the inspired leadership of Rabbi Polachek, a distinguished rabbinic faculty had gathered at RIETS to teach Talmud and Codes from the high school level through the Seminary Department. Among the faculty members was Rabbi Judah Weil, a disciple of the sainted Rabbi Israel Hacohen Kagan of Radun, Poland. Rabbi Weil was a *mashgiah* of the upper classes that studied in the Bet ha-Midrash. His small, emaciated body was almost hidden from sight as the taller students would gather around him seeking clarification of some difficult passage in the Commentaries or Codes. He was also a *bohen* (examiner), who tested the younger students regularly on their progress. His understanding and love for the *talmidei ha-yeshiva* (yeshiva students) were boundless. Of him, Dr. Samuel Belkin, a later president of RIETS, was to say reverently that "he was the Chafetz Chaim of America." On the festive day of Simhat Torah when the students danced with the Scrolls of the Law in the Bet ha-Midrash, or on Hanukkah when they held their annual celebration with food, song and often lampoons, it was always a highlight of the occasion when willing hands lifted Rabbi Weil's chair into the air and the *talmidei ha-yeshiva* sang and danced around him in an expression of their own appreciation.

Rabbi Benjamin Aranowitz,[67] a senior member of the faculty, Rabbi Samuel Gerstenfeld and Rabbi Joseph D. Levine, all taught Codes. Rabbi Sholom Rackovsky, Rabbi Aaron D. Burack (a former RIETS student) Rabbi Samuel Olishavsky, Rabbi Chaim Kaplan, Rabbi Chaim Shunfenthal, Rabbi Moses Aaron Poleyoff and Rabbi Ephraim M. Steinberg taught Talmud. Rabbi Abraham I. Selmanowitz[68] was also a *mashgiaḥ* in the Bet ha-Midrash. As the school grew larger, Rabbi Weil gave all his time to examining, including the administration of admissions and placement tests while Rabbi Selmanowitz remained as the sole *mashgiaḥ* of the older students.

Soon after Rabbi Polachek's death, Rabbi Moses Soloveitchek was called to serve the Yeshiva in the same capacity. Reb Moshe, as he was fondly called, was a scion of a rabbinic dynasty recognized the world over as representing the aristocracy of Jewish learning. His father was the illustrious Rabbi Chaim of Brisk, and his paternal grandfather was the great Rabbi Joseph Ber Soloveitchik. On the maternal side, his grandfather was Rabbi Raphael of Volozhin. The two names Volozhin and Brisk represented in Jewish intellectual circles what Oxford and Cambridge or Yale and Harvard stand for in the comparable world of secular knowledge. Reb Moshe had a rare intellect, a scalpel-sharp mind that cut through layers of law and precedents to elemental sources and principles, and an altogether brilliant memory. These qualities were characteristic of his forbears, the leaders of the two great European Jewish seats of learning.

There was a striking coincidence in Reb Moshe's appointment to succeed Rabbi Polachek. He was about a year his predecessor's junior, and he and Rabbi Polachek had both sat at the feet of the same great teacher, Rabbi Chaim Brisker. Like Rabbi Polachek, Reb Moshe had headed a rabbinical seminary, the Taḥkemoni Yeshiva in Warsaw, Poland, which was sponsored by the Mizrachi Organization of Poland.

Reb Moshe spent the years between 1920 and 1929 in Warsaw where his reputation grew and spread throughout the Jewish academic world. In 1929 he came to RIETS to continue Dr. Revel's tradition of having, it seemed, a genius in residence at the school. Rabbi Soloveitchik's daily *shiurim* in Talmud were masterpieces of logical construction. He was wont to present a talmudic opinion in the tractate under study and then refer to a contradictory statement in a different tractate. He would then analyze the legal sources for each statement, the position of the proponents of the statements and the opinions of the subsequent commentators. His mind—which scanned the vast Talmudic sea of rabbinic writings like a modern electronic calculator—rejected, accepted, collated and related all pertinent material. As he mounted block upon block of evidence and interpretation, two consistent streams of opinion and attitudes towards Jewish law were developed which stretched from the Biblical text and the Talmudic disputation to the most contemporary decision. What he made appear as a deceptively simple distinction between two points of view was based upon the marshalling of all studies on the subject developed over 2,000 years and reposing in hundreds of volumes, many of them obscure and relatively unknown. The same powers of ratiocination were used to reconcile apparently contradictory laws or opinions or inconsistencies within the teachings of a particular Talmudic sage. Hair-thin differences, almost imperceptible shadings in meaning, exegetical conclusions, all poured forth, tumbling over each other in an endless waterfall of knowledge and dialectic. The two-hour lecture over, a question had been resolved or a principle of law elucidated, burnished with a new shine. Permission to become a regular member of Reb Moshe's class was the crowning glory of a student's many years of study and tacit certification that he was already a *talmid ḥakham,* an accomplished scholar. To weather Rabbi Moses Soloveitchik's exacting standards and then to earn his signature on the *semicha* (certificate of ordination), was the highest accolade that could come to any student.

Reb Moshe's ministry at the Yeshiva, too, was unfortunately short-lived, lasting only twelve years. After a brief illness, he died on January 31, 1941. Thousands of his disciples attended his funeral in the Nathan Lamport Auditorium of Yeshiva College to hear the eulogies delivered. Among the representatives of the Yeshiva and rabbinic organizations who paid tribute to Reb Moshe was his eldest son and beloved disciple, Rabbi Joseph Ber Soloveitchik.[69]

Even as Dr. Revel had gathered a suitable rabbinic faculty to the Yeshiva, he brought together an equally well-known and capable faculty for the new College.[70] Among them were Dr. Shelley R. Safir, dean of the College and professor of Biology; Dr. Moses L. Isaacs, who taught chemistry; Dr. Jekuthiel Ginsburg, mathematics; Dr. Solomon A. Rhodes, French; Dr. Bernard Drachman, German; Dr. Nelson P. Mead, history of civilization; Dr. Isaac Husik, philosophy; Dr. Charles F. Horne, English; George M. Falion, Latin; Abraham B. Hurwitz, physical education; and Dr. Solomon Gandz, librarian. Serving on the Advisory Council of the College were Dr. Charles C. Torrey, Dr. David Eugene Smith and Dr. Nathan Isaacs.[71] Dr. Paul Klapper, later president of Queens College, was a friend and one of the prime advisers of Dr. Revel on matters of the College. Later Dr. Joseph Shipley, who was added to the English Department, was also of inestimable assistance.

Four years after the college was opened, its first graduation class of nineteen students received their diplomas. Of these, ten became rabbis, two became businessmen, two became professors at Yeshiva College, one the head of a national Jewish education service, one the president of another college, one a journalist, one entered the field of general education and one became a physician.[72]

First Years: Frustration and Glory

The first years of Yeshiva College, however, coincided with the Depression years, which brought heavy financial reverses to the supporters of the Yeshiva and had a consequent drastic effect on its financial situation. Only one building of the projected construction program had been completed. With the collapse of the general economy, many of the pledges made in good faith by friends of the college could not be redeemed.[73] There were heavy payments on the large $650,000 mortgage to be met, and with very little money coming in, all of the land other than that upon which the building stood was soon lost because of mortgage foreclosures; the master plan of a grand Yeshiva campus appeared doomed. It was only because of the great devotion of its faculties, which continued their loyal service although irregularly and inadequately paid, that the school managed to survive. During the middle thirties many instructors received no salary at all, and it is to their credit that not one faculty member resigned for this reason. Dr. Revel himself for years refused to accept any salary and was forced to direct his talents and efforts exclusively to the raising of funds for the pressing needs of the institution. He called scores of meetings of rich Jews in the City of New York and had them meet members of the faculty who described their own personal plight and the agony of the school. Other outstanding Jews made personal efforts to solicit funds for the school. But the response in all cases was minimal, for by this time, many of the old friends of Yeshiva had already passed on. Their liberal support had come because of their own intimate recollection of the great spiritual figures with whom the Yeshiva was identified, Rabbi Isaac Elchanan Spektor, Rabbi Chaim of Brisk, Rabbi Solomon Polachek. These early supporters were steeped in the tradition of the need to support the study of Torah. Their children had either been left financially unable to continue their parents' patronage or distracted by modern tensions from doing so. Only a few children of the school's pre-Depression supporters remained dedicated to the Yeshiva. The school needed new friends and supporters from among first and second generation Americans. And at this juncture in the history of the Jewish community, they were not yet available.

Among those whom Dr. Revel enlisted in the cause of Yeshiva was the illustrious Dr. Albert Einstein. In 1936, Dr. Einstein sent a number of letters to four prominent Jews. These letters were most revealing of his interest in Judaism and Jewish education and of his attitude towards Yeshiva. In one letter he wrote:

> I am taking the liberty to write you about Yeshiva College in New York. . . . We Jews do a great deal for our needy and unfortunate brethren, and this is very good. . . . Nevertheless, there are other more important obligations than this and one of the most important of these is the education of our youth. Our youth which

strives for higher education enter colleges which have no love for Jews or Judaism. Moreover, many of the colleges close their doors to them and, worse than all of this, is the alienation [of our youth] from the spirit of Judaism . . . because of the negative environment which is non-Jewish and estranges them from Judaism. Only a small segment of American Jews sees the seriousness of the danger which lurks for us in this direction. If they could see with their own eyes what had happened in Germany, they would realize better the symptoms of the disease. We are obligated to teach our youth to be proud Jews who are related to Judaism and we can achieve this only by educating them in a healthy Jewish environment.

We must establish schools of higher Jewish education in order to prevent the alienation of the best of our Jewish youth from Jewish tradition. In New York for the last eight years there is a college [Yeshiva College] that fills this purpose. This institution has earned . . . complete regard and recognition. . . . It is the first secular college administered in the Jewish religious spirit. It is engaged in a bitter battle for its very existence because the recognition of the need for Jewish cultural institutions has not yet found its way into the hearts of rich Jews. I, therefore, plead the cause of Yeshiva College with all my power because it has a higher purpose as the protector of the Jewish tradition.[74]

Dr. Einstein's appeal resulted in contributions of $50,000, a substantial sum in 1936 but hardly enough to make a serious impact on the financial problems of the Yeshiva. Nevertheless, Dr. Revel continued to strive for the greater expansion of the Yeshiva and initiated a graduate program in Jewish and Semitic studies in 1935, which was expanded into a full graduate school in 1937.

By now the pressures on Dr. Revel were becoming acute. The loss of the large parcel of the land which he had struggled so mightily to acquire for the Yeshiva was alone enough to break his heart. Frequently he stood at the window of his office and watched with agony first the excavation of the grounds, and then the construction of a block of apartment houses on the site. But in addition to the financial disappointments that beset him, his work at the Yeshiva and his personal duties were massive. When the new graduate school was opened, he offered a course in Rabbinic Codes while continuing the regular *shiurim* which he gave during the week to select classes. He also personally tested all the classes of the school at least twice a year, and a substantial portion of his time was devoted to giving examinations for ordination. On these occasions, with Rabbi Polachek, or later with Rabbi Soloveitchik and Rabbi Bernard L. Levinthal, the dean of the American rabbinate, he was involved in grueling hours of oral examination of each of the candidates.

Dr. Revel also maintained his very close relationship with all the students. He made the decisions on who was to be allotted a dormitory room, who was to receive a stipend, and how much was to be given. He passed on every promotion from one Talmud class to another and decided who was to be allowed to remain at the school for advanced study during the summer vacation. Often he would prohibit a student from remaining because he looked peaked or drawn, saying, "Go home and rest. You must recharge your batteries. Then you will come back fresh again." But Dr. Revel never took the time to rest and recharge his own batteries. A ceaseless scholar, he snatched several hours every day to devote to his own study and research and extensive writing in Semitics and rabbinic literature. Among his many writings were "Pseudo-Jonathan on the Pentateuch" and "Karaite Halakhah," as well as articles in the *Jewish Quarterly Review, Horeb, Dvir, Yagdil Torah, Ner Maaravi* and other scholarly publications. He was also associate editor of the Jewish Encyclopedia, *Otzar Yisroel.*

Dr. Revel also maintained a wide correspondence with other men of letters who visited the Yeshiva regularly. Among the great Talmudic personalities whom Dr. Revel brought to lecture at RIETS at different times during his tenure were Rabbi Abraham Kahane-Shapiro, chief rabbi of Kovno, Lithuania; Rabbi Moses Epstein and Rabbi Israel Sher, both of the Slabodka Yeshiva; Rabbi Abraham Bloch of the Telshe Yeshiva; Rabbi Joseph Kahanaman of the Ponovitz Yeshiva; Rabbi Joseph Hurwitz of the Meah Shearim Yeshiva in Israel; Rabbi Aaron Kotler of the Kletzk Yeshiva; Rabbi Baruch Ber Leibowitz of the Kaminetz Yeshiva; Rabbi Mayer Dan Plotski, the rabbi of Ostrov, Poland; Rabbi Mayer Shapiro of the Lublin Yeshiva, and Chief Rabbi Abraham Kook of Israel.

In the early years of the new building, Dr. Revel came to the

Yeshiva by taxi every morning. But as his family fortunes waned and the financial conditions of the Yeshiva worsened, Dr. Revel would come and go by subway. He used to say that this, too, was one of God's blessings, for now he gained additional time for his studies. Students who also used the subway found him regularly, often crushed between two wondering fellow riders, with his Talmud spread out on his knees, totally engrossed as if he were completely alone. Indeed his study habits were an inspiration to the students. No one ever presented himself in Dr. Revel's office without finding him deep in a volume. Behind his desk was a full wall of bookshelves containing hundreds of Talmudic works. While he talked on the telephone his hand was caressing, leafing through, or searching for some particular book. His greatest happiness was at the annual Hanukkah celebration, when he would come to the school dining room where the festivities took place, sing with the students, and address them in an inimitably erudite and inspiring manner. But these occasional pleasures were hardly sufficient to compensate for the strain, without vacation or rest, which sapped his energy and spent his strength. One day, while he was delivering his regular *shiur* to a senior rabbinic class, he sustained a stroke, collapsed and several days later, on December 1, 1940, died at the age of fifty-five.

Dr. Revel had been away from the Yeshiva only briefly during the entire twenty-five years of his association with it. During the quarter century in which he guided the Rabbi Isaac Elchanan Theological Seminary, it became a significant force in American Orthodox Jewry. Its survival and growth, confounded the dark critics who had declared that it had no legitimate place in the fabric of American existence. Dr. Revel's creation of the college proved that traditional Judaism and Western civilization could produce a productive educational synthesis. Yeshiva University stands today as a testament to Dr. Bernard Revel's vision, inspiration, and ceaseless toil.

CHAPTER 11. YESHIVA UNIVERSITY TODAY

For a quarter of a century, Dr. Revel had been a forceful and authoritative leader who held the reins of administration securely in his hands. His firmness, unyielding strength and great scholarship kept the school intact from within and protected from attack from without. With his death the school itself appeared on the threshold of a serious breakdown. No single individual on the faculty or in the administration seemed to have similar personal prestige and leadership qualities, and a very real problem of succession to the presidency confronted the Board of Directors.

At this time, a threat to the independence of RIETS came from the Agudat ha-Rabbanim, which had been closely related to RIETS in the early days of its history. Although it had applauded its teaching program and had supported the institution, the Agudat ha-Rabbanim had always sought to impose its authority on RIETS. As early as 1903, before RIETS moved to Henry Street, the Agudat ha-Rabbanim had urged that the new building become the headquarters of its organization as well and that it be called the Rabbinic Headquarters and Rabbi Isaac Elchanan Theological Seminary.[1] It also sought "the right to be included on the Board of Directors of the Yeshiva, to supervise the religious and secular studies and to watch over the behavior of the students . . ."[2] and to register all ordained students of RIETS.[3] This possessive attitude stemmed from the fact that the Agudat ha-Rabbanim zealously guarded the privilege of ordination and felt that the right to confer *semicha* should be retained by individual rabbis as it had been in the European yeshivot. At the very least, it was felt that the ordination should be in the hands of a rabbinic organization. Consequently, the Agudat ha-Rabbanim considered that Dr. Revel and RIETS had usurped its authority. Furthermore, the Agudat ha-Rabbanim had long challenged the desirability of a secular education for rabbis.

Thus, as RIETS grew in size and importance, the Agudat ha-Rabbanim began to reveal an open antagonism towards it. It opposed the placement of rabbis ordained by RIETS in communities where members of the Agudat ha-Rabbanim held pulpits and often forced Dr. Revel to withdraw such appointments. However, as long as Dr. Revel was alive, the incidents were contained and the friction was held to a minimum. With Dr. Revel's death, however, the opportunity for the Agudat ha-Rabbanim to assert its position seemed ripe, and it prepared to take over the administration of RIETS.

Rabbi Eliezer Silver of Cincinnati, president of the organization, sent a telegram to the Board of Directors informing them that he had appointed a committee of seven to assume the direction of the school. The prestige of the Agudat ha-Rabbanim was high and it was also logical that the Orthodox rabbinic leadership should be involved in directing a rabbinical school. But RIETS, which had developed without that close relationship, had often suffered from the animosity of individual member rabbis of the Agudat ha-Rabbanim. It was also now rooted in the wider Orthodox Jewish community which resented the strictures of the Agudat ha-Rabbanim against secular education. Thus, much as the directors regretted refusing the request of respected rabbis when the overtures towards a "takeover" by the Agudat ha-Rabbanim were made, Rabbi Moshe Soloveitchik, Rabbi Bernard Levinthal, himself a leading member of that group, and Samuel Levy led the directors to reject the proprietary claims of the Agudat ha-Rabbanim.

Challenges and Responsibilities

The Directors then organized an Executive Board to guide the school and recommend candidates for the presidency. The Executive Board was composed of Dr. Pinkhos Churgin, dean of the Teachers Institute; Samuel L. Sar, dean of men, Dr. Leo Jung, Rabbi Joseph H. Lookstein, Dr. Moses L. Isaacs, dean of the College; and Dr. Samuel Belkin. The members of the Executive Board had all been identified with RIETS for a long time, and as confidants of Dr.

Revel, they knew his wishes and were respected by the student body, the different faculties, and the directors. Each of the appointees also represented a special interest group within the school. Dr. Churgin was a representative of those faculty members who were concerned that the presidency should be passed to a scholarly figure. Mr. Sar had long been Dr. Revel's liaison with the fund-raising and financial side of the school. He also had strong positive relations with the Rabbinic Alumni of the institution. Rabbi Lookstein was one of the best known alumni of RIETS, a member of the Board of Directors and the rabbi of Congregation Kehillath Jeshurun in Manhattan, which had been the pulpit of Rabbi Moses S. Margolies, grandfather of Mrs. Lookstein. Rabbi Lookstein was also professor of homiletics at RIETS and influential among the supporters of the school.

Dr. Leo Jung was the rabbi of the Jewish Center in New York, which included some of the most important supporters of RIETS. When Yeshiva College was founded in 1928, the first classes were held at the Jewish Center. Dr. Jung was also a member of the board of directors and professor of ethics at the College.

Dr. Moses L. Isaacs, who was professor of chemistry from the very inception of the College, had replaced Dr. Shelley R. Safir as Dean of the College in 1940. Dr. Belkin, a young scholar who had come to the Yeshiva in 1936, was a favorite of Dr. Revel's because of his proficiency in Talmud and secular studies. In 1936 Dr. Belkin was asked by Dr. Revel to organize and head the Graduate School for Jewish Studies, founded a year earlier with courses leading to the degree of Doctor of Hebrew Literature.

The Executive Board was faced with three major responsibilities: to maintain the academic excellence of the school; to find a suitable replacement for Rabbi Moses Soloveitchik, who died two months after Dr. Revel, as head of the Talmud Department; and to screen candidates for the presidency, after a proper period of mourning for Dr. Revel had been observed.

The maintenance of the school program was a relatively simple matter. In this the Executive Board was aided by Norman B. Abrams, who was at the time administrative assistant of the Talmudical Academy High School. Mr. Abrams was graduated from the Teachers Institute in 1926 and had continued in various administrative positions in RIETS. Dr. Revel, during his tenure of office, had no presidential staff nor even a personal secretary assigned to him. But for specific projects he would coopt different members of the administration or faculty to assist him. Mr. Abrams had frequently served in this way and had in fact been acting as registrar of RIETS during the last years of Dr. Revel's life. Mr. Abrams now took over the administrative duties of the Talmud Department in addition to his obligation in the High School, while the deans supervised their respective divisions within the school.

Finding a replacement for Rabbi Moses Soloveitchik turned out to be the easiest task of the Executive Board. Among his other gifts to Yeshiva, Reb Moshe had left a son, Rabbi Joseph Ber Soloveitchik, who was soon to achieve an international reputation for Torah scholarship. In 1941, Rabbi Joseph B. Soloveitchik was appointed as professor of Talmud in his father's place and a member of the Ordination Board at RIETS, where he served with Dr. Belkin, Rabbi Benjamin Aranowitz and Rabbi Bernard L. Levinthal until the latter's death in 1952. Rabbi Soloveitchik was destined to exert an even greater influence than either his father or Rabbi Solomon Polachek before him. Although both of these latter scholars were not averse to secular learning, neither had formal training in the disciplines of science or in the liberal arts. Each was intellectually oriented exclusively in the tradition of Judaism. Halakhah was a broad mosaic composed of theology, philosophy, morals and ethics, law, the application of the precise categories of logic and social problems. Yet all were viewed as facets of the Torah, parts of the Jewish *anschauung* rather than as objective entities. None was accorded independent validity as a legitimate subject of study outside of the Torah. Neither Rabbi Polachek nor Rabbi M. Soloveitchik was seriously concerned with Plato, Aristotle or their successors. For them philosophers either corroborated the Torah or were found lacking when they denied it. Neither could interpret modern thought with authority or relate it to the general position of Judaism. Thus Reb Moshe, who was expositor par excellence of Maimonides' halakhic magnum opus, *Mishneh Torah,* had never so much as opened the covers of his master's philosophic classic *Moreh Nevukhim* (Guide for the Perplexed).

Rabbi Joseph Soloveitchek, however, had within himself marvelously harmonized secular and rabbinic learning. In his youth, under the personal tutelage of his father as well as others, he achieved the equivalent of a high school and junior college education. During this time, he absorbed the Talmud and the *Posekim* and dipped into the mysteries of *Habad* (the Lubavicher brand of Hasidism). In 1925, at the age of twenty-two, Rabbi Soloveitchik entered the University of Berlin. There he came under the influence of the neo-Kantian school of mathematic-scientific idealism led by Hermann Cohen of Marburg. In 1931 he completed his doctoral dissertation on the subject of Herman Cohen's epistemology and metaphysics. A year later, with his wife and first-born child, he emigrated to the United States and accepted the post of chief rabbi of Boston, which he still holds. In addition to his duties in the city of Boston, he gave courses in Jewish philosophy at RIETS until he assumed the position as head of the Talmud Department. Today he delivers two two-to-four-hour *shiurim* weekly and commutes regularly from his home in Boston. Rabbi Soloveitchik is the "Rav," the rabbi and accepted master of hundreds of *musmachim* (ordained rabbis) and is an acknowledged teacher without peer of Halakhah and Jewish lore. A gifted orator in Yiddish, Hebrew and English, he has lectured for as long as four hours with dramatic and rhetorical mastery that captivates scholar and layman alike.

Far beyond his predecessors, Rabbi Soloveitchik's influence has extended into the community at large. Known as the spokesman for Orthodox Judaism in America, he has delivered numerous public lectures. He is the honorary president of the Religious Zionists of America since 1946 (then known as the Mizrachi Organization of America); a member of the Advisory Committee on Humane Methods of Slaughter established by the Secretary of Agriculture; principal Jewish participant in a National Institute of Mental Health project undertaken jointly by Harvard University, Loyola and Yeshiva, to study religious attitudes towards psychological problems; a vital force in the Rabbinical Council of America. After the death in 1959 of the chief rabbi of Israel, the late Rabbi Isaac Halevi Herzog, Rabbi Soloveitchik was offered the position as chief rabbi, but this he declined in order to continue his teaching duties at Yeshiva and in order to be a free agent to press for the improvement of the religious and moral qualities of the State of Israel. In 1966, when Israel Rogosin, a noted industrialist, established the Israel Rogosin Center for Ethics and Human Values at Yeshiva, Rabbi Soloveitchik was appointed to conduct the pilot course in the program for the exploration of the ethical problems confronting modern man.[4]

With the selection of Reb Moshe's successor and with the academic problem of the school attended to, the Executive Board, by 1943, had fulfilled two of its three major obligations. During this time, too, the financial structure of the school had also been stabilized. The Endowment Fund, which had been founded by Mendel Gottesman with an initial gift of $50,000 in 1927,[5] had taken over the remaining mortgage indebtedness so that the fears of foreclosure on the building were eliminated. Current salaries were being paid on a regular basis and even back salaries were being restored to the employees and members of the faculty of RIETS who had waited so long and so loyally. The time was now ripe for the Executive Board to make its recommendation for the presidency.

During the three year interim period after Dr. Revel's death, the directors of RIETS and the Executive Board had been exposed to a great deal of lobbying and pressure in behalf and against a number of self-imposed or otherwise designated candidates for the office. Among those mentioned for the position were prominent and respected lay and rabbinic leaders whose candidacy deserved the most serious consideration. This was a delicate task. In addition to the merits of each candidate that had to be evaluated, there was also the influence of lifelong loyalties that the different directors had to friends and rabbis whose candidacies were being weighed. A further complication was the fact that the directors had different notions about what kind of president they were seeking. Some argued for an experienced fund raiser, others for a scholar of the highest achievements, others for a good administrator. Some, who despaired of finding one man who could continue to harmonize the two cultures represented by RIETS and the College, recommended separating the two and engaging two different presidents. By May 1943, the issues and the candidates had been sufficiently aired and debated and the directors announced the unanimous selection of Dr. Samuel Belkin to be the second president of RIETS.

Dr. Samuel Belkin and the Yeshiva of Today

Dr. Belkin was a young man of thirty-one, only fourteen years in the United States and hardly known to the Jewish community at large when he became president. But the members of the Executive Board, who knew Dr. Belkin intimately as a colleague and as a fellow teacher, as an administrator and as a scholar, aggressively submitted and supported his nomination. With a wisdom that seemed almost prophetic and that was vindicated over and over again, they had found a successor to Dr. Revel who would wear the mantle of leadership with a strength of character and vision of purpose that even his most ardent admirers could not have anticipated.

At age seventeen Dr. Belkin had been ordained at the Yeshiva of the Chafetz Chaim in Radun, Poland. A year later he came to the United States and was accepted into the home of Rabbi Bernard L. Levinthal in Philadelphia. In six years he mastered the English language, went through college, received a Ph.D. degree from Brown University, was elected to Phi Beta Kappa, wrote his doctoral dissertation in Hebrew, English, and Greek and was awarded an honorary fellowship at Brown. His doctoral thesis, *Philo and the Oral Law,* was published as Volume XI of the Harvard Semitics Series.

In 1935, Dr. Belkin, who seven years earlier spoke only Yiddish, Hebrew and Polish, came to Yeshiva College as an instructor of Greek. A year later, he was appointed a member of the Talmud faculty and soon became secretary of the faculty, instructor in Hellenistic literature at the Graduate School and finally its director. In 1940 he was named a full professor and, after the death of Dr. Revel, dean of the Rabbi Isaac Elchanan Theological Seminary.

In addition to his prodigious scholarship, Dr. Belkin demonstrated marked administrative ability, tireless energy and unusual leadership qualities. He was able to relate to his students with a warmth and compassion. Concerned with each young man, he provided help to those who needed it, visited them when they were sick, fed them at his home and worried about their needs. In return, his students revered him, confided in him and sought his advice and approbation. In addition to delivering his regular *shiur,* which was a marvel of logical exposition, incisive reasoning, and broad scholarship—and writing his many scholarly articles and books, Dr. Belkin, upon assuming the presidency, gave himself completely to blueprinting an expansion of the Yeshiva which even Dr. Revel could not have foreseen.

Dr. Revel's early preoccupation had been to establish the viable synthesis of religious and secular instruction under the aegis of a single institution. For many leaders and, certainly for Orthodox Jewry, this achievement might have been sufficient. No other segment of the Jewish community in any part of the world had accomplished even this much. Dr. Belkin, however, impatiently brushed aside the petty and sometimes prejudiced antagonism to synthesis. The critical years immediately following his assumption of office were characterized by the awareness of the terrible tragedy of the European holocaust, the annihilation of Jewish centers of study, and the death of millions of Jews and their scholarly leaders. The State of Israel was not yet in existence and Palestine could hardly be relied on to provide centers for Jewish learning. Dr. Belkin was determined that RIETS and Yeshiva College would carry at least the American Orthodox Jew to his complete educational fulfillment. Dr. Belkin planned that under Yeshiva's auspices men, and even women, who had hitherto been largely neglected in the field of higher religious education, would be inspired with moral dignity and spiritual strength to emerge as *yodei sefer* (scholarly personalities) and be able to enter every career and profession without losing an iota of their Jewishness. Social work, education, medicine, the sciences, fields where quotas on Jewish admissions or other difficulties had severly limited the Orthodox Jewish student, would now be opened to them. In short, Dr. Belkin, extending Dr. Revel's creation of the college, projected a blueprint for a broad and encompassing university program.

In 1945, the necessary foundation for the program was achieved when the New York State Board of Regents elevated Yeshiva to university status, which distinguished it as the first university in America under Jewish auspices. After Dr. Revel's death, the Graduate School, which he had founded, was expanded and named in his memory, the Bernard Revel Graduate School. In 1945 three new schools were founded, the Harry Fischel School for Higher Jewish Studies, another High School for Boys in Brooklyn and the Institute of Mathematics, now named the Belfer Graduate School of Science, after its patron, Arthur S. Belfer, a well-known Jewish communal leader. A new Science Center to house the Belfer Graduate School of Science is being built at the Main Center in Washington Heights. It will contain modern research laboratories, special classroom facilities, library, computer center, seminar rooms and other major facilities.

In 1945, too, the Community Service Division was set up to provide religious information and synagogue programming, and assist in the placement of rabbis, Hebrew teachers, cantors and center workers in communities all over the United States. This division also sponsors a Youth Bureau which offers Torah leadership seminars, a "Summer in Israel" program, and a summer camping program for young people. In 1954 a Cantorial Training Institute and an Israel Institute, devoted to the interpretation of the culture and spiritual significance of Israel, also were established.

In his overall plans for the University, Dr. Belkin had indicated his concern that women should be offered the same opportunities of yeshiva education as men, for while the graduate schools of Yeshiva University offered coed training, the college and high schools did not. More and more elementary yeshivot were being established which meant an ever increasing number of girls were able to continue their yeshiva education if the facilities were available. To fill this need, Yeshiva University in 1948 founded the first yeshiva high school for girls in the United States. It was located in Brooklyn.

Later another high school for girls was established in Manhattan. In 1952, further educational facilities for women were created with the establishment of the Teachers Institute for Women to parallel the program of the more than thirty-year-old Teachers Institute for men.

To aid the program of advanced religious education for women, Max Stern, a New York businessman, philanthropist and vice-chairman of the University's Board of Trustees, made a munificent gift in 1954. This enabled the founding of Stern College for Women, America's first college of liberal arts and sciences for women under Jewish auspices. With the advent of Stern College, it was possible for the first time to offer young women a collegiate program combined with a rich Jewish curriculum. Thirty-three young women, coming from all parts of the United States, constituted the first class in September 1954. In 1968 there were more than six hundred students enrolled in the College. In addition to the original building occupied by Stern College for Women at 35th Street and Lexington Avenue in midtown New York, the College possesses a residence hall accommodating 475 students. Development plans include the renovation of the present classroom building and dormitory as well as construction of a new classroom building.

In 1957, the Graduate School of Education and Community Administration, which had been established in 1948 with the assistance of a grant of $500,000 from the Ford Foundation's Fund for the Advancement of Education, was reorganized to form the Graduate School of Education. Today the school has been vastly expanded and is known as the Ferkauf Graduate School of Humanities and Social Sciences in appreciation of a generous gift in 1965 by Eugene and Estelle Ferkauf, who possessed a perceptive understanding of the value of education and the purposes of Yeshiva University. Also in 1957, the School of Social Work was created to train professional personnel for careers in Jewish and general social work. Its name was changed in 1962 to the Wurzweiler School of Social Work, deriving from a benefaction of the Gustav Wurzweiler Foundation. Both schools are housed in a nineteen-story building at Fifth Avenue and 12th Street in Manhattan.

These rapid changes and expansions within the University were due to the recognition that Yeshiva had been given by the general and academic community and to the imaginative blueprint for academic and physical expansion designed by Dr. Belkin. Referring to himself as a "rabbi who doesn't preach, a doctor who doesn't cure, and a professor who doesn't teach," Dr. Belkin traveled far and wide across the country, to assemble faculty, explain Yeshiva's ever-growing program and function and rally friends to its cause. Few men have led an American educational institution so far in so little time. In 1957, recognizing his prominence in higher education, the United States State Department invited Dr. Belkin, together with Presidents Nathan M. Pusey of Harvard, Rev. Theodore M. Hesburgh of Notre Dame and three other outstanding college presidents, to present the purposes of American education to the Russian people through *Amerika,* the Russian-language publication issued by the U.S. Information Agency in the Soviet Union.

Meanwhile Yeshiva, having achieved university rank during Dr. Belkin's administration, had added still another "first" to its record of achievements. In 1950, its charter had been amended to authorize granting the degrees of doctor of medicine and doctor of dental surgery. In 1951, an agreement between the University and the City of New York allowed the future medical school to provide the professional care of all the patients in the 1,400-bed Bronx Municipal Hospital Center. Students at the school were to utilize all the clinical materials available in the various medical services of the center. In 1955, the first class of students entered the newly constructed medical school, known as the Albert Einstein College of Medicine, the first medical school under Jewish auspices in the nation. In 1957, the Sue Golding Graduate Division of Medical Sciences was established, followed by the formation of the Ullmann Research Center for Health Sciences. In 1966, a twelve-story, 375-bed private hospital known as the Albert Einstein College Hospital was completed. The hospital includes two patient pavilions, the Charles H. Revson Diagnostic Treatment Center, the Evelyn and Joseph I. Lubin Rehabilitation Center and other units. In the following year, ground was broken for the Rose F. Kennedy Center for Research in Mental Retardation and Human Development, made possible to a large extent, by a major gift from the Joseph P. Kennedy, Jr. Foundation.[6] Also that year the Erna Michael College of Hebraic Studies, superseding the Teachers Institute for Men, was founded in recognition of the generosity of Jacob Michael in memory of his beloved wife.

At the end of 1968, too, the six-story, block-long Mendel Gottesman Central University Library, which will combine a number of the existing libraries, was completed at the Main Center in Washington Heights. It will house some 650,000 volumes and contain study cubicles, reading rooms, seminar rooms, archive facilities, manuscript and rare book room, museum and exhibition halls. It will also include the Pollack Library.

When the Stern College for Women was founded, Dr. Belkin had achieved his goal of creating parallel facilities of combined higher religious and secular studies for men and women from high school through college. In the main, students entering Yeshiva College or Stern College were graduates of one of the University's four high schools in the New York metropolitan area, the University's West Coast division in Los Angeles, or an equivalent high school in other parts of the country. Jewish youth of non-yeshiva high school background, however, who were interested in pursuing higher religious education and were brought to Yeshiva through the synagogues and youth movements identified with the University, were unable to qualify for admission to the College. To remedy this serious lack, Dr. Belkin, just as he had moved to open Yeshiva facilities to high school and college women, initiated, as well, a program for these deserving young students who otherwise would be denied the opportunity for an advanced religious education. In 1956 an experimental course was undertaken for forty-three students with only an elementary training in Jewish studies. The success of the program was immediate, and by 1968 there were 264 students enrolled. In 1965 the division was named the James Striar School of General Jewish Studies in memory of James Striar, an industrialist and communal worker from Bangor, Maine.

The measure of Dr. Belkin's contribution to the Yeshiva and the extent of its growth during his tenure of office are reflected in the

following: Yeshiva has attained university status and is now composed of thirteen schools and affiliates with libraries and publications
covering all the branches of the arts and sciences and Judaic and
Hebraic studies. Student enrollment has increased from 850 when
Dr. Belkin assumed office in 1943 to 7,500 in 1968, the faculty from
94 to 2,200 and the number of teaching centers from one to four.
In 1968, the physical plant was valued in excess of $75,000,000 and
the operating budget was $70,000,000, in contrast to the 1943 budget
of $444,000.

The impressive growth in budget, new schools and teaching centers is staggering in comparison to the humble beginnings of RIETS
and Yeshivat Etz Chaim. The $70,000,000 operating budget of 1968,
compared to the slightly more than $6,000 budget of RIETS for
1901,[7] is a convincing indication of the changes that have taken
place within Yeshiva's tent of Torah. Most dramatic is the expansion
into the exclusively secular areas of instruction through the Albert
Einstein College of Medicine, the Belfer Graduate School of Science,
and the Ferkauf Graduate School of Humanities and Social Sciences.
Yet, although RIETS followed in the tradition of the great American universities like Harvard and Princeton, which made their initial
appearances as divinity schools and then blossomed forth into the
many disciplines of modern education, the centrality of the purpose
of the religious schools in Yeshiva University has not been de-
emphasized. Dr. Belkin's major concern has been to maintain
supreme the Jewish nature of the university and the pre-eminence of
its Talmud and rabbinic instruction programs.

As of June 1968, the Rabbi Isaac Elchanan Theological Seminary
has ordained more than 1,000 rabbis, of whom about 400 were in
rabbinic pulpits and many others in religious teaching, administrative, and executive posts in cognate fields. Yeshiva College has
graduated 2,930 students and Stern College for Women, 629 students;
the Erna Michael College of Hebraic Studies has graduated 1,166
teachers and the Teachers Institute for Women, 300; the Albert
Einstein College of Medicine has graduated 847 doctors of medicine.
During World War II and since then, well over 100 rabbis ordained
by the Rabbi Isaac Elchanan Theological Seminary have served and

are continuing to serve as chaplains in the Armed Forces of the United States and Canada.

Yeshiva issues four scholarly journals: *Horeb,* a journal in Hebrew devoted to original studies in Jewish history and literature; *Scripta Mathematica,* a quarterly devoted to the research and expository aspects of mathematics; *Sura,* an annual in Hebrew designed to serve as a bridge between Jewish life in Israel and in the Diaspora, published jointly with the Sura Institute in Jerusalm; and *Talpioth,* a Hebrew quarterly dedicated to the exposition of Hebrew law, philosophy and ethics.

The existence of the Yeshiva during the past eighty years and the story of its institutional growth are a tribute to the adaptability and strength of American Orthodox Jewry, which at the time of the founding of Yeshivat Etz Chaim and of RIETS, was almost exclusively a weak, uprooted immigrant community. By faith, vision and courage, its founders and supporters created through the instrumentality of the Yeshiva first a rallying point for Orthodoxy and then a source of religious and educational leadership to bolster, teach and strengthen its adherents. Having realized its initial goals, the Yeshiva today fulfills further needs by its extended services to the community at large. Through its graduate schools, medical school, publications and special learned and scientific projects, it has made and continues to make a significant contribution to American culture as a whole. But its dedication to Orthodoxy—to maximum Jewish commitment and to maximum Jewish religious values—is its principal source of strength and hope for the future.

Notes

NOTES

Key to Frequently Cited Newspapers and Periodicals Referred to in Notes

American Hebrew	AH	*Jewish Forum*	JF
American Israelite	AI	*Jewish Leader (Boston)*	JL
American Jewish Chronicle	AJC	*Jewish Morning Journal*	
American Jewish Historical		*(Yiddish)*	JMJ
Quarterly	AJHQ	*Jewish Tribune*	JTrib.
Der Amerikaner (Yiddish)	DA	*Jüdische Gazetten*	
Ha-Ivri (Hebrew)	HI	*(Yiddish)*	JG
Ha-Yehudi (Hebrew)	HY	*Jüdisches Tageblatt*	JT
Jewish Day (Yiddish)	JD	*(Yiddish)*	
Jewish Daily Forward		*Jüdische Welt (Yiddish)*	JW
(Yiddish)	JDF	*New Warheit (Yiddish)*	NW
Jewish Exponent	JE		

Notes to Chapter 1 (pp. 1-16)

1. Samuel Joseph, *Jewish Immigration To the United States From 1881-1910* (New York: Columbia University Press, 1914), 174.

2. Moses Rischin, *The Promised City* (Cambridge, Mass.: Harvard University Press, 1962), 97-98.

3. *Ibid.,* 79.

4. Jacob Lestschinsky, "The Economic Development of the Jews in the United States," in *The Jewish People: Past and Present* (New York: Central Yiddish Culture Organization, 1946), I, 391.

5. *Ibid.,* Lestchinsky, "Jewish Migrations: 1840-1946," in *The Jews,* Louis Finkelstein, ed. (Philadelphia: Jewish Publication Society, 1949), IV, 1225; Rischin, *op. cit.,* 58.

6. Anita L. Lebeson, "The American Jewish Chronicle," in *The Jews,* I, 343.

7. Ben Zion Hoffman, *Fuftzig Yahr Cloakmacher Union* (New York: Cloak Operators Union, Local 117, 1936), 22.

8. Peter Wiernik, *History of the Jews in America* (New York: The Jewish Press Publishing Co., 1912), 268-69.

9. Harry Fischel, *Forty Years of Struggle for a Principle* (New York: Bloch Publishing Co., Inc., 1928), 12.

10. Alexander M. Dushkin, *Jewish Education in New York City* (New York: Bureau of Jewish Education, 1918), 69-72; Zvi Scharfstein, *History of Jewish Education in Modern Times* (New York: Ogen, 1947), II, 190. For a description of the public school system at this time see *The First Fifty Years, A Brief Review of Progress* (New York: New York Board of Education, 1949), 5-15.

11. Jeremiah J. Berman, "Jewish Education in New York City, 1860-1900," *YIVO Annual of Jewish Social Science, 1954,* IX, 272-74; Dushkin, *loc. cit.;* Zvi Scharfstein, "Le Tol'dot ha-Hinukh ha-Yehudi be-Artzot ha-B'rit," *Sefer Hashanah* (New York: Histadrut Ivrit of America, 1944), VII, 538-55.

Of all the Talmud Torahs for which founding dates are given in the *Jewish Communal Register of New York City* (New York: 1918), the Machzikei Talmud Torah, which was organized in 1883, is the only one listed that preceded the Yeshivat Etz Chaim. Israel Konovitz "Braishit ha-Hinukh ha-Ivri be-New York," in *Jubilee Book of the Hebrew Teachers Union of New York and Vicinity,* ed. Zvi Scharfstein (New York: 1944), sets the founding date of the Machzikei Talmud Torah in 1882.

12. Dushkin, *op. cit.,* 54.

13. *AH,* Aug, 13, 1889, 85, 90.

14. Even in 1906, Edmund J. James found that the Christian mission school "had become very active." Edmund J. James and others, *The Immigrant Jews in America* (New York: B. F. Buck and Co., 1906), 155.

See also an editoral in *JT,* Dec. 7, 1906, entitled "Soul Snatchers on the East Side," describing the renewed activities of the Episcopalian Mission Society and the "Chinatown" Mission House.

15. *AH,* Jan. 3, 1890, 202.

16. Moshe Davis, "Jewish Religious Life and Institutions in America," in *The Jews,* I, 407.

17. Dushkin, *op. cit.,* 54. For a further description of the various Mission Schools, see Appendix C, "Mission Schools in New York, 1896," Dushkin, 468-69.

18. *AH,* Jan. 3, 1890, 202; Dushkin, *op. cit.,* 54; Berman, *loc. cit.,* pp. 253-58.

19. Judah David Eisenstein, *Otzar Zikhronotai* (New York: J. D. Eisenstein, 1929), 66a.

20. *AH,* Dec. 12, 1879, 41.

21. Dushkin, *op. cit.,* 54-55.

22. Scharfstein, *op. cit.,* 194.

23. Dushkin, *op. cit.,* 53.

24. *Ibid.,* 59.

25. *Ibid.*

26. *AH,* Nov. 21, 1879, 3-4. In the entire city there were only 727 members supporting the movement. *AH,* Dec. 12, 1879, 49, 1177; Eisenstein, *op. cit.,* 66 a-b.

27. Dushkin, *op. cit.,* 52; Scharfstein, *op. cit.,* 172.

Earlier schools founded by the Jews in New York City in the eighteenth century (Hyman B. Grinstein, *The Rise of the Jewish Community of New York* [Philadelphia: Jewish Publication Society, 1947], 228), the day schools that flourished under the sponsorship of the German congregations between 1840 and 1870 (*Ibid.,* 231-46), and the "Mission Schools" of the Hebrew Free School Association in 1865 had also provided secular training with various degrees of emphasis, but it was an arrangement dictated by the fact that there was no public school system at that time. The quality of the religious education in these schools was rudimentary, and when opportunities for secular education became widespread and easily accessible, the schools soon closed down (*Ibid.,* 22ff. and 241; Berman, *loc. cit.;* and Dushkin, *op. cit.,* 42-59).

28. *AH,* Dec. 12, 1879, 41, and Dec. 26, 1879, 67.

29. Dushkin, *op cit.,* 57-58.

30. James, *op. cit.,* 192-93.

31. The word "Jewish" was omitted from its title to indicate the non-sectarian nature of the Alliance's program. Its president, Isidore Strauss, indicated: "On first blush our work may seem sectarian; it is nothing of the sort. It is educational, humanitarian, philanthropic and patriotic in its broadest sense." Quoted from *Educational Alliance, Fourth Annual Report, 1896,* 27, by Myron Berman, in "A New Spirit in the East Side: The Early History of Emanuel Brotherhood, 1903-1920" *AJHQ,* Sept. 1964, LIV, No. 1, 58 and note 20.

32. Uriah Z. Engelman, *Hebrew Education in America* (New York: Jewish Teachers' Seminary and People's University Press, 1947), 17.

33. See Jeremiah J. Berman, *loc. cit.,* 259.

34. *HI,* Sept. 11, 1896, 1b.

35. Isaac B. Berkson, *Theories of Americanization* (New York: Teachers College, Columbia University, 1923), 57 and note 1.

36. Leo L. Honor, "Jewish Education in the United States," in *The Jewish People: Past and Present* (New York: Central Yiddish Culture Organization, 1948), II, 157.

37. *HI,* Sept. 17, 1897. See also article in *HI,* Sept. 24, 1897, by Dr. Yehuda Levi Zinsler on the same subject.

38. Israel Friedlander, *Past and Present* (Cincinnati: Ark Publishing Co., 1919), 356ff.; Berkson, *op. cit.,* 97ff.

39. *The Jewish Communal Register* (New York: Kehillah, 1918), 89.

40. *Ibid.;* Dushkin, *op. cit.,* 486.

41. Joseph Jacobs, "United States," *Jewish Encyclopedia* (New York: Funk & Wagnall Co., Inc., 1906), XII, 373.

42. Nathan Goldberg, "The Jewish Population in the United States," *The Jewish People: Past and Present,* II, 105; Samuel Joseph, *op. cit.,* 174.

43. Jacob A. Riis, *How the Other Half Lives* (New York: Charles Scribner's Sons, 1897), 105; Rischin, *op. cit.,* 76-94.

44. *AH,* Dec. 12, 1879, 51.

45. In later years they were more successful. Eisenstein (*loc. cit.,* 66 a-b) says that at one time there was $60,000 in the treasury. See also Scharfstein, *op. cit.,* 175, and Berman, *op. cit.,* 259-71.

46. Further divisiveness was caused by petty loyalties to Landsmanshaften, according to Max H. Raisin, "Jews and Judaism in America," *Ha-Shiloah* (Berlin: 1898), IV, 468, 470. See also James, *op. cit.,* 149-50.

47. James, *op. cit.,* 150.

48. James, *op. cit.,* 151. Although Jacob Riis wrote (*op. cit.,* 112-13), that "attached to many of the synagogues are Talmudic schools that absorbed a share of the growing youth," he probably was referring to the informal groups that met to study in the *Beth Hamidrash* (small synagogue or chapel used as a place of study) of the various synagogues. Certainly, there were no "Talmudic Schools."

Rabbi Moses Weinberger, describing the education scene in New York in 1887, does not mention even one Hebrew school attached to a congregation. See beginning of *Sefer ha-Yehudim veha-Yahadut be-New York* (New York: Dr. Morris Wechsler, Printer, 1887), I.

49. Dushkin, *op. cit.,* 66.

50. Honor, *loc. cit.*

51. *Weekly Bulletin of the Department of Health,* New York City, Apr. 17, 1915, IV, No. 16, 129; *JT,* April 28, 1915, 10c-d.

52. James, *op. cit.,* 150-51.

53. Honor, *loc. cit.*

54. Dushkin, *op. cit.,* 68.

55. James, *loc. cit.*

56. Dushkin, *loc. cit.*

57. Ezekiel Lifschutz, "Jewish Immigrant Life in American Memoirs," *YIVO Annual of Jewish Social Science,* 1950, V, 223.

58. James, *loc. cit.*

59. Lifschutz, *op cit.,* 223.

60. Sampson Lederhendler, "The Religious Unrest," *New Era Illustrated Magazine,* February 1905, VI, No. 3, 289.

61. Friedlander, *op. cit.,* 286-87.

62. Honor, *loc. cit.;* Jacob Lestschinsky, "Jewish Migrations: 1840-1946," *The Jews,* IV, 1225.

63. Dushkin, *op. cit.,* 63.
64. Honor, *loc. cit.*

Notes to Chapter 2 (pp. 17-33)

1. See the Certificate of Incorporation of the Chebra Machsika Ishiwas Eitz Chaim [sic], Appendix II, and the Program of Exercises of Rabbinical College, Appendix VI; Alexander M. Dushkin, *Jewish Education in New York City,* 73-75; *Hebrew American Directory and Universal Guide* (New York: Gordon Publishing Co., 1892), 139; Jacob I. Hartstein, "The Yeshiva Looks Back over Fifty Years," *Jewish Education* (April-June 1937), IV, 53.

Minutes of the meetings of the Directors of Yeshivat Etz Chaim were recorded by a Mr. Lifshitz (interview with Dr. Mordecai M. Kaplan); by Aryeh Leib Rosenthal, who was Secretary from 1892 to 1900 (interview with his son, Rabbi Moses Rosenthal, and *JT,* Jan. 31, 1897), and by Eliezer Lipnick, who succeeded Rosenthal at the end of the century (interview with Jacob L. Andron, and *JMJ,* Feb. 1, 1912). However, all the record books have been lost.

Abraham Cahan, (*Bleter fun Mein Leben* [New York: Forward Association, 1926] II, 361) bears witness to the meager resources, but great determination of the founders of the Yeshiva.

Moses Weinberger, a contemporary of Cahan, in his book *Sefer ha-Yehudim veha-Yahadut be-New York* (New York: Dr. Morris Wechsler, Printer, 1887, 23ff.), reported on the news that the Yeshivat Etz Chaim was being organized and that about 15,000 individuals were ready to support such an institution. He expressed great enthusiasm at the prospect of the founding in this country of a yeshiva where Mishnah and Talmud would be taught.

2. See Note 11 Chapter 1.

3. Jeremiah J. Berman, "Jewish Education in New York City, 1860-1900," *YIVO Annual of Social Science, 1954,* IX, 27; Dushkin, *loc. cit.*

4. See Announcement of formation of RIETS, Appendix IV. Although Dushkin, *loc. cit.,* p. 73, claims RIETS was first formed at 47 East Broadway, there may have been several organizing meetings at different locations. Harry Fischel, in his *Forty Years of Struggle for a Principle* (New York: Bloch Publishing Co., Inc., 1928), claims (p. 36) that Etz Chaim started at 1 Canal Street.

5. Cahan, *loc. cit.;* Dushkin, *loc. cit.;* personal interview with Dr. Mordecai M. Kaplan; announcement of Etz Chaim in *JG,* Feb. 5, 1897.

The building was acquired on Nov. 15, 1898, at a cost of $15,500 (see note 55 this chapter). Previously, Etz Chaim had apparently entered into abortive negotiations to acquire a new building. On Feb. 24, 1888, the directors announced that they "had bought a magnificent 5 story brownstone house at 150 Henry Street near Rutgers Street . . . It is the finest house on the finest block." (*JT*, Feb. 24, 1888.) After another similar announcement (*JT*, Feb. 28, 1888), this location was never referred to again.

6. Hyman B. Grinstein, *The Rise of the Jewish Community of New York* (Philadelphia: The Jewish Publication Society, 1947), 228.

7. *Ibid.*, 231-46.

8. *Ibid.*, 229 and 241.

9. For a study of the sponsorship of the "German" schools see Grinstein, *op. cit.*, 231ff.

10. See Certificate of Incorporation of the Chebra Machsika Ishiwas Eitz Chaim [sic], Appendix II.

11. Constitution of Yeshiva Etz Chaim, Appendix I.

12. See Solomon Th. Hurwitz, "Three Epochs of Jewish Education in America," *AJC*, Feb. 3, 1917, p. 392.

13. About Morris Bernstein see "A Message from Mr. Bernard Bernstein," *Hedenu: Student Organization of the Rabbi Isaac Elchanan Theological Seminary* (New York: May 1936), 13. In the *New York City Directory* (*NYCD*) for the year 1886-1887, there are eight persons listed by this name with various occupations such as "clerk," "pedlar," "segarmaker," "shoes." Samuel Waxman was listed in *NYCD* as dealing in clothing at 74 Baxter Street for the year 1886-87. There is an Abraham Rubenowitz in *NYCD* for 1886-87, as a tailor at 9 Forsyth Street. Rachmiel Witman is not listed in *NYCD* for 1886-87, although several other persons with the surname "Wittman" are listed. *NYCD* for the year 1886-87 lists a Henry W. Greenberg, living on the Lower East Side, who dealt in real estate, but for the year 1887-88 the name appears as Henry M. Greenberg, who dealt in real estate and was located at a different address in the same neighborhood on the Lower East Side.

The name Julius D. Bernstein does not appear in *NYCD* for the years 1886-87 or 1887-88. There are three persons listed in these directories bearing the name of "Julius Bernstein." In *JG*, Jan. 15, 1897, Rabbi Yehuda David Bernstein is referred to as the founder of Yeshivat Etz Chaim as well as a founder of the Rabbi Isaac Elchanan Theological Seminary. His name also appears on the Certificate of Incorporation of the Rabbi Isaac Elchanan Theological Seminary Association, Appendix III. Moses Heller is not listed in *NYCD* for the year 1886-87. However, there is a Morris Heller listed as a tailor at 60 Mulberry Street.

Falk Berman is listed, *NYCD* 1886-87, as a tailor at 15 Chrystie Street. Louis Shapiro is listed as a "pedlar" at 140 East Broadway. Information about Rabbi Ratkowsky was received in an interview with Mrs. Charlotte Chazin, his granddaughter. According to another source he was a furrier (see Note 68, Chapter 4). He is not listed in the *NYCD* for 1886-87 or for 1887-88. Louis Siegelstein is in *NYCD* for the year 1886-87, as a peddler at 71½ Division Street. See also Appendix II.

Baruch P. Liberman is not listed in *NYCD* for the year 1886-87 or for 1887-88. However, there is some biographical data concerning him in the *Hebrew American Directory and Universal Guide* (New York: 1892), 139. His full name, given there, is Baruch Pinchas Liberman.

See also *AH*, May 11, 1883, quoted in Jeremiah Berman, *op. cit.*, 273; and Judah David Eisenstein, *Otzar Zikhronotai* (New York: J. D. Eisenstein, 1929), 25b.

When Jonah Ginsberg died, the Yeshiva placed an obituary notice in the press stating that he had been an active worker for and founder of Etz Chaim (*JMJ*, Feb. 12, 1912, p. 10c); Rothstein is cited in Cahan, *op. cit.*, II, 358.

Moses Isaac Bernstein may be identical with Morris Bernstein, one of the incorporators.

14. Cahan, *op. cit.*, 361. For an account of the organization of the Association of the American Orthodox Hebrew Congregations and the career of the Chief Rabbi, see Abraham J. Karp, "New York Chooses a Chief Rabbi," *AJHQ*, 44, No. 3 (March 1955), 129-98.

15. *Hebrew American Directory and Universal Guide*, 139; *JT*, Jan. 31, 1897. For biographical information on Roggen see *JT*, Nov. 25, 1915, p. 16, and Isaac Rosengarten, "A Pioneer in American Orthodox Jewry," *JF*, VIII, No. 3 (April 1925), 146. Personal interviews held with Schlang's son Isidore (Yechezkael Schlang's death was announced in *JT*, Sept. 3, 1912, p. 8d), and with Jacob L. Andron, on Shamai Rosenthal. For biographical information on Alexander and his business see *JT*, Nov. 25, 1915, p. 39.

16. Cahan, *loc. cit.*

17. *JT*, May 4, 1888, p. 2.

18. Moses Weinberger, *Sefer ha-Yehudim veha-Yahadut be-New York* (New York: Dr. Morris Wechsler, Printer, 1887), 17-25.

19. *JG*, Nov. 19, 1897, p. 16.

20. The school advertised its thanks to the "Society of Daughters of Israel Malbish Arumim" who "clothe the students of Yeshiva Etz Chaim . . . and support the Yeshiva to the extent of $25 per month . . . last week they contributed $100 which the Yeshiva needed desperately to pay the interest due on the building . . ." (*JT*, May 16, 1897, p. 6).

The group continued at least until 1912 as evidenced by obituary notices published in memory of Mrs. Berman of 1964 E. 94th Street, "a long time member of the Beth Israel Malbish Arumim Society of Yeshivat Etz Chaim" (*JT*, April 26, 1908, p. 8); Mrs. Amelia Rubinsky (*JMJ*, March 15, 1912, p. 10); Mrs. Esther Abrams (*JMJ*, March 25, 1912, p. 10); Mrs. Feige Freedlander (*JMJ*, June 9, 1912, p. 8. President of the Society in 1912 was a Mrs. Gellis (*JMJ*, March 25, 1912, p. 10).

21. *JT*, May 16, 1897, p. 6.

22. Constitution of Yeshivat Etz Chaim, Appendix I.

23. *JT*, Jan. 31, 1897.

24. *Ibid.*

25. Personal interview with Hillel Rogoff.

26. *Ibid.*

27. *JT*, Jan. 31, 1897.

28. Aryeh Leib Rosenthal was the secretary in 1897 (*JT*, Jan. 31, 1897, and *JG*, Feb. 5, 1897, p. 2). A Mr. Lifshitz was secretary prior to him (interview with Mordecai M. Kaplan). By 1900 Eliezer Lipnick was the secretary (interview with Jacob L. Andron, and *JMJ*, Feb. 1, 1912, p. 5c).

29. Joseph Boylen was the collector in 1897 (*JT*, Jan. 31, 1897).

30. Personal interview with Dr. Mordecai M. Kaplan.

31. Cahan, *op. cit.*, 358.

32. *Ibid.*; interview with Mordecai M. Kaplan; *JG*, Nov. 19, 1897.

33. Cahan, *op. cit.*, 360.

34. *Ibid.*, 359.

35. *Ibid.*

36. *JT*, July 27, 1888. Other choice descriptions were used as well.

37. *JT*, Aug. 1, 1888, p. 2.

38. Cahan, *op. cit.*, 369.

39. It is not known who replaced Cahan. According to Jacob L. Andron, a Nathan Mussar was employed as an English teacher in the 1890's.

40. Personal interview with Mordecai M. Kaplan; interview with Mrs. Charlotte Chazin, Rabbi Ratkowsky's granddaughter, and letters from her in author's possession.

41. Personal interview with Mordecai M. Kaplan.

42. Personal interview with Hillel Rogoff.

43. *JT*, April 23, 1888.

44. *Ibid.*

45. *JT*, May 4, 1888.

46. *JT*, July 27, 1888, p. 1.

47. *JT*, April 23, 1888.

48. *JT*, Dec. 25, 1888, p. 2.

49. *HI*, July 3, 1896, p. 1e.

50. Personal interview with Jacob L. Andron.

51. *HI, loc. cit.*

52. Personal interview with Jacob L. Andron and Mordecai M. Kaplan. Harris was later associated with the firm of Lewis and Harris of 27 W. 3rd Street, New York City. The Bernsteins were in the silk and satin business at 40 W. 17th Street, New York City (*JMJ*, Jan. 12, 1912).

53. *JT*, July 14, 1905, p. 2b.

54. Personal interview with Jacob L. Andron.

55. Recorded Nov. 28, 1898, in New York County, Liber 48 of *Conveyances*, 367.

56. One hundred students were reported in attendance in 1892, in *Hebrew American Directory and Universal Guide,* 139.

57. Sampson Lederhendler, "The New York Yeshibath," *New Era Illustrated Magazine* (March-April, 1905), VI, 344.

58. Judah D. Eisenstein, "Yeshibah," *Jewish Encyclopedia* (New York: Funk & Wagnalls Co., 1906), XII, 600.

59. Interview with Mordecai M. Kaplan.

60. *JT,* Nov. 3, 1904, p. 26.

61. *JT,* Dec. 10, 1906, p. 2b.

62. *JT,* Dec. 18, 1908, p. 8b.

63. *JT,* Dec. 28, 1908, p. 6b.

64. *JT,* Sept. 25, 1908, p. 10a and *JMJ,* Jan. 16, 1911, p. 7f.

65. *JT,* Dec. 18, 1908, p. 8b, and Jan. 9, 1910, p. 8c.

66. The following account is based on an interview with Dr. Harry Barash, a New York City physician.

67. *JT,* Dec. 18, 1908, p. 8b.

68. *JT,* Sept. 25, 1908, p. 10a.

69. *JT,* Oct. 2, 1910, p. 10b. A. C. Rosenberg writing about the need for devotion to Judaism reported that he had visited Yeshivat Etz Chaim and described the students as "children that will remain ever loyal to our people" and as "cultured" with "true Jewish hearts." He was also proud that "many of them have entered directly into City College." (*JT,* Oct. 3, 1910, p. 8a-b).

70. Interview with Dr. Harry Barash.

71. *JT,* Dec. 25, 1908, p. 6b.

72. *JT,* Dec. 25, 1908, p. 6b; *JMJ,* Jan. 13, 1911, p. 7b.

Notes to Chapter 3 (pp. 34-47)

1. Moses Rischin, *The Promised City* (Cambridge, Mass.: Harvard University Press, 1962), 97-98.

2. *HI,* July 2, 1897, p. 1a-b.

3. *Jüdische Gazetten,* Jan. 6, 1899, p. 5f; Rischin, *op. cit.,* 148.

4. Eisenstein, *Otzar Zikhronotai,* 252b.

5. *Ha-Tzefirah,* No. 83 (1887), p. 3.

6. Dr. Wise put the matter very simply in May 1874: "Either we must educate young men for the pulpit, or expect to close up the temples and synagogues in the next generation. A cause which has no expounders, no pleaders, must vanish . . . *We must educate our rabbis or have none.*" Quoted in Dena Wilansky, *Sinai to Cincinnati* (New York: Renaissance Book Co., 1937), 73.

7. Bernard Drachman, *The Unfailing Light* (New York: Rabbinical Council of America, 1948), 177-80.

8. For a description of the founders of the Jewish Theological Seminary and early Conservative Judaism, see Drachman, *loc. cit.,* and Moshe Davis, "Biographical Sketches," *The Emergence of Conservative Judaism: The Historical School in Nineteenth Century America* (Philadelphia: Jewish Publication Society, 1963), 329ff.

9. *JT,* March 18, 1888, p. 1.

10. Drachman's position in the Jewish Theological Seminary was anomalous. He was a devoted Orthodox Jew who could not subscribe to the religious changes that evolved in the Seminary. See the account of his association with the Seminary in his autobiography, *The Unfailing Light.* The Yiddish press also dealt kindly with him because of his identification with all orthodox endeavors. In the interim period between Morais and Schechter, he apparently headed the Seminary faculty. *Die Jüdische Welt* (July 2, 1902, p. 1a) called him the "Acting Head" of the Seminary in 1902. With Schechter's assumption of the presidency, Drachman was eased out of his position on the faculty.

11. See Letter 2 and note 1 in Meir Ben Horin "Solomon Schechter to Judge Mayer Sulzberger, Part II. Letters from the Seminary Period (1902-1915)" in *Jewish Social Studies* (April, 1965), XVII, No. 2, p. 76. Note 1 in this article also sheds light on note 10, this chapter.

12. *HI,* Aug. 13, 1897, and Aug. 6, 1897, p. 1a.

13. *HI,* Sept. 17, 1897, p. 1a.

14. *HI,* Oct. 15, 1897, p. 1e.

15. *Ibid.*

16. Ezekiel Levit, "What We Need," *JT,* Feb. 5, 1903, p. 5c.

17. *HI,* July 30, 1897, p. 1d-e; *JT,* Sept. 22, 1888; *Ha-Tzefirah,* 1893, No. 77, p. 319.

18. See, for example, report in *JW,* Feb. 1903 (p. 3a), of the examination conducted by Rabbi Gershon Lesser of Cincinnati of the students of RIETS and his glowing comment.

19. *HI,* Aug. 27, 1897, p. 1e.

20. *JG,* Dec. 24, 1897.

21. *HI,* Dec. 18, 1896.

22. *HI,* Aug. 6, 1897, p. 1a.

23. Solomon Schechter, Morais' successor as president of the faculty of the Jewish Theological Seminary, continued Morais' prejudice against Yiddish. "Though he [Schechter] knew it would incite them [the Yiddish enthusiasts and the Yiddish press], he refused to give any favor to the Yiddish tongue, and would not admit it as a language of instruction in the Seminary. He had a scorn for that distorted Jewish patriotism which held Yiddish to be a bond." (Norman Bentwich, *Solomon Schechter* [Philadelphia: Jewish Publication Society, 1948], 213.)

24. Solomon Goldman, "The Portrait of a Teacher," in *Louis Ginzberg*

Jubilee Volume (New York: The American Academy for Jewish Research, 1945), English section, p. 1.

25. *JT*, April 4, 1905, English page.

26. *JW*, July 3, 1902, p. 4.

27. *Ibid.*

28. *HI*, July 2, 1897, p. 1a-b.

29. *JT*, March 9, 1908, p. 4b.

30. In connection with the Jewish Theological Seminary, the *Tageblatt* had pronounced: "The truth is that the East Side is still unwilling to affiliate itself with the institutions in which the uptowners are the leaders and have the power owing to their large donations . . ." (*JT*, Nov. 23, 1902, English page.)

31. I. M. Wise commented on this contempt on the part of the immigrants, whom he called "those Russian refugees." He said: ". . . they, by their public organs, constantly denounce and coarsely insult us as 'reformers' under which they understand a class of Israelites who stand far below them and outside the pale of Judaism. Have we not done enough good for those for whom we are not good enough?" (Wilansky, *op. cit.*, 78.)

32. As far as reform was concerned, the Yiddish press summed up its attitude by saying, "The reform movement for the East Side is a tremendous blunder." (*JT*, Feb. 4, 1904, English page.)

33. *JT* of Dec. 2, 1896 (p. 2a-b) carried the following editorial comment: "All Russian rabbis are called upon to support this [Jewish Theological Seminary] important institution . . . and to encourage their congregations to support the building, where pure American Judaism, the Judaism which has not denied the Sabbath, holidays and kashruth is being taught and strengthened . . ."

34. In 1905, Dr. Mendes, who was very active in the newly organized Union of Orthodox Jewish Congregations, and a past president, repeated the lament: "It seems strange," he said at a meeting of the New York Branch of the Jewish Theological Seminary, "that the Seminary is not supported by the part of the community most interested in its success. The downtown Jews, those usually called ultar-orthodox, display no interest in our efforts. They don't come to us. We must, therefore, go to them and show them that the future of traditional Judaism in America lies in this institution." (*JT*, Apr. 4, 1905, English page.)

35. *JG*, June 25, 1897, p. 1; *HI*, Dec. 18, 1896, for example.

36. Israel Friedlander, *Past and Present* (Cincinnati: Ark Publishing Co., 1919), 256-57.

37. With great insight, the *Jüdische Welt* in its first issue carried an English column entitled "The Conflict of Ideals" which defined the problem as follows: "A battle is being waged at the present moment in the City of New York as severe and protracted as any that have occurred in the history of humanity. No blood is shed, no physical wounds are given, but the anguish and misery caused is nevertheless severe, because they inflict wounds of the

spirit. The conflict between the old and the new generation is the natural price that is paid for progress throughout the world, but, in the instance we are thinking of, the contest is intensified by the abnormal conditions in the Jewish population of the East Side.

"Here the east and west meet on the same soil and in the same households. Europe—one might even say half Asia—and America are found with their diverse ideals within one same family, and the conflict that ensues is unending and the more bitter because it is between the nearest and dearest. The Russian Jew comes here with his reverence for the law, with his Old World notions of submission, and lo! within a few years there grows up around him a set of young people more American than the Americans, with reverence for nothing and submission to nothing but their own desires. Each side thinks the other is wrong. The bitterness that is thus infused into the holiest of human relations is as sad a condition of affairs as we can think of . . . The tragedy of the situation is obscured by its frequency in our city of today, but its intensity and bitterness is not mitigated by these repetitions . . ." (June 27, 1902, p. 12.)

38. For the life of Rabbi Illowy, see Henry Illowy, *Sefer Milhamot Elohim* (Berlin: M. Poppelauer, 1914).

39. *HI,* March 20, 1896, p. 20.

40. As late as in 1906, the cry was still for leadership, and in an article addressed "To Those Jews Who Want To Remain Jews," the following analysis is found in the *Jüdische Gazetten:* "What is lacking is an organized strength that will unite all the sparks [of the Jewish effort]. We need representatives . . . who will know how to utilize American methods and to spread Jewish agitation in the way that will lead to the immediate accomplishment of the goal . . ." (Dec. 7, 1906, p. 11d.)

41. *JT,* March 6, 1888, p 1

42. *JT,* June 25, 1897, p. 12; *JG,* June 25, 1897, p. 1; *HI,* Jan. 13, 1895, p. 1c; *HI,* Feb. 14, 1896, p. 2.

43. Rabbi Duber Abramowitz, in an introductory article to the initial issue of the Hebrew rabbinic monthly, *Bet Vaad le-Hakhamim* (Shevat, 1903), I, 1-2.

44. S. Rosenfeld, "Ha-Dat veha-Hinukh," *Ha-Shiloah* (Berlin: 1897), 266.

45. *JG,* Jan. 13, 1899, p. 8d-f; Abraham J. Karp "New York Chooses a Chief Rabbi," *Publications American Jewish Historical Society,* XLIV, No. 3 (March 1955), 162ff.

Notes to Chapter 4 (pp. 48-72)

1. See a letter headed "How Long Shall The Tail Wag The Dog," in *Die Jüdische Welt* (July 23, 1902, p. 8c) for a typical East Side evaluation of the "uptowners." Also, correspondence in *JW,* July 30, 1902, p. 8b, and *JW,* Aug. 3, 1902, p. 8c; Moses Rischin, *The Promised City* (Cambridge, Mass.: Harvard

University Press, 1962), 95-98; Jeremiah J. Berman, "Jewish Education in New York City, 1860-1900," *YIVO Annual of Jewish Social Science, 1954,* IX, 248-49, 252-53.

2. *JG, January 15, 1897.* The Synagogue was apparently also known as the Vizohner Synagogue. In recalling the history of the Machzikei Talmud Torah, the *Jüdisches Tageblatt* (Mar. 1, 1908, p. 8c-d) referred to its first meeting held on Sunday, March 7, 1886, at the Vizohner Synagogue, 44 East Broadway. See also note 26, this chapter.

3. I. Cohen, "Yeshiva Rabbi Isaac Elchanan," *Aspaklaria* (Adar, 1907), p. 40.

4. From statement in leaflet certifying the *kashrut* of the Kosher Wurst Fabric, Brooklyn, N.Y., in possession of Louis Matlin, son of Rabbi Matlin.

5. Interview with Rabbi Henry Guterman.

6. *JG,* Sept. 15, 1905, p. 15a, and Oct. 6, 1905, p. 10.

7. For short biography of Rabbi Bernstein, see Ben Zion Eisenstadt, *Israel's Scholars in America* (New York: Rosenberg, 1903), p. 20.

8. Personal interviews with Rabbis Jacob Bosniak and David Rackman.

9. Personal interview with Rabbi Henry Guterman.

10. *JG,* Sept. 17, 1897 and *JG,* Apr. 6, 1900, Section II, p. 3. Germansky died Dec. 3, 1914 (*JT,* Dec. 4, 1914, p. 4b).

11. Personal interview with Jacob L. Andron.

12. *JT,* Dec. 1, 1902, p. 4a.

13. I. Cohen, *op. cit.,* 42.

14. See text of Certificate of Incorporation, Appendix III.

15. Dushkin, *Jewish Education in New York City* (New York: Bureau of Education, 1918) 76-78. This is contradicted by Jacob L. Andron, who, in a personal interview, denied that RIETS ever was located in the Etz Chaim building.

16. Judah David Eisenstein, *Otzar Zikhronotai* (New York: J. D. Eisenstein, 1929), 81b. A writer of a later date gives the first location of RIETS as "Ludlow Street." See Moshe Rivlin, "Yeshivas Rabbi Isaac Elchanan," *DA,* April 4, 1927, p. 2; Elias Hershman ("Immigrant M. Hurewitz True Founder of Y.U.," *Commentator* [undergraduate publication of Yeshiva College] March 12, 1956) claims that the first meeting place was at 156 Henry Street. This address may be confused with the location which RIETS occupied later, in 1904.

17. The claim that RIETS was founded at the Mariampol Synagogue was later substantiated in a short historical account of the Machzikei Talmud Torah found in the *Tageblatt* on the occasion of its 25th anniversary (*JT,* March 1, 1908, p. 8c-d).

18. See also article on RIETS by P. Einbinder, "Fifty Years Since the Founding of the First Yeshiva in America," *Jewish Daily Forward,* Sept. 11, 1936, p. 9b.

19. Personal interview with Louis Matlin. According to Jacob L. Andron's recollection, however, Rabbi Matlin found asylum for his class in a synagogue at 34 Ludlow Street first and then moved to the Mariampol Synagogue.

20. For details of life and accomplishments of Rabbi Isaac Elchanan Spektor, see Ephraim Shimoff, *Rabbi Isaac Elchanan Spektor* (New York: Yeshiva University, 1959).

21. This was commonly done in memory of a great rabbi. In Kovno, for example, a home for poor orphans was built and given Rabbi Isaac Elchanan's name (*JW*, March 9, 1903). The Beth Sefer Tifereth Yerushalayim in New York City was similarly named after New York's Chief Rabbi, when he died in 1902. It is now known as The Rabbi Jacob Joseph School. The Yeshiva Tifereth Bachurim, in Brooklyn, N.Y., took on the new name of Rabbi Chaim Berlin soon after his death. (*JT*, Oct. 13, 1912, p. 6d, and Oct. 18, 1912, p. 8a.)

Daughters of Nathan Lamport, Mrs. Charles Cohen and Mrs. Alexander Lamport, recall that their father insisted that the school be named after Rabbi Isaac Elchanan because he was inspired by his father's stories of the great sage. Mr. Lamport's father, Zvi Hirsch, was one of the favorite students of Rabbi Isaac Elchanan. Jacob L. Andron, however, recalls that it was Rabbi Y. D. Bernstein who suggested the name.

The tradition of naming an Academy of Torah study after a great scholar is found in the Babylonian Talmud, Baba Kamma 16b and 17a, where the rabbis interpret the verse referring to King Hezekiah: "And they did him honor at his death" (II *Chron.* 32:33), as signifying "that they set up a *yeshiva* near his sepulchre." This suggestion as to the origin of the name of RIETS is borne out by announcement issued in connection with a *yahrzeit* observance scheduled in memory of Rabbi Isaac Elchanan in 1913, which said in part, as follows: ". . . it is now 17 years since the death of . . . Rabbi Isaac Elchanan . . . and 16 years since a memorial was set at his selpulchre, which is the holy Yeshiva Rabbi Isaac Elchanan." (*JT*, Mar. 26, 1913, p. 6b.) Note the similarity in language between the Talmudic text and the announcement.

22. Fischel, *Forty Years of Struggle for a Principle* (New York: Bloch Publishing Co., Inc., 1928), 36.

23. *JG*, Aug. 13, 1897.

24. For a description of this area see Rischin, *op. cit.*, 76-84.

25. This does not explain why RIETS did not move with Etz Chaim to its new home.

26. An article in *Ha-Ivri*, Sept. 17, 1897, states that RIETS met at Congregation Beth Telfillas Israel at this same location, 44 East Broadway. There is also a reference to a Vizohner Synagogue (*JT*, Mar. 30, 1903, p. 1e and March 1, 1908, p. 8c-d) and a Ḥebra B'nai Emes (*JT*, June 11, 1905, p. 2b) at this

same address. Several synagogues may have been holding their services on different floors of the same building. Jacob L. Andron contends that while the official organization of RIETS may have taken place at the Mariampol Synagogue, classes were not actually located there until later. He recalls that the students met at 34 Ludlow Street even after the official organization.

27. *JT*, Feb. 8, 1904, p. 1g.

28. *JG*, June 29, 1900, Section II, p. 3a and personal interviews with Jacob L. Andron and Hillel Rogoff.

29. *JG*, June 29, 1900, Section II, p. 3a. In 1899, it was estimated that there were 20 students at RIETS. *JG*, June 30, 1899, p. 4b.

30. Mr. Bramson was the owner of a butcher shop at 10 Suffolk Street. Interview with Moshe (Marks) Hurewitz.

31. *JG*, June 29, 1900, Section II, p. 3a.

32. *JT*, Nov. 17, 1901, p. 4b.

33. *JT*, July 3, 1902, p. 4a.

34. *JT*, Nov. 21, 1902, p. 16 and English page.

35. *JT*, Nov. 17, 1901, p. 4b, and Apr. 27, 1903, p. 1f.

36. *JT*, Nov. 24, 1902, English page.

37. *JT*, May 5, 1904, English page, and see also *JW*, Feb. 2, 1903, English page.

38. *Ibid.*

39. *JG*, Mar. 8, 1901, p. 9f.

40. Masliansky was late relected to the executive of the Jewish Theological Seminary (*JT*, April 4, 1905, English page).

41. *JT*, Oct. 28, 1902, p. 4b.

42. *JT*, Oct. 28, 1902, p. 4b.

43. *JG*, June 29, 1900, Section II, p. 3a.

44. *Ibid.*

45. *Ibid.;* see also installment of book in *Hadoar*, 3 Kislev, 1941.

46. *JG*, June 17, 1901, p. 10f; Ephraim E. Lisitsky, *Eleh Toldot Adam* (Jerulalem: Mossad Bialik, 1956), p. 90. The Congregation was also known as B'nai Chesed Anshei Kalvarier (*JT*, Apr. 16, 1903, English page) and as Ḥebra Kadisha B'nai Israel Kalvarier Congregation (*Jewish Communal Register*, 180).

47. For a short history of the Kalvarier Synagogue and references of RIETS stay at the synagogue see *JMJ*, Mar. 10, 1912, pp. 4e-g, and March 12, 1912, p. 4a-b; *JT*, April 16, 1903, English page, Dec. 5, 1901, p. 4f, and Nov. 24, 1901, p. 6c. See also *JT*, Nov. 6, 1901, p. 2f and Sept. 16, 1902, p. 2; and *JW*, Dec. 23, 1902, p. 2a, and Feb. 15, 1903, p. 3a.

48. *JT*, Dec. 26, 1901, p. 2f.

49. Rabbi Alperstein is known to have spoken on behalf of RIETS at the Mariampol Synagogue on Saturday, Jan. 24, 1903, (*JT*, Jan. 22, 1903, p. 2g)

and during the following month at Congregation Nachalat Zvi at 170 East 114th Street (*JT*, Feb. 19, 1903, p. 2). For a brief biography of Rabbi Alperstein, see Ben Zion Eisenstadt, *Anshei Ha-Sheim be-Artzot ha-B'rit* (St. Louis, Mo.: Moinester Press, 1933), biography No. 97, p. 41.

50. On Rabbi Litwin see *JT*, Nov. 6, 1901, p. 2f, and Aug. 6, 1905, p. 6c. Rabbi Litwin remained with RIETS until 1910, after which, in 1913, he took a similar position with Yeshivat Rabbi Chaim Berlin in Brooklyn (*JT*, Jan. 15, 1913, p. 8g). On Rabbi Shapiro, *JT*, Dec. 2, 1901, p. 2f, and Aug. 18, 1905, p. 2a. In the middle of 1905, Rabbi Shapiro accepted a rabbinical position in Sioux City, Iowa, and terminated his affiliation wth RIETS. He was replaced at that time by Rabbi Abraham Gelerinter (*JT*, Aug. 18, 1905, p. 2a). We do not know how long Rabbi Gelerinter was with RIETS. In 1910 he was the rabbi of Congregation Anshei Bialystok and also sold *etrogim* before the Sukkot holidays (*JT*, Sept. 26, 1910, p. 7a). In 1913, he was appearing as a *maggid*, itinerant preacher and free lance speaker, at different synagogues (*JT*, May 9, 1913, p. 8a, and June 10, 1913, p. 11e). See also Eisenstadt, *op. cit.*, 35, for a brief biographical sketch of Rabbi Gelerinter.

On the procedures of the collectors see *JT*, Dec. 9, 1903, p. 2g, and several issues thereafter.

51. A visit of Rabbi Litwin's to Rochester is recorded in which the rabbi of the city, Rabbi Yitzchak Isaac Ginsberg, introduced him to the congregation and supported the request for funds on the grounds that "there was a Rochester young man studying at RIETS and receiving $3 per week in addition to clothes and other necessaries" (*JT*, Jan. 19, 1904, p. 2b).

52. The later support of the *Agudat ha-Rabbanim*, the Union of Orothodox Rabbis, was very significant for RIETS in this connection because that rabbinical organization called upon its members to extend all courtesies to the solicitors and to help them in their mission.

53. *JT*, Jan. 22, 1903, p. 2g.

54. *JW*, Jan. 28, 1903, p. 2e.

55. *JT*, Dec. 5, 1901, p. 2f.

56. *Bet Vaad Le-Hakhamin* (New York, 1903), I, 12-15.

57. *JT*, Dec. 5, 1901, p. 2f.

58. *JT*, June 28, 1905, p. 2b.

59. *JT*, Oct. 29, 1905, p. 6a.

60. Now known as David Rackman. Rabbi Rackman was later extolled by Rabbi Israel Rosenberg's congregation in Bayonne following a visit to the vice-president of RIETS (*JT*, May 28, 1906, p. 7f).

61. *JT*, Oct. 29, 1905, p. 6a.

62. *JT*, Dec. 15, 1905, p. 6g.

63. *JT*, May 29, 1906, p. 2b.

64. *JT*, Dec. 26, 1901, p. 2f. It is not clear how long Rabbi Leibowitz was

with RIETS. In 1905, an ad in the *Tageblatt* speaks of him as having been engaged to serve the Sabbath Cooperative Association at 87 East Broadway. (See also *JG,* Aug. 24, 1906, p. 15g.) He traveled at the time in the New England States (*JT,* July 11, 1905, p. 7f). In 1913 he became a *maggid,* an itinerant preacher (*JT,* June 6, 1913, p. 10d; June 13, 1913, p. 11e; and June 27, 1913, p. 12g). He finally became a solicitor for the Rabbi Jacob Joseph School (*JT,* Jan. 1, 1914, p. 4a).

65. *JT,* Dec. 26, 1901, p. 2f. Elias Hershman in the *Commentator* article previously cited (note 16, this chapter), states that "Moshe Hurewitz was the original founder of what today is Yeshiva University" and that he was president of the school from its inception in 1896 until Dr. Philip Hillel Klein succeeded him. This contradicts the newspaper references to H. Bramson as president (note 31, this chapter) and the absence of Moshe Hurewitz as a signatory to the Petition of Incorporation.

66. *Hebrew American Directory and Universal Guide* (New York: Gordon Publishing Co., 1892) 139.

67. Mr. Dubowsky was a *shohet.* Interview with Jacob L. Andron.

68. Mr. Ratkowsky was a furrier. Interview with Mrs. Charles Cohen and Mrs. Alexander Lamport.

69. Died in Feb. 1903 (*JT,* Feb. 27, 1903, p. 2).

70. *JG,* May 17, 1901, p. 10f.

71. *JT,* Dec. 26, 1901, p. 26.

72. *Ibid.* See complete budget 1901-1902, Appendix V.

73. See detailed budget 1901-1902, Appendix V. Another account appearing only three days after the publication of the budget credits Rabbi Litwin with $1,190 and Rabbi Shapiro with $285 (*JW,* Aug. 27, 1902, p. 5b).

74. *JW,* Aug. 24, 1902, p. 6d. See detailed budget of year 1901-1902 in Appendix V.

75. *JT,* Sept. 26, 1902, p. 6c.

76. *JT,* July 2, 1902, p. 2.

77. We have no information as to what was meant by the "middle class" or whether such a teacher was actually engaged.

78. The new Kalvarier Synagogue was to be a three-story building and basement, built on a 54 ft. frontage and 82 ft. deep, at a cost of $75,000. (*JW,* April 15, 1903, English page, and *JT,* April 14, 1903, p. 2c.) It was reopened on March 13, 1904 (*JT,* March 14, 1904, p. 4a). By that time, the new quarters at 156 Henry Street had already been acquired. In the following year, Lucas' classes were back at the Pike Street Synagogue (*JT,* Jan. 17, 1905, English page).

79. Biographical sources for Dr. Klein are: Eisenstadt, *op. cit.,* 88-89; Morris Engleman, ed., *In Memoriam—Rev. Dr. and Mrs. Philip Klein* (New York: Ference Press, 1926), issued on the occasion of the death of Dr. Klein

and his wife, Julie Hirsch Klein; *Universal Jewish Encyclopedia,* VI, 415.

80. Bernard Revel, "Tribute," *In Memoriam—Rev. Dr. and Mrs. Philip Klein.*

81. Dr. Klein was not "the first president" of RIETS, as erroneously recorded in the *In Memoriam* volume on the first Hebrew page of the publication. He was preceded by H. Bramson and M. Hurewitz as indicated above. The election is reported in *JT*, Aug. 20, 1902, p. 2b. See also *JW*, Aug. 24, 1902, p. 2c.

Moshe Hurewitz was elected vice-president, Baruch Pinchas Liberman continued as treasurer, and David Abramowitz remained as secretary (*JW*, Feb. 13, 1903, p. 3a). The directors were: Rabbi Avraham Eliezer Alperstein, Rabbi Moses Mayer Matlin, Rabbi Baruch Zalmon Ziv, Rabbi Zalman Cohen, Rabbi Yehuda David Bernstein, Baruch Pinchas Liberman, Samuel Yitzchak Shpransky, Jacob Quint, David Abramowitz, Elias Ratkowsky, Mendel Zuckerman, Samuel Yitzchak Andron, Aaron Leib Dubowsky, Isaiah Bramson (it is not clear whether he was the H. Bramson who had been president of RIETS in 1900), Yechiel Dov Shapiro, David Brener, Samuel Silberstein, Joseph Stern, Chaim Sklamberg, a Mr. Shidlowsky, Eliezer Zev Eppner, Chaim Robinson, Gershon Brener, Yechiel Bronstein (*JT*, Aug. 20, 1902, p. 2b). Mr. Harry Altshul of Jersey City was added to the board later (*JT*, May 21, 1903, p. 5e), followed by Rabbi Baruch Cohen, 29 Canal Street (*JT*, Aug. 21, 1902, p. 2). Chaim Sklamberg, who was a wholesale grocer and purveyor to hotels (*JT*, July 17, 1913, p. 8g, and *JT* [Brooklyn edition], July 14, 1916, p. 9a-b) later became president of the Kalvarier Synagogue (*JT*, March 13, 1905, p. 2b). David Brener died Oct. 17, 1905 (*JT*, Oct. 17, 1905, p. 6a).

82. *JT*, Sept. 16, 1902, p. 2.

83. *JW*, Feb. 13, 1903, p. 3a.

84. *JW*, Dec. 23, 1902, p. 2a.

85. *JW*, Feb. 13, 1903, p. 3a.

86. *JT*, Sept. 26, 1902, p. 6c. Two gifts of $100 and $50 each by unnamed donors were also announced at that time.

87. *JT*, Jan. 21, 1904, p. 2c. When Mrs. Manheim died, RIETS recorded its sympathy in the press saying that "hers was the first $1,000 contribution towards buying the building of the Yeshiva . . . [she] . . . spent a fortune for Torah." As a mark of respect, only Yeshiva students were permitted to bear her coffin (*JMJ*, March 1, 1911, p. 8b).

88. The men's auxiliary was to supplement the dues paying members of the institution itself. The 1901-1902 budget reports income from dues of members "to be $950 for that year." See budget in Appendix V.

89. A ladies' group must have been active prior to this date, although there are a few references to it until 1904. An early reference to a ladies' group was found in 1899, when the *Tageblatt* reprinted the content of a postcard, reading

as follows: "Sisters, you are invited to be present at a special meeting on Monday, January 23, at 8:00 P.M., at 10 Jefferson Street. The purpose of the meeting is to negotiate peace with the men [sic] and to arrange that our money should be used in the proper ways. Respectfully, Esther Zelikowitz, President" (*JT*, Jan. 23, 1899, p. 1). No heading was attached to the card and there is no further indication as to name, size or purpose of the organization. Another reference is found in the 1901-1902 budget which attributes the donation of $275 through "dues of the ladies branch." See budget in Appendix V.

90. *JT*, Feb. 21, 1904, p. 2a.

91. *JT*, Dec. 26, 1901, p. 2f.

92. *JT*, Jan. 19, 1904, p. 7g.

93. *JT*, Jan. 21, 1904, p. 2c.

94. *JT*, Jan. 3, 1904, p. 2e; Feb. 1, 1904, p. 2b; Mar. 13, 1903, p. 8f; and June 14, 1903.

95. *JT*, Jan. 19, 1904, p. 7g.

96. *JT*, Feb. 21, 1904, p. 2a.

97. *Ibid.*

98. *JT*, Jan. 6, 1905, p. 2b. The Women's Organization of Pri Etz Chaim of Yeshivat Meah Shearim in Jerusalem, donated many volumes for student use (*JT*, Oct. 20, 1904, p. 2). Rachel Schwartz also gave sets of books (*JT*, Dec. 10, 1905, p. 2a), and a Sefer Torah was given by Toba Greenfield (*Ibid.*), and by Mr. and Mrs. Zephania Polsky of Lincoln, Neb. (*JT*, Sept. 1, 1905, p. 2a).

99. *JT*, Jan. 26, 1904, p. 2b.

100. *JT*, May 19, 1904, p. 2b.

101. *JT*, March 13, 1904, p. 2b.

102. *JT*, Jan. 10, 1904, p. 7f.

103. *JT*, Feb. 17, 1905, p. 2b. The directors promised that *Kaddish* would be said in Mr. Epstein's memory at his *Yahrzeit*.

104. *JT*, Dec. 20, 1905, p. 2c. An additional $10 came during this time as a bequest of a Dr. Mandelstam (*JT*, June 23, 1905, p. 7g).

105. *JT*, May 21, 1903, p. 5e.

106. *Ibid.*

107. *JT*, Nov. 17, 1904, p. 2b.

108. *JT*, April 29, 1904, p. 2b, and May 1, 1904, p. 2b.

109. *JT*, May 9, 1904, p. 2b.

110. *JT*, May 17, 1904, p. 7g.

111. *JT*, Sept. 11, 1905, p. 7d. Montreal seemed to be responsive to RIETS' needs. The following year, Rabbi Joseph S. Singer of Ottawa collected $135 in that community, again with the assistance of Rabbi Cohen and others (*JT*, Aug. 10, 1906, p. 6).

112. *JT*, Sept. 11, 1905, p. 7d.

113. *JT*, Nov. 29, 1905, p. 6g. When Rabbi Rosenberg left Bayonne for Burlington, Vt., the directors again expressed deep and "public thanks for the great work which he did for the material and spiritual good of the Yeshiva while he was here" (*JG*, Feb. 19, 1907, p. 13f).

114. *JT*, March 27, 1905, p. 2b.

115. *JT*, Jan. 20, 1905, p. 6a. Rabbi Duber Shapiro was very successful in his collections. There is a record of a visit to Dayton, Ohio, where he addressed the members of Congregation Beth Jacob. So impressive was his message that the congregation sent a donation to RIETS immediately and assumed an annual obligation. They also were so inspired by his exhortations that they decided to build a Hebrew School (*JW*, Feb. 15, 1903, p. 3a).

116. Secretary Abramowitz advertised for "an honest man" with "good references or security" to solicit members (*JT*, Aug. 7, 1905, p. 2g).

117. *JT*, Jan. 31, 1905, p. 2b, and several issues thereafter. Sampson Lederhendler, "The New York Yeshibath," *New Era Illustrated Magazine*, VI, No. 4 (March and April, 1905), 344.

118. *JT*, Nov. 22, 1902, p. 2f.

119. *JT*, March 27, 1905, p. 6c.

120. *JT*, April 10, 1905, p. 6b.

121. *JT*, March 3, 1903, p. 2f.

122. Rabbi Alperstein later became the rabbi of Congregation Mishkan Israel Anshei Suwalk of 55 Christie Street (*JT*, July 14, 1905, p. 2b and 2e).

123. *JT*, Oct. 3, 1901, p. 2b.

124. *JT*, Aug. 20, 1903, p. 2b, and *JW*, Nov. 14, 1902, p. 2a.

125. *JT*, Jan. 19, 1904, p. 7g, and Jan. 21, 1904, p. 2c.

126. *Ibid*.

127. The actual recording date of the deed of sale was on April 29, 1904. The property was bought in the name of the Rabbi Isaac Elchanan Theological Seminary Association from the executors of the estate of Louis Michael. Manheim and Manheim, the sons of Yora Manheim, were attorneys for RIETS, serving without fee.

128. *JT*, Jan. 29, 1904, p. 2b, and repeated at various intervals until March 2, 1904, p. 7f.

129. Saul Schenker, a student of that day, placed the time of removal during the latter part of 1904. Dr. David H. Barash, however, who taught English at RIETS at the time, recollects that RIETS was already at 156 Henry Street when he began to teach there in July, 1904.

130. *JT*, March 16, 1903, p. 4a.

131. The Yeshiva Committee had been set up by the Agudat ha-Rabbanim in 1902 and was composed of eleven members: Rabbis Alperstein, Bernstein, Levinthal, Margolies, Peikes, Rabbiner, Rabinowitz, Rappaport, Silver, Wien and Yaffe. Their function was to help systematize the curricula of the various

yeshivot and to urge that the English language and the sciences should be taught at the schools (*JT*, Aug. 6, 1902, p. 1c).

132. The *Takanot Agudat ha-Rabbanim* (Philadelphia: Joseph Judah Shur) make it appear that Rabbi Bernstein was not speaking for himself but that he was conveying the plea of the director of RIETS. Page 3 of the *Takanot* indicates that the action was taken "on the request of the directors of RIETS that the Agudat ha-Rabbanim take the conduct of the Yeshiva under its direction . . ." See also *JT*, Aug. 1, 1904, p. 6a and report in the *American Jewish Year Book* (Philadelphia: Jewish Publication Society, 1903), 160.

133. *JT*, Aug. 28, 1903, p. 2b.

134. *JT*, Aug. 1, 1904, pp. 5d and 6a.

135. *JT*, Aug. 15, 1905, p. 5d; *JG*, Aug. 25, 1905.

136. *JT*, Aug. 28, 1903, p. 2b; also *Takanot Agudat ha-Rabbanim*, p. 10. The pogroms in Kishineff and Odessa in 1905 climaxed the persecution against Jews in Eastern Europe. From the beginning of the century, the pressure of students escaping to the U.S. was felt by the directors of RIETS.

137. The resolution of the *Agudat ha-Rabbanim* contained an additional provision not mentioned in the newspapers. In general, the resolutions as published in *Takanot Agudat ha-Rabbanim* are not identical to those published in the press. However, only those of 1903 and 1904 are to be found in the *Takanot*. A meeting held during the month of Heshvan (corresponds generally to the month of November) 1903 at RIETS at 32 Rutgers Street indicated that the rabbis' interest went beyond acquiring a building for the school alone. They suggested that the house become a center for the *Agudat Ha-Rabbanim* as well. The name was to be *Bet de-Rabbanim u-Bet Mesivta d'Rabbeinu Yitzchok Elchanan, Zal* (Rabbinic Headquarters and Rabbi Isaac Elchanan Theological Seminary). Throughout the early years, the *Agudat ha-Rabbanim* showed a proprietary interest in RIETS. Later, they instructed their Yeshiva Committee to seek "the right to be represented on the Board of Directors of the Yeshiva, to supervise the religious and secular studies and to watch over the behavior of the students, etc., also to help maintain them" (*JG*, Aug. 25, 1905, English page).

138. *JT*, July 11, 1904, English page. This resolution touched off a heated exchange between J. D. Eisenstein and the *American Hebrew* (July 1, 1904, p. 180, and June 7, 1904, p. 130). Dr. Schechter may have been defending the position of the Seminary when he said at a meeting of the New York Branch of the Jewish Theological Seminary on April 2, 1905: "It is not necessary to emphasize that this is an Orthodox seminary; it is also a Jewish seminary. Of course, it is Orthodox" (*JT*, April 4, 1905, English page).

139. See citations in note 138.

140. *Sefer ha-Yovel shel Agudat ha-Rabbanim he-Ortodoksim* (New York: Orion Press, 1928), 373b.

141. *JG*, July 19, 1907, p. 14f. In a letter to the *Jüdische Gazetten* on the subject of the Jewish Theological Seminary, Rabbi Jacob Gutman of Jersey City, an old friend of RIETS, explained this decision of the Agudat ha-Rabbanim in the following words: "We give our full respect to the Seminary, to its leaders and its professors . . . for their deeds and accomplishments, but we can never give it [the Jewish Theological Seminary] the credit which it has not earned, namely the authority to give its students the right to decide and judge Jewish law . . . Have you ever heard of a man becoming an authority on the four sections of the *Shulḥan Arukh* without ever having studied them . . ." (*JG*, Sept. 6, 1907, p. 4e).

Rabbi Shalom Rabinowitz expressed the same idea two years later in a letter referring to a *Tageblatt* article reporting that "Five Rabbis Receive Semicha [ordination]" at the Seminary. He pointed out that they could not have received *semicha* because they had no knowledge of the Halakha and because "Schechter himself has no semicha and, therefore, cannot bestow it upon others." To this the editor replied that the Jewish Theological Seminary never awarded the degree of *semicha,* only the title of "preacher and teacher of moral Judaism" and therefore was not subject to this criticism (*JT*, June 25, 1909, p. 11f). (According to the *American Jewish Year Book, 1904-1905* [Philadelphia: Jewish Publication Society, 1904, p. 181], Dr. Schechter was "graduated a rabbi in Vienna." Norman Bentwich in his biography *Solomon Schechter* [Philadelphia: Jewish Publication Society, 1948, p. 41] also states that Schechter was ordained. Neither source, however, indicates when and by whom.)

Dr. Israel Freidlander gave substance to the position of the Agudat ha-Rabbanim. Interviewed by the *London Jewish Chronicle* (June 22, 1906, p. 21), he was asked whether the ordination granted by the Jewish Theological Seminary "Is . . . the same as what we understand by the 'Hatorat Horaah' [traditional ordination]? Does it contain the formula 'Yoreh Yoreh, Yodin Yodin'?" Dr. Friedlander responded: "No. In the modern congregations of America there is little demand for the exercise of such functions. The people who want to ask ritualistic and legalistic questions would go to a Russian Rav . . ."

142. A resolution favoring *yeshivot* had also been adopted as early as 1900 by the newly formed Union of Orthodox Jewish Congregations. On Dec. 28, 1900, they convened at the Eldridge Street Synagogue and adopted a series of resolutions. The fourth resolution stated that "Synagogues sponsoring Yeshivas must be supported," (*JG*, Jan. 4, 1901, p. 3). But this exhortation was directed toward supporting the sponsoring synagogues rather than the *yeshivot* and made no specific reference to RIETS.

143. The school was determined to raise funds from any source. In August, 1904, it advertised that it had for sale at 156 Henry Street, "Bathtubs, stoves, boilers, mirrors, mantelpieces and bric-a-brac." These furnishings apparently

were stripped from the new building and unnecessary for the purposes of the school, were worth some money. The directors also offered the premises for rent to a "Ḥebra" or "congregation" that might want to use one of the rooms as a synagogue on the Sabbaths and Holidays. *JT*, Aug. 7, 1904, p. 2d.

At least one Ḥebra is known to have rented the synagogue facilities of the building. In a listing of a funeral service, the "Minsker Synagogue" sponsored by the Minsker Old Men's Benevolent Association was mentioned as being at 156 Henry Street, *JMJ*, Jan. 23, 1906, p. 4g.

144. *JT*, Nov. 1, 1904, p. 2b.

145. *JT*, Nov. 9, 1904, p. 2b.

146. *JT*, Nov. 1, 1904, p. 2b.

147. *JT*, Nov. 17, 1904, p. 2b.

148. *Ibid.*, and *JT*, Oct. 19, 1904, p. 6d.

149. *JT*, Oct. 25, 1904, p. 6e.

150. *JT*, Aug. 13, 1905, p. 6a. It was at this time that Rabbi Rosenberg began to travel on behalf of RIETS.

151. *JG*, July 26, 1907, p. 12e.

152. Proclaiming their happiness, the directors announced "to all lovers of Torah that 156 Henry Street has left the realm of the secular and entered the realm of the sacred and is now owned by RIETS . . . and let the mockers no longer say that with the orthodox Jews, the Torah is hidden in a corner and wanders from house to house like an uninvited guest . . . Blessed are all who helped, for they removed a blot from Israel" (*JT*, May 9, 1904, p. 2b).

Notes to Chapter 5 (pp. 73-92)

1. *HY*, May 14, 1908, p. 2.

2. *Ibid*.

3. I. Cohen, "Yeshiva Rabbi Isaac Elchanan," *Aspaḳlaria* (Adar, 1907), 42.

4. *Ha-Ivri*, Sept. 17, 1897.

5. Judah D. Eisenstein, *Otzar Ziḳhronotai* (New York: J. D. Eisenstein, 1929), 81b.

6. See Chap. 4, p. 57.

7. See Chap. 4, p. 61.

8. *Jüdische Welt*, Jan. 28, 1903, p. 2e.

9. *Jüdisches Tageblatt*, Dec. 5, 1901, p. 2f.

10. *Ibid*.

11. See Chap. 4, p. 65.

12. Interview with Rabbis David Rackman and Chaim Moseson.

13. *Jüdische Gazetten*, May 8, 1906, p. 14c.

14. Cohen, *op. cit.*, 42-44.

15. *HY*, May 14, 1908, p. 13; Cohen, *loc. cit.* The insignificant increase

of students between 1906 and 1908 does not show lack of growth. The lower classes continued to grow at a fair rate; the low over-all enrollment, however, was due to the loss of students during the strike of 1908. The upper class was depleted but the loss was made up by new enrollments in the lower division.

16. Despite the fact that RIETS advertised for a "good Rosh Yeshiva" to teach the "middle class" of RIETS (see p. 64) none of the students of that day have any recollection of there being more than one class. When Dr. Klein was elected as president of RIETS in 1902, he stated that it was necessary to separate the older and younger students and "perhaps even a third class [should be] created" (*JT*, Sept. 26, 1902, p. 6c). However, there is no indication that such a class actually was created or even that two classes were formed.

Nevertheless, in 1901, President Moshe Hurewitz reported that there were two Roshei Yeshiva (lecturers in Talmudic studies) and one *mashgiah* in the Hebrew Department, and three teachers in the English Department (*JT*, Dec. 26, 1901, p. 2f). In 1900, President H. Bramson had announced that there was one English teacher for the eighteen students (*JG*, June 29, 1900, Section **II,** p. 3a).

Several months after Dr. Klein's statement about a "third class," RIETS in an appeal for funds, stated that there was a staff of four Roshei Yeshiva and one *mashgiah* who taught the students in the Hebrew Department, and four teachers in the English Department (*JW*, Dec. 23, 1902, p. 2a).

In view of Dr. Barash's recollection that he was the first English teacher at RIETS (see p. 78) and the recollection of the early students, it seems highly improbable that the claims in the appeals issued by RIETS were correct. The facts may have been exaggerated, in the case of both the Hebrew and the English staffs, in order to stimulate a better response. In the absence of any concrete evidence, and because of the large amount of negative evidence, we shall assume that there were no English classes and only one regular Talmud group in RIETS prior to 1904.

As far as the English staff is concerned, the reference may have been to *private* teachers who were engaged by the school to tutor *some* students. This would explain the item in the 1901-1902 budget (Appendix V) of $240 expended for "teachers." A good many private lessons at 25 cents or so could have been had for this sum.

The fact that there was no teaching of secular subjects under the roof of RIETS is further borne out by the item of $100 for "*heder*" to teach English. *Heder* could have been used to mean elementary instruction.

17. One article in the *Tageblatt* reported that the students were between the ages of fourteen years and twenty (*JT*, Nov. 24, 1901, p. 6c). But personal recollections of the early students, as well as the comments about the advanced scholarship of the students, indicate that they were older than fourteen.

18. According to his brother Louis and his wife Rebecca, Akiva Matlin's

studies were interrupted by a delicate religious problem. The Matlins were *Kohanim*, of priestly descent, who according to Jewish law are prohibited from being exposed to corpses. When Akiva wrote his father that he had reached the stage where he was already dissecting cadavers, Rabbi Matlin was horrified. Akiva was ordered home immediately and found a job as a bookkeeper in a slaughterhouse.

19. Dr. Isadore Singer, editor of the *Jewish Encyclopedia* to which Lederhendler was a contributor, called him "the Israel Zangwill of the East Side." Lederhendler was an autodidact who used all his free time to memorize the dictionary. He studied English at Cooper Union and mastered it sufficiently to teach foreigners and later to become a reporter for the *Sun* and other periodicals.

20. His first pulpit was in Syracuse, New York (*JW,* Jan. 2, 1903, p. 2d).

21. *HI,* Sept. 17, 1897.

22. Ephraim Lisitsky, *Eleh Tol'dot Adam* (Jerusalem: Mossad Bialik, 1956), 92.

23. Newcomers to New York City, "greenhorns," were often taken on as "apprentices" for a nominal wage or none at all. Some impoverished Jews earned 50 cents a day, others earned a few dollars weekly, while some hard working pushcart peddlers earned 15 to 20 dollars weekly (Rischin, *The Promised City* [Cambridge, Mass., Harvard University Press, 1962], 52-67).

24. See Chap. 4, p. 62.

25. The name of the student is not revealed, but a newspaper story tells of a visit of the collector, Rabbi Duber Shapiro, to Rochester, where he appeals for funds on the basis that one of the local boys "is studying at RIETS and receiving $3 per week plus clothes, etc." (*JT,* Jan. 19, 1904, p. 2b).

26. Cohen, *loc. cit.,* 42.

27. *Ibid.,* 43.

28. In the budgetary year 1901-1902, the secretary received $120, the penny collectors and Rabbi Shapiro received $616, and the entire teaching staff, $763. See Budget in Appendix VI.

29. Personal interview with Jacob L. Andron.

30. *JT,* Dec. 26, 1901, p. 26. The official budget for 1901-1902 shows that $3,196.50 was collected in the boxes during that year. See Appendix V.

31. Interview with Rabbi Joseph H. Lookstein.

32. Interview with Rabbi Jacob Bosniak.

33. *JT,* Nov. 30, 1906, and Dec. 2, 1906.

34. Cohen, *loc. cit.,* 43.

35. *JT,* Oct. 3, 1901, p. 2b; personal interview with Jacob L. Andron.

36. *JMJ,* Jan. 23, 1911, p. 4b.

37. Personal interview with Jacob L. Andron. Rabbi Isserson was called to

the congregation in 1906 (*JT*, Dec. 11, 1906). He died five years later (*JT*, July 24, 1910, p. 8c). At that time he was the rabbi of Beth Midrash Tifereth Jerusalem (*JT*, Sept. 27, 1910, p. 8c) at 240 Madison Street.

38. *JT*, Sept. 27, 1910.

39. Personal interview with Hillel Rogoff.

40. Personal interview with Dr. Mordecai M. Kaplan.

41. Personal interview with Rabbi Jacob Bosniak. Rabbi Vidrevitz died in 1911 at the age of seventy-five (*JT*, May 10, 1911, p. 1a-b).

42. Jacob I. Hartstein ("Yeshiva University" in *American Jewish Year Book 1946* [Philadelphia: Jewish Publication Society], 74) says that Rabbi Benjamin Aronowitz was the "one-man faculty" at Henry Street.

Moshe Davis ("Jewish Religious Life and Institutions in America," *The Jews*, I, 391), repeats this statement, saying: "The supervisor, or one-man faculty . . . was Rabbi Benjamin Aronowitz." This is not so. The only time that RIETS had a "one-man faculty" was when Rabbi Baron was the *mashgiah*.

Rabbi Aronowitz did not come to RIETS until after 1909, possibly after Rabbi Baron had already returned to Russia. In 1909, there were several teachers employed at RIETS. See note 54, this chapter.

43. An erroneous statement was made in the *Tageblatt* (JT, Nov. 24, 1901, p. 6c), to the effect that while RIETS was located at the Kalvarier Synagogue, Rabbi Nahum Dan Baron was "connected with the congregation." Rabbi Baron was never connected with any congregation, but served RIETS exclusively.

44. See report of resolution adopted at the Convention of Agudat ha-Rabbanim, commending Rabbi Baron for his ten years of "tireless service" to RIETS and "devotion" to the students (*JT*, July 30, 1908, p. 8e).

45. Lisitzky, *op. cit.*, 90-91.

46. *Ibid*.

47. See report of resolution (*JT, loc. cit.*).

48. The resolution was adopted in August of 1908. As late as July of that year his name appears among those of the officers and staff of RIETS as signatories to an announcement in *JT*, June 12, 1908, p. 10e. Thus we know that until the middle of 1908 he was still with RIETS.

49. Lisitzky, *loc. cit.*

50. Cohen, *loc. cit.*, 42; personal interviews with Hillel Rogoff and Rabbi David Rackman.

51. Cohen, *loc. cit.*

52. Rabbi Shapiro died in November, 1908. He was eulogized in his own synagogue on Sunday, Nov. 15, 1908, by Rabbi Z. H. Orliansky (*JT*, Nov. 13, 1908, p. 8d). See also *Jewish Morning Journal*, Nov. 15, 1908.

53. Personal interview with Rabbi David Rackman.

54. In early 1908 Rabbi Nahum Dan Baron, Rabbi Moshe Sobol, and Rabbi

David Rackman constituted the teaching staff. Their names appear as signatories on a congratulatory statement to Rabbi Samuel Glick on the occasion of his appointment to the pulpit of a synagogue in Lynn, Mass. (*JT*, May 29, 1908, p. 10f). Again their names appear side by side with the officers of RIETS in congratulating David Abramowitz on the occasion of his daughter's marriage (*JT*, June 12, 1908, p. 10e).

55. Address of Simon Wolf, president of Executive Committee of B'nai B'rith at Grand Lodge Conference in New Orleans, quoted in "Editorial Survey," *New Era Illustrated Magazine* (March and April 1905), VI, No. 4, 424.

56. *JT*, July 3, 1902, English section, p. 1a.

57. Editorial in *JT*, May 11, 1908, p. 4b.

58. Address of Simon Wolf reported in *JT*, May 11, 1908.

59. The budget for 1901-1902 (Appendix V), shows an item of $240 for "Teachers" which apparently refers to teachers of English subjects, and an expenditure of $60 for a general item of *"sforim,* books, etc." The "books" probably refers to texts for English subjects. What fraction of that general item was allotted specifically for "books" is not established.

According to Dr. Morris Robinson, who attended RIETS between 1901 and 1903, the son of one of the directors who was attending a secular high school or college volunteered his services twice weekly for a short time. Only four or five students, however, attended. See also note 16, this chapter.

60. Instruction apparently was resumed later. In 1907, Mr. Pressman, a twenty-year-old student at Cooper Union, was the English tutor. Lessons were given from 6 to 8 P.M. in the evenings for the younger students. The course of study was most elementary. Rabbi David Aronson recalls that the textbooks used bore the imprint of the New York Board of Education. Meager as these studies were, they sufficed to stimulate the students to continue their education. Many a folio of the Talmud was covered with scribbled sums and equations as the students used the time and books assigned for Hebrew studies to improve their knowledge of mathematics and to prepare for the Regents examinations (personal interview with Rabbi David Aronson).

61. This account is based on an interview with the New York physician Dr. David Harry Barash, whose youthful experience at Yeshiva Etz Chaim has been recounted in Chap. 2.

62. Personal interview with Rabbi Jacob Bosniak.

63. Among the requirements was the provision that upon successful completion of the tests, the candidate's name was to be entered in the records of the Agudat ha-Rabbanim as having earning the degree. The actual diploma, however, was to be awarded only when the candidate was married. At that time, a special committee to deal with Yeshiva matters was created. It consisted of Rabbis A. Gordon, Yehuda David Bernstein, Israel Rosenberg, Gutman, and M. L. Bernstein. (Proceedings of the 8th session of the Third Annual

Convention of the Agudat ha-Rabbanim held on Sunday, July 31, 1904 [*YT*, Aug. 1, 1904, p. 5d].)

64. Cohen, *loc. cit.*, 42.

65. Rabbi Guterman received his *semicha* from Dr. Philip H. Klein late in October 1906, and from Rabbi Moses S. Margolies and Rabbi Samuel Z. Wien in November 1906.

66. Neither Rabbi Guterman nor Rabbi Miller recalls his name. The newspapers do not carry the information either.

67. Cohen, *loc. cit.*

68. Among the other directors were Rabbi Avraham Eliezer Alperstein, Harrry Altshuler, Chaim Dolinsky, Moshe Hurewitz, Nathan Lamport, Chaim Robinson, who was treasurer, and Mr. Abramowitz, who was secretary (Cohen, *loc. cit.*, 44). Rabbi Yehuda David Bernstein was the vice-president (*JT*, Oct. 19, 1904, p. 6d).

69. Cohen, *loc. cit.*, 45.

70. Personal interview with Louis Rabinowitz.

71. *HY*, May 14, 1908, p. 13; *JG*, May 8, 1906, p. 14c.

Notes to Chapter 6 (pp. 93-110)

1. As in the case of Congregation Adath Yeshurun of Yassy at 58-60 Rivington Street (see editorial in *Jüdisches Tageblatt*, Oct. 28, 1908, p. 4a). The synagogue was finally sold under foreclosure for $2,017.

2. See editorial in *JT*, Feb. 27, 1908, p. 4a.

3. *Ibid.*

4. *JT*, Dec. 1, 1908, p. 2e. Prospective buyers were referred to David Abramowitz, secretary of RIETS.

5. *JT*, March 23, 1909, p. 15d.

6. *JT*, Nov. 17, 1904, p. 2b.

7. See Chap. 4, p. 72 and quote in *JT*, Aug. 13, 1905, p. 6a.

8. See Chap. 4, p. 72 and quote in *JT*, July 26, 1907, p. 12e.

9. See Chap. 4, p. 72.

10. *JT*, Jan. 18, 1906, p. 4a-c, and *Jüdische Gazetten*, Jan. 26, 1906.

11. *Ibid.* The editorial comment of both the *Tageblatt* and the *Gazetten* was as expected. It read as follows:

"The essence of this statement of the students of the Yeshiva is that they want more secular studies since without culture they cannot accept a pulpit in America.

"They are entirely justified in these demands! Jewish scholars without American education arrive daily on every ship . . . [on the other hand] cultured students without Jewish scholarship are to be found in the [Jewish Theological] Seminary and in all colleges. The Yeshiva in Henry Street must be the common ground where Torah and culture can be blended."

12. *Ibid.*

13. The quoted demands appeared under the heading "The Yeshiva Students Write" in *JT*, Jan. 26, 1906, p. 7g.

14. Under this title the "Observer" of the *Tageblatt* wrote the long article referred to here (*JT*, Jan. 26, 1906, English page).

15. The columnist implied a conspiracy of silence to keep the Jewish public ignorant of the events at RIETS. He called the *mashgiaḥ* "the foreman in the sweatshop of the Talmud," and referring to the directors as "politicians and holy grafters," accused them of being "linked with the Catholic priesthood in thinking the Bible a dangerous book, and in essaying to restrict its influence." Ephraim Deinard, in his letter to *Ha-Ivri,* also had some uncomplimentary remarks to make about the directors. For source, see note 26, chapter 7.

16. *JT*, Jan. 26, 1906, English page. An early student of RIETS, Sampson Lederhendler, had previously made a similar observation out of his personal experience. In comparing RIETS with the Jewish Theological Seminary ("The New York Yeshibath," *New Era Illustrated Magazine,* VI, No. 4 [March and April, 1905] p. 344), he wrote:

"The latter is better managed . . . but the former has better material in its charges. The students of the Yeshiva are more earnest, more sincere, more Jewish . . . If the Yeshiva should be taken over by men of intelligence who are abreast of the twentieth century, it might possibly become an unequalled force for good in American Judaism."

17. Dushkin, *Jewish Education in New York City,* 76-78.

18. *JT*, Feb. 23, 1906, p. 2c. The following were elected to the Board of Directors: Rabbis Avraham E. Alperstein, Bayevsky, Gutman, Solomon E. Jaffe, Moses M. Matlin, and Samuel Z. Wien, and Messrs. Moshe Abramowitz (president of Mariampol Synagogue, *JT*, June 3, 1906, p. 5b), Jacob L. Andron, Gershon Brener, Zalman Cohen, Chaim Dolinsky, Abraham Dubowsky, Meyer Freiman, Moshe Hurewitz, Nathan Lamport, Baruch Pinchas Liberman, Shamai Rosenthal, Samuel Silberstein, Tennenbaum, and Mendel Zuckerman. For some details of the life of Rabbi Margolies see note 16, Chap. 10.

19. *JT*, Jan. 26, 1906, English page.

20. At the end of the year it was estimated that the weekly budget was $400. *JT*, Dec. 27, 1908, p. 8f. This proportion was consistent with the unpublished 1901-1902 budget which listed the total expenditure for the year at $6,242.01 and the amount spent for student support at $4,398.21. See Appendix V.

21. *JG*, May 8, 1908, p. 14c.

22. *Ibid.* Chaim R. Rabinowitz, a student at RIETS during the strike, has recently written a personal recollection of those days, "60 Shana le-Shvitot be-Yeshivat Rabbeinu Yitzchok Elchanan," *Hadoar,* June 14, 1968, Vol. 47, No. 30, pp. 552-54.

23. Quoted from editorial in *JT*, May 6, 1908, p. 4a-b and *JG*, May 5, 1908, p. 4a.

24. *Ibid.*

25. Editorial, *JMJ*, May 5, 1908, p. 7a.

26. *Ibid.*

27. *Ibid.*

28. Editorial, *JMJ*, May 6, 1908, p. 4a.

29. *HY*, May 14, 1908, p. 2.

30. *HY*, May 28, 1908, p. 2.

31. *Ibid.*

32. *Ibid.*

33. See the humorous editorial treatment in the *Tageblatt* and *Gazetten* of a representative of the New York press who described his visit to RIETS. He claimed that he found all the fifteen classes of RIETS engaged in a sympathy strike in behalf of the teachers who had "walked out" because they were not paid their salaries. The reporter concluded his account with the statement that Rabbi Isaac Elchanan, the principal of the school, had remained silent and refused any comment on the nature of the strike (*JT*, Sept. 3, 1908, p. 4b, and *JG*, Sept. 11, 1908, p. 4c).

34. *JMJ*, May 8, 1908, p. 7g.

35. They spoke at the following synagogues respectively: Sennier Synagogue, Olia Synagogue, Kalvarier Synagogue, Christie Street Synagogue, Kahal Adath Jeshurun and Adas B'nai Israel (*Ibid.*, and *JT*, May 8, 1908, p. 8c).

36. *JT*, May 10, 1908, p. 8a.

37. *JT*, May 14, 1908, p. 4a-b.

38. *JT*, May 11, 1908, p. 4a-b.

39. *JT*, May 12, 1908, p. 4b.

40. *JG*, May 15, 1908, p. 13d.

41. *JMJ*, May 14, 1908, p. 1f-g.

42. *Ibid.*, and *JT*, May 13, 1908, p. 1e.

43. *JMJ*, loc. cit.

44. *JT*, May 13, 1908, p. 1e.

45. *JMJ*, loc. cit.

46. *Ibid.*

47. *JT*, May 12, 1908, p. 4b.

48. *JMJ*, May 14, 1908, p. 1e.

49. *Ibid.*

50. *Ibid.*

51. According to the findings of the finance committee, at least one week was owed. The *JMJ*, however, reported (May 15, 1908, p. 10) that stipends of four weeks were overdue.

52. Announcements of the meeting appeared in *JT*, May 13, 1908, p. 6c, and May 14, 1908, p. 6e. The report of the meeting appears in *JT*, May 15, 1908, p. 8a, and *JMJ*, June 23, 1908, p. 1d.

53. For some biographical notes on Rabbi Levinthal see *Kevod Hakhamim*

(Philadelphia: 1935), issued on the occasion of the Rabbi's 70th birthday celebration. See also C. David Matt, "Rabbi Bernard Louis Levinthal," *JE*, May 17,
1935; Ben-Zion Eisenstadt, *Israel's Scholars in America* (New York: Rosenberg, 1903), p. 66; and Alex Goldman, *Giants of Faith* (New York: Citadel
Press, 1964) pp. 160-176.

54. The most specific report of this meeting is found in *JMJ*, June 23,
1908, p. 1d.

55. *JT*, May 15, 1908, p. 8a.

56. *JMJ*, June 23, 1908, p. 1d.

57. *JMJ*, June 24, 1908, p. 7d.

58. *JMJ*, loc. cit.

59. *JT*, June 23, 1908, p. 8d, and *JG*, June 26, 1908, p. 15a.

60. *Ibid*.

61. Editorial in *JT*, Apr. 14, 1908, p. 4a.

Notes to Chapter 7 (pp. 111-119)

1. *JT*, July 28, 1908, p. 8e.

2. *Ibid*.

3. *JT*, July 30, 1908, p. 8e.

4. *Ibid*. Rabbi Levinthal was to go to Washington, D.C., and Baltimore;
Rabbi Bachrach to Worcester; Rabbi Ginzberg to Syracuse; Rabbi Gutman
to Trenton; Rabbi Gordon to Utica; Rabbi Horowitz to New Haven; Rabbi
Israelite to Cleveland; Rabbi Radisky to California; Rabbi Rosen to Providence;
Rabbi Rosenberg to Troy and Albany; Rabbi Seltzer to Maine; Rabbi Turman
to Scranton and Wilkes Barre, and Rabbi Sivitz to Philadelphia.

5. *JT*, July 31, 1908, p. 8e.

6. *Ibid*.

7. *Ibid.*, p. 7e.

8. *JMJ*, Aug. 21, 1908, p. 8d. Editorial in *JT*, Aug. 23, 1908, p. 4b.

9. *JMJ*, Aug. 21, 1908, p. 8d.

10. Editorial in *JMJ*, Aug. 23, 1908, p. 4a.

11. *JT*, Aug. 23, 1908, p. 4b.

12. *Ibid*.

13. *Ibid*.

14. *Ibid*.

15. The report of this meeting as condensed in the text is found in *JT*,
Sept. 1, 1908, p. 8e.

16. *Ibid*.

17. *JT*, Sept. 4, 1908, p. 10b.

18. *Ibid*.

19. *JT*, Sept. 18, 1908, p. 8e. The meeting was to be held on Sunday, Sept.
20, 1908, at 2:00 P.M. at RIETS.

20. The meeting was held on Tuesday night (second day *Hol Ha-Moed Sukkot*) Oct. 13, 1908 at 6:00 P.M. at RIETS (*JT*, Oct. 15, 1908, p. 6c).

21. Quoted from a letter by A. Rosenberg to *HI*, Dec. 17, 1908, p. 5. Mr. Wilner had had previous experiences in fulfilling presidential duties at RIETS. There is no clear picture as to the presidential succession between February 1906, when Rabbi Margolies was called to head RIETS, and Mr. Wilner's election in the late fall of 1908. A year after Rabbi Margolies was elected, Mr. Wilner's name was listed as president in a newspaper article (*JG*, Feb. 19, 1907, p. 13f). In June 1908, less than two weeks prior to Rabbi Levinthal's election, Nathan Lamport's name was similarly listed (*JT*, June 12, 1908, p. 10e). It is possible that because Rabbi Margolies was elected as a result of an emergency during the middle of the normal presidential term, which extended from late summer to late summer, he only completed the unfinished period until August 1906. Wilner may then have been elected to serve until August 1907, when Nathan Lamport took over. The latter was president during the strike in early 1908.

Wilner also signed the papers for the sale of the Henry Street building in April 1904 in the capacity of president of RIETS. This sale took place after Dr. Klein had been elected president.

22. *JT*, Dec. 27, 1908, p. 8f.

23. The signatories were Nathan Lamport, president; Rabbis Samuel Z. Wien, Bernard L. Levinthal, Moses S. Margolies, Abraham A. Yudelovitch, B. Cohen, Isaac W. Wendrofsky, Chaim Y. Vidrevitz, Moses M. Matlin, and Yehudah D. Bernstein; and Messrs. Y. D. Shapiro, Gershon Brener, Chaim Dolinsky, Chaim Robinson, Jacob L. Andron (*JMJ*, Sept. 13, 1908, p. 5d).

24. Rabbi Baron was succeeded by Rabbi Abraham Aaron Yudelovitch, one of the outstanding authorities on the *Shulḥan Arukh* of his day.

25. The following directors were elected: Rabbis Yehuda David Bernstein, Gutman of Jersey City, Kaminetsky, Philip H. Klein, Bernard L. Levinthal, Abraham Marin, Moses S. Margolies, Moses Mayer Matlin, Zvi Hirsch Orliansky*, Israel Rosenberg of Bayonne, Shabsai Rosenberg, Moshe Zev Shocher, Samuel Z. Wien, Isaac W. Wendrofsky, Abraham A. Yudelovitch, and Moses S. Sivitz.

The following laymen were elected: Messrs. David Abramowitz, Moshe Abramowitz, Harry Altschul, Samuel J. Andron (president of Yeshiva Rabbi Jacob Joseph)*, Birkhan, Gershon Brener (president of Talmud Torah Tifereth Jerusalem [*JG*, April 2, 1909, p. 4c]), David Cohen, Zalman Cohen, Chaim Dolinsky, (president of Congregation Tifereth Jerusalem, [*JT*, April 2, 1909, p. 4c]), Aaron Leib Dubowsky, Harry Fischel*, Maier Freiman, Samuel Golda, Aaron Goodman, C. M. Greenberg, Moshe Hurewitz, Nathan Hutkoff, David Kaplan, Nathan Lamport*, C. I. Lass, Abraham Levy, Lazarus Levy, Baruch Pinchas Liberman, Meyer London, Kalman Mahl, H. Mandelbaum, M.

Michelover, Jacob Ritzman, Chaim Robinson, Abraham Shmuel Rosenberg, Shamai Rosenthal (died in November 1908)*, Jacob Saperstein of the *Jewish Morning Journal,* Jonathan Schepp, Shmuel Silberstein, Joseph Spektorsky, Samuel Wilner, M. R. Wolowitz, Asher Yarmulowsky and Mendel Zuckerman (*JT,* Oct. 15, 1908, p. 6c).

26. Only a month later, Ephraim Deinard, writing to *Ha-Ivri,* said that "... there is almost no memory left of RIETS ... All the students have already left it ..." (*HI,* Nov. 12, 1908, p. 3c). Among the students who left during 1908 to attend the Jewish Theological Seminary were Jacob Bosniak, Solomon Goldman, Yechiel Kaplan and David Aaronson. Earlier during the 1906 strike, the following students were known to have left: Israel Bettan, Sam Cohen, and Abraham A. Newman. Louis Epstein and his brother, later to become a pediatrician, left in 1907. (Personal interview with Rabbi Jacob Bosniak and Rabbi David Aaronson.)

27. *JG,* Dec. 25, 1908, p. 16b.

28. *JT,* Dec. 27, 1908, p. 8f.

29. *JT,* Aug. 28, 1908, p. 8a.

30. *JT,* Aug. 30, 1908, p. 4a, and personal interview with Rabbi Chaim Moseson.

31. *JT,* Aug. 28, 1908, p. 8a.

32. *JT,* Aug. 30, 1908, p. 4a.

33. *JT,* Sept. 18, 1908, p. 8e.

34. *JT,* Sept. 25, 1908, p. 8e.

35. *JT,* Oct. 9, 1908, p. 4d. The meeting was set for Oct. 11, 1908.

36. *JT,* Dec. 27, 1908, p. 6a.

37. *JT,* Oct. 20, 1908, p. 2e, until Nov. 2; again *JT,* Nov. 30, 1908, p. 2e.

38. The address 213 East Broadway has the same numerals as that in 123 East Broadway, the address of the Adas B'nai Israel, where the first meeting was held. A newspaper misprint may have been responsible for the "213."

39. *JT,* Nov. 16, 1908, p. 8g.

40. *JT,* Dec. 27, 1908, p. 8f.

41. *JG,* Feb. 19, 1909, p. 13f.

42. Apparently a class was organized to meet at the Adas B'nai Israel Synagogue under Rabbi Jaffe (personal interview with Rabbi Chaim Moseson).

43. *JG,* Jan. 29, 1909, p. 16d.

44. *JG,* Jan. 29, 1909, p. 16d.

Notes to Chapter 8 (pp. 120-130)

1. *Jüdische Welt,* Aug. 6, 1902, p. 1d.

2. Nathan Lamport reported that sixteen students went to the Jewish Theo-

* Also directors or officers of Yeshiva Rabbi Jacob Joseph.

logical Seminary in 1911, while others gave up their careers altogether (*JMJ*, March 13, 1911, p. 4g).

3. *JT*, Sept. 6, 1912, p. 8d. At the beginning of the year the enrollment was only 45 (*JMJ*, Jan. 8, 1912, p. 4f-g).

4. They were divided into three classes. The two lower classes had regular teachers; the upper class was under the supervision of a *mashgiaḥ* (*JT*, Sept. 14, 1913, p. 6a).

5. Rabbi Levinthal's resolution to condemn the Jewish Theological Seminary as non-Orthodox was followed by a stormy session in which much heat was generated; it was climaxed by Rabbi Baruch Cohen's query: "How can we condemn the Jewish Theological Seminary when sons of our own member rabbis attended and graduated from that institution?" (*JT*, May 22, 1914, p. 10a-e, and *Sefer ha-Yovel shel Agudat ha-Rabbanim* [New York: Oriom Press, 1928], p. 52a).

6. *JT*, May 21, 1914, p. 8a-b.

7. The Executive Committee of the Agudat ha-Rabbanim, meeting on June 10, 1914 to consider the questions referred to it by the convention, decided to appoint a Yeshiva Education Committee to strengthen existing yeshivot and to help raise funds for them. Such committees had been appointed often in the past. This one was composed of the following rabbis: Solomon E. Jaffe, chairman, and Moses S. Margolies, Philip H. Klein, Israel Rosenberg, A. Ginzberg, Moses S. Sivitz, M. L. Preil, Avraham E. Alperstein, Kaliditsky, Hirshenson, Isaac Siegel, Elias Inselbuch, Samuel H. Glick, Benjamin B. Guth and I. Isaacson (*JT*, June 12, 1914, p. 10b).

8. As for example, *JT*, Sept. 3, 1911, p. 8b, and Oct. 10, 1913, p. 56.

9. Registered in record of the Supreme Court of New York County No. 23306/1915.

10. *JT*, May 3, 1910, p. 80.

11. *JT*, Aug. 3, 1914, p. 5g.

12. Report of Jewish Theological Seminary biennial meeting in *JMJ*, March 25, 1912, p. 4f.

13. *JT*, Oct. 6, 1910, p. 8b-c.

14. A week later the debt had been reduced to $3,000 (*JT*, Oct. 11, 1910, p. 8d), probably with the new mortgage money.

15. This particular drive brought in a total of $480 (*JT*, June 23, 1911, p. 14b).

16. *JT*, Aug. 12, 1910, p. 8b; *JMJ*, Aug. 14, 1910, p. 8c.

17. *JT*, Aug. 21, 1910, p. 8d.

18. *JT*, Sept. 30, 1910, p. 14c.

19. *JT*, Sept. 6, 1911, p. 8f.

20. For the history and scope of the Jewish Kehillah, see *The Jewish Communal Register* (New York: Jewish Kehillah, 1918).

21. Details of David Cohen's life were given in the press at the time of his death (*JMJ*, April 21, 1911, p. 1d).

22. *JMJ*, Aug. 12, 1910, p. 7d.

23. *JMJ*, March 9, 1911, p. 7g; *JT*, March 9, 1911, p. 8a.

24. *JMJ*, March 3, 1911, p. 4g.

25. *Ibid.*

26. *JMJ*, March 12, 1911, p. 4a.

27. *JT*, Sept. 15, 1911, p. 6a.

28. *JMJ*, May 13, 1912, p. 8e. This claim was repeated regularly (*JT*, Oct. 10, 1913, p. 12d, and Nov. 16, 1913, p. 4d-e).

29. *JT*, Oct. 7, 1912, p. 8d.

30. *JT*, July 11, 1912, p. 1f.

31. *JMJ*, April 9, 1911, p. 9f.

32. *JMJ*, April 12, 1911, p. 7b.

33. For an account of David Cohen's funeral, see *JMJ*, April 21, 1911, p. 1d, and April 23, 1911, p. 5a and editorial p. 4b.

Notes to Chapter 9 (pp. 131-148)

1. The other officers were: vice-president, Baruch P. Liberman; secretary, M. Shapiro; treasurer, Jonathan Scheff. Trustees were Samuel Wilner, A. Zalinsky and Elias Cohen. Directors were David Abramowitz, Harry Altschul, Rabbi Yehuda D. Bernstein, Gershon Brener, S. Cohen, Chaim Dolinsky, A. Dubowsky, Harry Fischel, S. Golde, Moshe Hurewitz, M. Hutkoff, S. Jarmulowsky, Leon Kamaiky, Dr. Philip H. Klein, Rabbi Moses S. Margolies, Nathan Lamport, H. Lass, Abraham M. Levy, Baruch P. Liberman, K. Mohol, J. Richman, Chaim Robinson, Jonathan Scheff, J. Saperstein, Rabbi S. Wise, Samuel Wilner, Rabbi Isaac W. Wendrofsky, Peter H. Wiernick, Mendel Zuckerman (*Jewish Communal Directory,* 92-93).

2. *JMJ*, June 9, 1912, p. 4e.

3. *Ibid.*

4. *JT,* Sept. 28, 1915, p. 4c.

5. Registered in record of the Supreme Court of New York County No. 23306/1915.

6. A newspaper advertisement in March 1915, announcing the annual observance of the *yahrzeit* of Rabbi Isaac Elchanan carried the joint signatures of the directors of RIETS and Etz Chaim, over the address of 85 Henry Street (*JT*, March 5, 1915, p. 5e).

7. Harry Fischel, *Forty Years of Struggle for a Principle* (New York: Bloch Publishing Co., Inc., 1928), 161.

8. *Ibid.,* 36.

9. For this and further material, see Fischel, *op. cit.*

10. Program of Dedication of Rabbinical College, Appendix VIII.

11. *JT*, Dec. 6, 1915, p. 1c-d. Jacob Hecht and Nathan Roggen had privately bought the property for the school on July 1, 1914. The cost is not specified, but the purchase was subject to two mortgages aggregating $23,000 (*Liber 150 of Conveyances*, p. 180). On Oct. 10, 1915, they resold the property to Yeshivat Etz Chaim, presumably at the same price, but subject to three mortgages aggregating $26,000 (*Liber 156 of Conveyances*, p. 286).

12. *JT*, June 27, 1915, p. 5a-b; *JMJ*, June 27, 1915, p. 8b-c.

13. *JT*, July 2, 1915, p. 1 and 8c; *JMJ*, July 2, 1915, p. 5a-b-c; Fischel, *op. cit.*, 162ff.

14. For list of donors, see Fischel, *ibid*. See also *JT*, July 2, 1915, p. 8c and *JMJ*, July 2, 1915, p. 5a-b-c.

15. *JT*, June 27, 1915, p. 5a-b.

16. Fischel, *op. cit.*, 167. The amount apparently was $16,250 (*JMJ*, Dec. 6, 1915, p. 1g) or $16,259 (*JT*, Dec. 6, 1915, p. 1c, and *Hebrew Standard*, Dec. 10, 1915).

17. *JT*, June 27, 1915, and Ephraim Caplan in *JMJ*, Dec. 14, 1915, p. 4c-d-e.

18. Fischel, *op. cit.*, 166.

19. *Register*, Appendix VII, and *JT*, Dec. 1, 1915, p. 4g.

20. Appendix VI, Fischel erroneously reports the date as Dec. 15 (*op. cit.*, 163).

21. Appendix VI, and *New York Times*, Dec. 4, 1915, for members of committee.

22. See, for example, Fischel's address, quoted from the *Hebrew Standard* in his autobiography (p. 166).

23. Editorial, *JT*, Dec. 5, 1915, p. 6a-b.

24. *JT*, June 27, 1915, p. 5a-b.

25. *New York Tribune*, Dec. 6, 1915.

26. *JMJ*, Dec. 5, 1915, p. 4c-e.

27. *JMJ*, Dec. 3, 1915, p. 4c-e, and Appendix VI.

28. The ordained rabbis were: Baruch Davidson, Joseph Drevy, Nachman Ebin, Benjamin Fleischer, Samuel H. Glick, Jacob Granowitz, Redach Gulka, Henry Guterman, Joshua Aaron Horowitz, Mordecai Aaron Kaplan, Zadok Kapner, Harry Karp, Issachar Levin, Chaim Moseson, Ben Zion Pearl, David Rackman (Rachmilewitz), Romanov, Joseph Naphtali Rosenberg, Jacob Sachs, Baruch Shapiro, David B. Swirin, Benjamin Wendrowsky, Yarmis, Solomon Zimmerman and Drs. Moshe Robinson and Hyman Rosenberg. An additional five rabbis, already ordained although still studying at RIETS, were Rabbis Aaron Burack, D. Esrog, Meyer Kaplan, Wolf Roggen and Yallin (*JT*, Feb. 1, 1915, p. 4c, and Dec. 12, 1915, p. 1g; *JMJ*, Dec. 3, 1915, p. 4c-d-e; and Appendix VII).

29. Quoted in *American Hebrew*, Dec. 10, 1915.

30. *JMJ*, Dec. 6, 1915, p. 1g.

31. Caplan was generally critical even of the officers of the Rabbinical College, noting that during the banquet that followed Dr. Revel's induction, they all disappeared, leaving only Chaim Robinson, Harry Altschul and Nathan Lamport at the dinner. He also satirized the banquet as having taken place around long rough tables and benches with "the lack of order of chassidic *shalosh seudos* [traditional Sabbath "third meal" generally eaten in the synagogue immediately before the evening service] at which the unwieldy plates and rusty flatware destroyed the appetite for an otherwise good meal" (*JMJ*, Dec. 14, 1915, p. 4c-e).

32. Editorial, *JMJ*, Dec. 7, 1915, p. 4a-b.

33. Israel Friedlander, *Past and Present*, p. 299.

34. Quoted in *AJC*, May 10, 1908, p. 2.

35. *Ibid.*, p. 315.

36. For details of the life of Dr. Bernard Revel, see Leo Jung, "Bernard Revel," *Eidenu: Memorial Publication in Honor of Dr. Bernard Revel* (New York: Students of the Rabbi Isaac Elchanan Theological Seminary, 1942) 6-14, and Hirschel Revel, "Rabbi Dr. Bernard Revel," *ibid.*, 15-18.

For a bibliography of the writings of Dr. Revel, see Hirschel Revel, "Bibliography of the Writings of Rabbi Dr. Bernard Revel," *ibid.*, 21-26, and in *Horeb, VI* (November 1941), pp. 200-204. This does not include unpublished manuscripts which are in the possession of his widow, Mrs. Sarah Revel.

See also Pinkhos Churgin, "Horav Dr. Dov Revel Ve-Yezirato," *Horeb, op. cit.*, 1-8, Menachem Ribalow's obituary in *Hadoar*, Vol. 21, No. 6 (Dec. 6, 1940), p. 81; Aaron Shurin, *Keshet Gibborim* (Jerusalem: Mossad Harav Kook, 1964), 270-74; and Alex J. Goldman, *Giants of Faith* (New York, Citadel Press, 1964), 216-34.

A broad appreciation of Dr. Revel, his scholarship and personality, is found in Sidney B. Hoenig, *The Scholarship of Dr. Bernard Revel* (New York: Yeshiva University Press), 1968.

For a full study of Dr. Revel's life and accomplishments see Aaron Rothkoff, *Vision and Fulfillment: The Life of Rabbi Dr. Bernard Revel*, an unpublished doctoral dissertation at Yeshiva University, 1966.

37. Dated Jan. 8, 1908 to and in possession of Rabbi David Rackman.

38. *The Dropsie College for Hebrew and Cognate Learning Register 1963-1964* (Philadelphia: 1963), 64.

39. *JT*, July 13, 1915, p. 7c.

40. *JT*, Sept. 28, 1915, p. 4c.

41. Letter cited in note 37, this chapter.

42. Letter to Rabbi Rackman, Mar. 6, 1908.

43. *JT*, July 1, 1915, p. 4c-d.

44. Quoted in *Jewish Forum*, I, 1 (Jan. 27, 1919), p. 717.

45. *JT*, Dec. 12, 1915, English page.

46. See Appendix VII, and *Jewish Communal Register*, 1201ff.

47. *JT* (Brooklyn edition), Aug. 20, 1916, p. 8e; Aug. 22, 1916, English page; Sept. 3, 1916, English page; Sept. 15, 1916, English page; and Shelley R. Safir, "Ten Years of the Talmudical Academy," *Tenth Anniversary Souvenir Journal of the Talmudical Academy Alumni Association* (New York, 1926).

48. *Ibid., Jewish Communal Register*, pp. 1202ff., and Appendix VII.

49. Safir, *op cit.*

50. Safir, *op. cit.*

51. *Jewish Communal Register*, 1201 ff.

52. For references to Rabbi Berlin as president of RIETS see Samuel L. Sar, "Rabbi Berlin As President of the Rabbi Isaac Elchanan Theological Seminary," *Der Mizrachi Weg*, XVI, 9 (June, 1952), p. 6; *Hebrew Standard*, June 25 and June 30, 1922; and *Jewish Daily News*, March 29, 1922. See also Rabbi Jacob Levinson's article in *Talpioth*, note 54, this chapter. For reference to Rabbi Israel Rosenberg, see *Eduth le-Yisroel* (New York: Ezras Torah Fund, 1949), 9, 10.

53. The author has relied on personal interviews with Dr. Meyer Waxman and Dr. Hyman B. Grinstein and on a tape recording made by Dr. Pinkhos Churgin on March 29, 1955 describing the development of the Teachers Institute. See also *JMJ*, Jan. 16 and Feb. 13, 1925, and the *Jewish Courier* (Chicago), May 19, 1927; Hyman B. Grinstein, "Teachers Institute for Men— Bet Medrash Lemorim," *Alumni Review of Yeshiva University* (New York: 1962, fall issue); Norman B. Abrams "Bet Medrash Lemorim," *Nir: Student Publication of the Teachers Institute* (New York: 1926), 26-33; and Isidor Margolis, *Jewish Teachers Training Schools in the United States* (New York: National Council for Torah Education of Mizrachi-Hapoel-Mizrachi, 1964), 135-87.

54. Rabbi Berlin was born in 1880 in Volozhin and died in 1949 in Jerusalem. For biographical details see Rabbi Jacob Levinson, "In Memory of Rabbi Meir Bar-Ilan (Berlin)," *Talpioth*, V, 3-4 (Jan. 1952), 389-91; and "Autobiographical Sketch," *ibid.*, 392. For an evaluation of Rabbi Berlin see Pinkhos Churgin, "The Man of Wide Horizons," *ibid.*, 407-10.

55. For a report of the reorganization plans see Norman B. Abrams, *op. cit.; JT*, Nov. 15, 1921; *Hebrew Standard* and *American Hebrew*, both Nov. 18, 1921. According to the newspaper accounts, the Teachers Institute was meeting at 133 East Second Street, New York City. Nathan Lamport was president, Harry Fischel and Samuel Bayer were vice-presidents, Philip Luria was treasurer, and Rabbi Herbert S. Goldstein was honorary secretary. The Board of Education was composed of Rabbi Moses S. Margolies, chairman; Rabbi Meyer Berlin, vice-chairman, and Rabbi Bernard L. Levinthal, Rabbi Jacob Levinson, Rabbi Herbert S. Goldstein, Dr. Meyer Waxman, Samuel Wilner, Moses Stoll and Dr. Blaustein.

56. The building was dedicated on Sunday, Apr. 3, 1921, Fischel, *op. cit.,* 223-25 and Jacob I. Hartstein, "A Half Century of Torah in America," *Hedenu: Jubilee Publication of the Student Organization of the Rabbi Isaac Elchanan Theological Seminary* [New York 1936], 26. See also J. L. Brill, "The Work of Pioneers," *JT*, May 20, 1925, and *Jewish Courier* (Chicago), May, 19, 1927.

57. Abraham Soyer, in *JT*, May 18, 1924. See also *New York Graphic*, Feb. 1, 1926.

58. On Feb. 1, 1922, one year after the new building was acquired, the deficit in the budget was $33,500. This was reported by Samuel L. Sar at annual meeting of the Rabbi Isaac Elchanan Theological Seminary held under the chairmanship of Jacob Hecht. The Directors were Harris Altschul, Leon Kamaiky, Samuel Bayer, Harry Fischel, Mendel Gottesman, Peter Wiernick, Abraham Levy, J. L. Lubell, L. Kopiet, Jacob Hecht, Jacob H. Schiff, Nathan Roggen, Samuel Wilner, M. W. Levin, David Berg, Nathan Lamport, N. S. Roth, Joseph Friedman, Hyman Krarus, S. Gulistein, Samuel Rothenberg, Israel M. Horowitz, Joseph Lamport, Louis Gottesman, Joseph Polstein, H. D. Weil, Abe Levitan, Morris Friedman, and Rabbis Moses S. Margolies, Meir Berlin, Bernard L. Levinthal, Israel Rosenberg, Herbert S. Goldstein, Philip Hillel Klein, Davidson, Silver, and Preil.

59. The Ladies' Branch of the Rabbi Isaac Elchanan Theological Seminary provided the food and volunteer maintenance of the kitchen and dining room and the linens and supplies for the dormitory. Its president was Pesha Elka Dolinsky and its secretary, Sara Taub (*JMJ*, Dec. 2, 1924). A branch of the women's group was founded in Brooklyn. The officers were: president, Mrs. Chana Silverman; vice-presidents, Mrs. Ida Kaplan and Mrs. Patt; treasurer, Mrs. Sylvia Lefkowitz; trustee, Mrs. Adolf Fruchthandler; secretary, Adolf Fruchthandler (*DA*, Feb. 27, 1925 and *JT*, March 1, 1925). See also *JF*, VIII, 10 (Dec. 1925), 558.

60. *The Jewish World* (Philadelphia), Feb. 17, 1925.

61. A number of collectors traveled widely on behalf of the Seminary. Rev. Meyer Fried of Worcester, Mass. visited Minneapolis for the school (*American Jewish World* [Minneapolis], April 10, 1925). In 1926, he came to serve as "field secretary and acting manager of the Rabbi Isaac Elchanan Theological Seminary in place of S. L. Sar who is in Europe" (*Telegram* [Worcester], July 26, 1926). He remained with the Yeshiva after Mr. Sar's return. Rabbi Abraham Bender traveled to Pittsburgh (*Jewish Indicator* [Pittsburgh], Feb. 20, 1925) and Buffalo (*Jewish Review* [Buffalo], Nov. 26, 1926). Rabbi Curland visited Philadelphia (*Jewish World* [Philadelphia], Feb. 17, 1925). Rabbi M. H. Karplander spent a month in Detroit (*Jewish Chronicle* [Detroit], Sept. 11, 1925). Harris L. Selig visited Cleveland, Chicago, and Detroit (*Jewish Courier* [Chicago], July 12, 1926 and *Jewish Chronicle* [Detroit], July 16, 1926).

Many former students also volunteered their services. Rabbi Ben Zion Pearl visited South Norwalk, Conn. (*Sentinel* [South Norwalk], Aug. 12, 1925); Rabbis Nachman Ebin, Aaron Burack and Simon Borodkin addressed a dinner at the Brooklyn Jewish Center in New York City, where $100,000 was pledged (*JMJ*, Feb. 5, 1925); a list of rabbis who spoke on behalf of the institution during the Passover Holiday of 1925 is found in *JT*, March 27, 1925; and twenty-two rabbis, parents of students at the school, also appealed for funds during Passover that same year (*Light of Israel* [New York], April 3, 1925).

62. For example, Rabbi Mordecai E. Stern went to Congregation B'nai Abraham in Brooklyn (*JMJ*, Sept. 12, 1924); Rabbi Moshe Mintz went to Ottawa (*JT*, Oct. 9, 1924); Rabbi Mordecai Schuchatowitz went to Congregation Adath Jeshurun, Roxbury, Mass. (*Jewish Advocate and Hebrew Record* [Boston], Nov. 19, 1925); Rabbi Herman Rosen went to Congregation Agudath Achim, Altoona, Pa. (*JT*, July 14, 1925); Rabbi Zvi H. Glickman went to Adas Israel Synagogue, Elmhurst, Queens (*JT*, Aug. 10, 1925). Rabbi Isidore Goodman went to Congregation Beth El, Indianapolis; Rabbi Mordecai Rabinowitz, to Congregation Har Zion, Baltimore; Rabbi H. Schuchatowitz, to Peekskill, New York; Rabbi Jechiel M. Charlop went to the Bronx Jewish Center, New York City (*Review Observer* [Cleveland], Sept. 11, 1925). Rabbi Joseph Hagler went to Congregation Linas Hatzedek Anshei Sfard in the Bronx (*JMJ*, April 2, 1925); Rabbi Isaac Tendler went to Congregation Kochov Jacob, Manhattan (*AI*, March 5, 1925); Rabbi Jacob Lebowitz, to Beth Judah Center of Rochester (*Jewish Courier* [Chicago] May 3, 1925); Rabbi Max J. Mintz, to Congregation Beth Israel of Milwaukee (*Wisconsin Jewish Chronicle* [Milwaukee] Feb. 12, 1926). Rabbi Isaac Miller went to Congregation Emanuel, Youngstown, Ohio; Rabbi Abraham Rosenfeld went to the Maspeth Jewish Center, Queens; Rabbi Benjamin Axelman went to Richmond, Va.; Rabbi M. Romm went to Minneapolis (*Jewish Chronicle* [Brooklyn] June 4, 1926). Rabbi Meyer Cohen went to Colchester, Conn.; Rabbi Philip Greenstein, to Shamokin, Pa.; Rabbi Joseph H. Lookstein to Congregation Kehillath Jeshurun, New York City; Rabbi Alexander Rosenberg, to Congregation Ohab Zedek, Yonkers, New York; Rabbi D. Essrig, to Congregation Beth Israel, Los Angeles, (*AI*, June 10, 1926); Rabbi Shepherd Z. Baum, to Syracuse, and Rabbi Benzion Rosenbloom, to Torath Moshe Congregation (*Jewish Independent* [Cleveland], Aug. 27, 1926).

63. For biographical details of the life of Samuel L. Sar see Abraham Zuroff "My Father-in-Law," *Talpiot*, VIII, 3-4 (April, 1963), 245-48, and Aaron Shurin, *op. cit.*, 101-106.

64. An appeal was made by the Yeshiva "to all Jews to donate volumes to the library" (*JD*, July 6, 1924).

65. *Jewish Courier* (Chicago) Dec. 28, 1926, and *New York Graphic*, Dec. 9, 1926. Earlier, several thousand other volumes had been purchased as well (*JD*, April 4, 1925).

66. *JD*, Sept. 24, 1924, and Reuben Izeland, *JD.*, Nov. 27, 1924; *JDF*, Nov. 2, 1924; *Jewish World* (Philadelphia), Feb. 17, 1925; and the *New York Times*, Aug. 24, 1925.

67. *AI*, Sept. 3, 1925, and *Jewish News* (Denver), Aug. 27, 1925.

68. *JMJ*, Jan. 16, 1925 and Feb. 13, 1925, the next year a temporary dormitory annex was opened at 286 East Broadway for thirty-one additional out-of-town students. Mrs. Leo Jung was chairman of the program marking the opening (*Jewish Transcript* [Seattle], Dec. 28, 1926).

69. *Jewish World* (Philadelphia), Feb. 17, 1925.

70. *JT*, June 2, 1925.

71. *Ibid.*, and Sept. 14, 1925. See also *Jewish World* (Philadelphia), Feb. 17, 1925.

72. Rabbi Mordecai Hirschprung, "Short History of Rabbi Isaac Elchanan Theological Seminary," *JMJ*, May 14, 1925.

73. *Light of Israel* (New York), Sept. 5, 1924; *JT*, June 23, 1925; *Observer* (Hoboken), June 12, 1925, and *JT*, Sept. 26, 1924 and May 8, 1925.

74. The student who came from Shanghai was named A. Einhorn (*Jewish Review* [Buffalo], July 23, 1926).

75. *Journal of Commerce*, Jan. 26, 1905, report of the testimony of Congressman Samuel Dickstein before a congressional committee. An anonymous rabbi testifying before this committee on behalf of the exemption was asked "Why import rabbis when a great yeshiva like the Rabbi Isaac Elchanan Theological Seminary is producing them?" His response was that the Seminary was still too young to produce as many or as experienced rabbis 'as we need' " (*JMJ*, Feb. 15, 1925).

Notes to Chapter 10 (pp. 149-170)

1. Bernard Revel, "America's First Jewish College," *Daily Jewish Bulletin*, May 31, 1925. For other references to the aims of the college, see statement by Dr. Revel in Henry Beaumont Herts, "The Architecture of the Yeshiva," *JTrib.*, Dec. 7, 1928; "Yeshiva College Dedicates a New Building," *American Hebrew*, Dec. 7, 1928; and I. L. Brill, "The Yeshiva College," *JD*, Dec. 8, 1928. See also Harris L. Selig's exposition in the *Eagle* (Montreal), May 15, 1925, and the *Jewish Leader* (Boston), May 28, 1925.

2. *AH*, Jan. 18, 1924.

3. *American Israelite*, May 10, 1908. See p. 136. Later it cast a slur on the students of the Yeshiva as well, saying that the "larger majority of the Yeshibah [sic] students are only kept there because of the pittance of support that is given and which is the only means of keeping them away from the sweatshops." (Quoted in *American Jewish Chronicle*, July 21, 1916, p. 323.)

4. Editorial. *AI*. April 30, 1935.

5. "Timeo Danaos et Dona Ferentes," *AI*, May 28, 1925.

6. *AI*, April 30, 1925, and *Jewish Forum* VIII, 12 (December 1925), 558.

7. See a series of observations on the Rabbi Isaac Elchanan Theological Seminary by Louis Marshall in Charles Reznikoff, *Louis Marshall: Champion of Liberty* (Philadelphia: Jewish Publication Society, 1957), II, 888-93.

8. *AI*, Mar. 12, 1925.

9. S. M. Melamed, "From Extreme to Extreme," *NW*, March 18, 1925.

10. *NW*, March 25, 1925; *Jewish Chronicle* (Detroit), April 17, 1925.

11. *NW*, March 18, 1925.

12. *Ibid.*

13. A. Levinthal, "Letters to the Editor," *NW*, March 28, 1925. See also statement by Lewis E. Miller and a defense of the Rabbi Isaac Elchanan Theological Seminary by Jacob Porush, *ibid.;* and *Freiheit*, May 30, 1925.

14. Letter by A. Levinthal, *NW*, March 28, 1925.

15. *NW*, March 25, 1925; *JC* (Detroit), April 17, 1925.

16. For a sampling of contemporary biographical material about the leading supporters of Yeshiva College, see: on Nathan Lamport, Maurice A. Bregman, "Keeping Young at Seventy," *Jewish Advocate and Connecticut Hebrew Record*, Jan. 20, 1927, and "The Man Behind the Yeshiva," *Israel's Messenger* (Shanghai), March 4, 1927; on Harry Fischel, *B'nai B'rith Messenger* (Los Angeles), Aug. 10, 1928; on Benjamin Winter, article by Leo Robbins, *JDF*, March 3, 1926; on Louis Gold, Maurice A. Bregman, "The Man Who Built 9,000 Homes," *JTRIB*, Nov. 19, 1926; on Rabbi Moses S. Margolies, *JD*, May 31, 1925, and *Sefer ha-Yovel ha-Pardes* (New York: 1951) ed. S. Elberg pp. 458-461, and obituary in *New York Times*, Aug. 26, 1963; on Nathan Roggen, H. Schneiderman, "Nathan Roggen—Builder of Jewish Institutions," *Light of Israel*, Nov. 25, 1925.

17. B. Shelvin wrote, ". . . more and more, indications grow that Jewish Orthodoxy is awakening and achieving maturity . . . and the best indication is its relationship to the Rabbi Isaac Elchanan Theological Seminary in New York." ("Jewish Orthodoxy in America," *JMJ*, Jan. 1, 1925). See also *Der Amerikaner*, Jan. 2, 1925; A. A. Roback, "The Rise of Orthodox Jewish Influence in America," *Jewish Transcript* (Seattle), Sept. 18, 1925, and *Jewish Forum*, VIII, 8 (Sept. 1925) 395.

18. Dr. Hirsch L. Gordon, "Our Wealth in America," *Hadoar*, IV, 6 (Dec. 19, 1924), 6.

19. Ephraim Caplan in *Eagle* (Montreal) May 19, 1924.

20. *JMJ*, May 16, 1924.

21. See Rabbi Mordecai Hirschprung, *op. cit.*

22. Caplan in *Eagle* (Montreal), May 19, 1924; *JF*, VII, 12 (December, 1924), 759.

23. November 1928; see also Editorial in *Jewish World* (Philadelphia), March 31, 1925.

24. Amendment to Charter of the Rabbi Isaac Elchanan Theological Seminary Association, March 27, 1924; see also *Jewish World* (Philadelphia), May 29, 1924.

25. See article by B. Rossman in *JDF* May 31, 1924, and *JDF* June 4, 1924; see also comment by Ben Zion Goldberg, *JD*, June 4, 1924.

26. *JMJ*, May 27, 1924.

27. Caplan, *Eagle*, June 20, 1925.

28. *Jewish Exponent*, April 17, 1925. See comments by President Nicholas Murray Butler, Columbia University, and President Sidney E. Mezes, College of the City of New York, in *AI*, April 30, 1925, and *JE*, May 8, 1925; by Presidents Walter Dill Scott, Northwestern University; William Lowe Bryant, University of Indiana; Frank Aydelotte, Swarthmore College; Henry McCracken, Vassar College; Ray Lyman Wilbur, Leland Stanford University; and Frank L. Speare, Northeastern University; and Provost J. H. Penniman, University of Pennsylvania, and Dr. Israel Schapiro, Chief of the Semitic and Oriental Division of the Library of Congress in the *New York World*, Nov. 20, 1925; and by Dr. Charles Parkes Cadman, President of the Federal Council of Churches of Christ in America, *ibid.*, Feb. 11, 1925.

See also *Jewish World* (Cleveland), May 30, 1924; *Cleveland Plain Dealer*, May 2, 1925; *New York Evening Sun*, May 16, 1925; *JMJ*, May 16, 1925, and an article by Ephraim Caplan in the same issue; also "The Yeshiva College," *JF*, XI, 7 (July, 1928), 358 ff., for later comments by Dr. Edward Chauncey Baldwin, University of Illinois, and Dr. Solomon Solis-Cohen of Philadelphia.

29. *Jewish Leader* (Boston), May 28, 1925.

30. *JMJ*, March 18, 1925.

31. *JMJ*, May 16, 1924, July 1, 1924, Sept. 22, 1924, Sept. 25, 1924, and Feb. 5, 1925; *JT*, March 27, 1925 and April 28, 1925; *Light of Israel*, April 3, 1925; *New York Telegraph*, May 15, 1925; *New York American*, Nov. 14, 1926; *Times* (Brooklyn), Nov. 1, 1926.

32. *JT*, April 28, 1925.

33. *Jewish World* (Philadelphia), Dec. 13, 1924.

34. The Union of Orthodox Jewish Congregations guaranteed to the Regents of the University of the State of New York the minimum annual income of 4 percent of $500,000 necessary for institutions conferring higher degrees. A condition for the agreement was that the Seminary would give precedence in placing its graduates as rabbis in pulpits of member congregations of the Union. The agreement with Yeshiva was signed on February 27, 1924. (Herbert S. Goldstein, "A Year of Orthodoxy," *JF*, III, 10 [Dec. 1925].) See also *New York Times*, Dec. 3, 1923, which reported the initial announcement of the Union's support. Rabbi Herbert S. Goldstein explained the importance of the Yeshiva because "American Jewry has not produced a single great rabbi or great Jewish scholar in the true sense of greatness [and] we can no longer depend upon Europe for our rabbis, for it is no longer possible to

secure them from abroad." See also resolution adopted at the Convention of the Union of Orthodox Congregations to support the campaign of the Yeshiva (*Light of Israel,* Oct. 26, 1925).

35. *Jewish World* (Philadelphia), Dec. 13, 1924. Rabbi Goldstein replaced Dr. H. Pereira Mendes, minister of the Spanish and Portuguese Synagogue, as professor of Homiletics when the latter retired. (Joseph H. Lookstein, "Dr. Revel and Homiletics: A Page of Yeshiva Memoirs," *Hedenu,* 62.)

36. Other members of the campaign committee were Judge Otto Rosalsky, Dr. Bernard Drachman, Rabbi Meyer Berlin (Bar-Ilan), Mendel Gottesman, Leon Kamaiky, Dr. Philip Hillel Klein, Nathan Lamport, Rev. Zvi Hirsch Masliansky, Dr. Henry Pereira Mendes, Joseph Polstein, Nathan Roggen, Gustave Roth and Abraham Levy. Other members of the building committee were Samuel Beyer, Elias A. Cohen, Louis Gold, Saul Herring, Mendel Gottesman, Albert Herskowitz, A. A. Israel, Nathan Lamport, Jacob Leitner, Abraham Levy, Sam Minskoff, Joseph Polstein, and Harry Roggen. (*JMJ,* Sept. 24, 1924; and *JT,* May 14, 1924 and Sept. 25, 1924.) Harris L. Selig resigned as of January 1, 1929 (*New York Home News* and *Jewish Independent* [Cleveland], both of Dec. 28, 1928).

37. *JMJ,* Sept. 24, 1924 and Dec. 17, 1924. It was purchased for the Seminary by Harry Fischel. (*New York American,* Sept. 20, 1924). See also *JT,* Sept. 25, 1924; *Herald Tribune,* Mar. 17, 1925; and *New York American,* March 10, 1928.

38. *New York Times,* Oct. 26, 1924.

39. This purchase represented nineteen additional building lots (*JMJ,* Dec. 8, 1924; *DA,* Dec. 12, 1924; *Jewish Leader* (Boston), Dec. 7, 1924; *Jewish Indicator* (Pittsburgh), Dec. 5, 1924).

40. *JDF,* May 15, 1927.

41. From a speech by Dr. Revel, reported in the *Jewish Leader* (Boston), May 28, 1926.

42. *JMJ,* Sept. 24, 1924 and Dec. 18, 1924; *JDF,* Sept. 25, 1924 and Dec. 25, 1924; *Jewish Chronicle* (Detroit), and *Jewish Review* (Buffalo), both Dec. 7, 1928.

43. *JMJ,* June 20, 1924, and *Jewish World* (Cleveland), June 25, 1924. For earlier pledges see *New York Evening Post,* Dec. 3, 1923.

44. *JMJ,* Dec. 17, 1924.

45. *AH,* Dec. 26, 1924, and *JMJ,* Dec. 30, 1924; and *New York Times* and *JD,* both Dec. 22, 1924. *JT* (Dec. 26, 1924) reported an extensive list of contributors and the amounts subscribed. See also *Jewish Times* (Baltimore), Jan. 9, 1925. *JD* (Dec. 22, 1924) had set the amount raised at one million dollars, but Harris L. Selig confirmed that the total amount was $800,000 ("Letter to the Editor," *Evening World,* Jan. 17, 1925).

46. Harris L. Selig, *ibid.*

47. *AH*, Dec. 26, 1924. Nathan Lamport died at age 74 on August 13, 1928. After being in the United States for more than 54 years, he had amassed, it was reported almost two million dollars, of which he left half to charity (*Jewish Transcript* [Seattle], Aug. 24, 1928). See also *JTrib.*, Dec. 20 and Dec. 24, 1926; and *JT*, June 29, 1924.

When Lamport fell ill, his feeling for the Rabbi Isaac Elchanan Theological Seminary was such that he wrote a letter to his son asking him to attend the dedication of the new building in his place. The letter reflects his dedication to the Yeshiva and is reminiscent of the great ethical wills of the Middle Ages:

> My dear Sonny,
>
> You will be at the Yeshiva dedication. My limbs are getting weaker—my pulse is getting low—my eyes keep growing dim. I fear that the Almighty will not let me participate personally in this occasion. . . .
>
> I'm not complaining about God's dictum, but I want all of . . . my good brothers to know I love them.
>
> I love them for the earnest desire they always showed to give their efforts for our Yeshiva. . . . They are all men who deserve our affection and appreciation; many are there whose names are rarely publicly mentioned. . . .
>
> Oh, my boy, you will be with them when the great glory of our efforts will be crowned in the towering domes of our magnificent Yeshiva Building.
>
> Those beautiful domes, this magnificent edifice, stand proudly on the heights of our city and proclaim proudly to all of America the great contribution that we are bringing at the altar of liberty. . . .
>
> What could we find more happiness in, what can there possibly be more comfort and joy in, than settling our Torah permanently on the soil of our own America?

The complete text of the letter is to be found in *The Hebrew*, Dec. 28, 1928. See also *American Hebrew News*, Dec. 28, 1929.

48. *JF*, IX, 9 (Sept. 1928), 430.

49. The dinner took place on April 26, 1925 (*New York World*, May 25, 1925). For progress reports, donors and pre-dinner activities, see *New York Times*, March 12, 1925; *Jewish Leader* (Boston), March 16, 1925; *Brooklyn Citizen*, March 8, 1925; *World*, Feb. 15, 1925 and March 29, 1925; *Brooklyn Times*, Feb. 24, 1924; and *Hebrew Record* (Boston), April 2, 1925. See also *JT*, May 21, 1925, and *Jewish Chronicle* (Brooklyn), May 29, 1925. J. L. Brill ("The World of Pioneers," *JT*, May 20, 1925) reported, however, that only $1,026,000 was raised at the dinner.

50. *JD*, May 26, 1925.

51. Quoted in *Jewish Chronicle* (Brooklyn), June 12, 1925.

52. *JT*, June 17, 1925. The *NW*, still outraged by this form of Orthodox philanthropy, chastised New York Jewry for contributing only $700,000 during the same year to Keren Hayesod (the Jewish National Fund), while a group of Jews raised twice as much for a yeshiva (May 13, 1925).

53. *JF*, VII, 4 (April, 1924), 231, and *JTrib.*, Sept. 18, 1925. The first parlor meeting was held at the home of Mrs. Abraham Levy at 777 West End

Avenue, New York City. Another was held at the home of Mrs. Max Levine of 302 W. 92nd Street, New York City (*JD*, May 28, 1924). A later meeting at the Astor Hotel found 36 women giving a total of $40,000 (*JMJ*, Jan. 14, 1925, and *New Journal* [Brooklyn], Jan. 16, 1925). Another group met at Congregation Ohab Zedek at 18 West 116 Street (*JMJ*, Jan. 3, 1925). See also *Jewish Chronicle* (Brooklyn), April 10, 1925, and *Jewish Courier* (Chicago), April 6, 1925.

54. *Evening Sun*, May 16, 1925.

55. *Home News*, Jan. 18, 1926, and *Times*, Jan. 31, 1926, and May 9, July 19 and July 27, 1925.

56. The Festival was held on May 23, 1926 (*Jewish Theatrical News*, June 1, 1926). For details of the evening, contributors and committees, see *Jewish Theatrical News*, May 11, 1926; *Times*, April 29 and May 23, 1926; *JTrib.*, May 7 and 11, 1926; *Telegram*, May 19 and 24, 1926; *Herald Tribune*, May 23, 1926, and *World*, May 26, 1926.

57. Jacob I. Hartstein, *Hedenu*, 28. See also *Jewish Daily Bulletin*, Feb. 11, 1927; *Times*, Feb. 13, 1927; *Jewish Review Observer* (Cleveland), March 11, 1927; *Jewish World* (Philadelphia), March, 13, 1927; *Jewish Times* (Baltimore), March 25, 1927; and *Rochester Democratic-Chronicle*, March 27, 1927. *Times* and *Daily News*, April 24, 1927; *New York Graphic*, *New York Evening Post*, and *Herald-Tribune* of May 2, 1927; *St. Louis Dispatch*, May 3, 1927; *Jewish World* (Philadelphia), May 5, 1927; *JTrib.*, May 6, 1927; *JDF*, May 15, 1927; and *Zionist Record* (Johannesburg, South Africa), June 17, 1927.

58. *Jewish Courier* (Chicago), May 19, 1927.

59. The following text of the letter, dated April 29, 1927, from President Calvin Coolidge was reproduced in *JE*, May 13, 1927:

> I regret that it is impossible for me to be present at the laying of the cornerstone of the new buildings of the Yeshiva Rabbi Isaac Elchanan. Marking as they do a new era in the development of your institution of higher education, which stands for culture, learning and scholarship, and for religious training so vitally essential to the welfare of our country, the exercises on Sunday have a peculiar significance to all true Americans. Long eminent in philanthropic, social and communal work, the Jews of America, through the increased advantages at the disposal of the Yeshiva, will be able to broaden their field for training of scholars and religious leaders for their people. This is of importance not only to them, but to our national life as a whole.
>
> I send my congratulations, greetings and best wishes.
>
> Calvin Coolidge.

60. *JF*, V, 1 (January 1922), 5.

61. Interview with Harold Levy, son of Abraham Levy, member of the Board of Trustees of RIETS in the 1920's and 1930's. I am grateful, too, to Rabbi Aaron Rothkoff for furnishing Dr. Revel's quotations and some of the details of the merger talks. See his *Vision and Fulfillment: The Life of Rabbi*

Dr. Bernard Revel, an unpublished doctoral dissertation at Yeshiva University, 1966. For Marshall's quotation, see note 7, this chapter.

62. Amendment to the Charter of the Rabbi Isaac Elchanan Theological Seminary Association changing the name of the corporation to the Rabbi Isaac Elchanan Theological Seminary Association and Yeshiva College, granted by the Board of Regents on March 28, 1928. See also *Jewish Courier* (Chicago), April 10, 1928, and *Jewish Criterion* (Pittsburgh), April 13, 1928.

63. *Home News* and *Evening Telegram,* Sept. 27, 1928.

64. For Program of Dedication, see *Times,* Dec. 10 and Dec. 12, 1928; *Home News, Herald-Tribune* and *Standard Union* (Brooklyn) of Dec. 10, 1928. See also *Record* (Philadelphia), Dec. 9, 1928 and *JTrib, JE* and *Jewish Criterion* of Dec. 14, 1928. The building on East Broadway was sold to the Home of Old Israel, Inc., for $82,000 (*Times,* July 23, 1927).

65. *Herald Tribune* and *Home News* both of Dec. 16, 1928. Mayor James J. Walker, Rabbi Moses S. Margolies, Rabbi Bernard L. Levinthal, Dr. Fredrick C. Robinson, president of the College of the City of New York; Dr. Henry Noble McCracken, president of Vassar College, Judge Otto A. Rosalsky and others participated in the program.

66. For details of Rabbi Polachek's life and death, see *Eidenu: Memorial Volume Published by the Students of the Rabbi Isaac Elchanan Theological Seminary in Memory of Rabbi Solomon Polachek* (New York: 1928); and the *Herald-Tribune,* July 10, 1928; *Times,* July 10 and 11, 1928; *AI,* July 20, 1928; and *B'nai B'rith Messenger* (Los Angeles), July 20, 1928.

See also Meyer Berlin, *Fun Volozhin biz Yerushalayim* (New York: 1933), II, 252-59; Hirsch L. Gordon, "The Meitscheter Illui," *Eidenu, op. cit.,* 204 and ff., and expanded article under same title in *Hadoar,* March 5, 1965; also preface in *Hidushe ha-Illui mi-Meitschet* (New York: 1947), xxi-xxx; Rabbi Samuel K. Mirsky, "Dedication," *Talpioth,* VI, 1-2 (March, 1952), 1; Nissan Waxman, "Rabbi Shlomo Poliachek: A Portrait," *Talpioth, loc. cit.,* 3-34; O. Feuchtwanger, "The Majeter Illuy" in *Righteous Lives* (New York: Bloch Publishing Co., 1965), 119-121; and Aaron Rothkoff," "The Meitsheter Illui," *Jewish Life,* 35, 2 (Nov.-Dec., 1967), 29-35. Also *JMJ,* Aug. 6, 1924; *Evening Post,* July 10, 1928; *Jewish Press* (Omaha), July 20, 1928.

67. For some details about Rabbi Aranowitz see *Ha-Zedek: Yeshiva Student Publication,* Dec. 21, 1939, p. 2.

68. For obituary notice of Rabbi Selmanowitz, see *JMJ,* Oct. 6, 1946.

69. See *JTrib.,* Nov. 28, 1928; *Times,* July 10 and 11, 1928; *Jewish Independent* (Cleveland), Nov. 30, 1928; *Jewish Times* (Philadelphia), Nov. 10, 1928, and two obituary articles in *Hadoar* XXI, 15, Feb. 7, 1941, 234 and 245. See also Shurin, *op. cit.,* 200-207.

70. "The First Jewish University," *Jewish Chronicle* (Newark), Dec. 28, 1928.

71. See *Yeshiva College Catalogue* (New York, 1928), 5-6; *New York Home News,* and *Herald Tribune,* both of Oct. 19, 1928; *Jewish Independent* (Cleveland) and *AI,* both of Oct. 19, 1928; *Reform Advocate* (Chicago), Oct. 20, 1928, and *B'nai B'rith Messenger* (Los Angeles), Nov. 9, 1928.

72. The students had been tested by Dr. H. E. Garrett, professor of psychology at Columbia University, for "mental alertness and prospective academic performance." The results were described as "truly astonishing" by Dr. Garrett in view of the heavy load of their religious program in addition to their curriculum of secular studies. Of 137 colleges similarly tested, only Wells College, Dartmouth College, and Haverford College rated higher than the Yeshiva College score (*JF,* XV, 3 [March 1932], 67).

73. It was reported that $1,275,000 in unpaid pledges was outstanding early in 1928. For details of the unpaid pledges and the mortgage, see *Times,* Jan. 31 and March 9 and 10, 1928.

74. Aron, William "Einstein: The Jew and His Judaism," *Hadoar,* April 9, 1965.

Notes to Chapter 11 (pp. 171-184)

1. See Note 137, Chapter 4.
2. *Ibid.*
3. See Note 63, Chapter 5.
4. For biographical sketch and work evaluation of Rabbi Joseph B. Soloveitchik, see Aharon Lichtenstein, "Joseph Soloveitchik," in *Great Jewish Thinkers of the Twentieth Century,* Simon Noveck, ed. (Washington: B'nai B'rith Department of Adult Jewish Education, 1963), 281-297. See also Eugene B. Borowitz, "The Typological Theology of Rabbi Joseph B. Soloveitchik," *Judaism,* XV, 2 (Spring 1966), 203-10, and Chaim R. Rabinowitz, "Ha-Rav Yosef Dov Soloveitchik ke-Darshan" in *Hadoar,* 47, 25, May 12, 1967, 467-69.
5. *JF,* XI, 9 (Sept. 1928), 467, and *Herald Tribune,* Nov. 11, 1927.
6. For some details on the variety of studies and accomplishments of the Albert Einstein College of Medicine see *The First Decade: A Progress Report* (New York: The Albert Einstein College of Medicine, 1966), and *Ten Brave Years (1955-1965)* (New York: The Albert Einstein College of Medicine, 1966).
7. See Appendix V.

Appendices

APPENDIX I: CONSTITUTION OF THE SOCIETY MACHZEKI JESHIBATH ETZ CHAIEM ORGANIZED 5646

ARTICLE I
NAME AND LANGUAGE

Sec. 1. This Academy shall always bear the name of
MACHZEKI JESHIBATH ETZ CHAIEM.

Sec. 2. All business and transactions shall be made in the Jewish language, especially the Minute Book which shall be in the Hebrew Language (Loshon Hakodosh).

Sec. 3. This Academy can never be dissolved and must exist so long as ten creditable members keep themselves together.

ARTICLE II
PURPOSE

Sec. 1. The purpose of this Academy shall be to give free instruction to poor Hebrew Children in the Hebrew language and the Hebrew Law—Talmud, Bible and Sulchon Aurach during the whole day from nine in the morning until four in the afternoon. Also from four in the afternoon, two hours shall be devoted to teach the native language, English, and one hour to teach Hebrew—Loshon Hakodosh and Jargon to read and write.

Sec. 2. This Academy shall be guided according to the strict Orthodox and Talmudical Law and the custom of Poland and Russia.

ARTICLE III
MEMBERSHIP

Sec. 1. Every Hebrew can become a member of this Academy.

Sec. 2. The dues shall be from three dollars a year and upwards.

Sec. 3. When a member gives to this Academy a hundred dollars at one time, he remains a member during his whole life time.

ARTICLE IV
OFFICERS

Sec. 1. This Academy shall be governed by fourteen officers, namely: one President; one Vice-President; one Treasurer; one Secretary and ten Directors.

Sec. 2. The ten Directors shall be divided into the following committees:—

One Committee consisting of four Directors, named Trustees, whose duty it is to superintend the house and money affairs, such as to repair the house when it is necessary, to make programmes, to appoint Hebrew and English teachers, to buy books and everything which belongs to it, according to the income of the time.

Sec. 3. Another Committee consisting of six members who shall be called Leaders—Mnahalim, shall superintend the course of study in Talmud, Bible and Shulchon Aurach to appoint Hebrew teachers, and also in some occurrence to be a Hebrew teacher, and to discharge one if they have sufficient reason for it.

Sec. 4. If all the six leaders agree on some point, they can act according to their opinion, if they disagree they must bring the matter before the President and the Board of Trustees.

ARTICLE XII
TEACHERS

Sec. 1. It is the duty of the Teachers to teach according to the Programme of the Board of Leaders.

Sec. 2. They must be found in the Academy every day in the week in the right time according to the Programme of the Board of Leaders.

ARTICLE XIII
EXAMINATIONS

Sec. 1. The principal examination shall take place on the fifteenth day of Shebat and on the fifteenth day of Ab.

Sec. 2. Ordinary examinations shall be made by the Leaders from time to time according to their opinion.

SEC. 3. Excepting the Leaders and the Officers of the Academy, no one has the right to come in the Academy and examine the children without the permission of the Superintendent of the Academy.

ARTICLE XIV
BENEFIT

SEC. 1. When an officer becomes sick and this is reported to the Secretary, a Director shall visit him daily.

SEC. 2. When a Director dies, the Secretary shall send notice to all the Officers that they shall pay the last honor to the deceased.

SEC. 3. The Academy shall send a carriage and also a committee of four, to the cemetery.

SEC. 4. Ten children from every class shall attend the funeral and say Psalms.

SEC. 5. When anyone was a Director or any other officer during the three years following the establishment of the Academy, he shall be entitled to all this during his whole life, provided that he obeys the Jewish Law and is interested in the benefit of the Academy.

SEC. 6. The Directors shall assemble in the Academy every morning to pray jointly. Also a chapter of Mishna shall be learned every day, together with the prayer beginning with "Anna" and "Kadish" . . . "for the rising of his soul."

SEC. 7. "Hazkoras Nshamos" (Memorial Prayer) shall be made every Saturday and Holiday of the first year.

SEC. 8. The same shall be made every "Yahrzeit" day as long as the Academy exists.

SEC. 9. If any man not an officer of the Academy should have given a Hundred dollars at one time to the Academy, "Hazkoras Nshamos" shall be made every Saturday and Holiday of the first year of his death.

SEC. 10. When any one gave $500 at one time or left that sum to the Academy, "Hazkoras Nshamos" shall be made during the first year, and a "Neir Nishmas" (Candle for his soul), shall be lighted on the "Yahrzeit Day" during the first ten years.

SEC. 11. When any man left $1000, "Hazkoras Nshamos" shall be made during the first year, and the twenty years following his death, a candle shall be lighted on the "Yahrzeit" day.

Sec. 12. When any man gives more than a $1000, then all the above things shall be made and as long as the Academy exists the "Yahrzeit" shall be held and a chapter of "Mishna" shall be learned on that day.

Sec. 13. When such donations are given to the Academy, the names of the donators shall be inscribed on a tablet of the Academy, to be remembered forever.

APPENDIX II: CERTIFICATE OF INCORPORATION, CHEBRAH MACHSIKA ISHIWAS ETZ CHAIM

State of New York
County of New York }   ss:
City of New York

We the undersigned,

MORRIS BERNSTEIN[1]
SAMUEL WAXMAN[2]
ABRAM RUBENOWITZ[3]
RACHMIEL WITMAN[4] and
HENRY M. GREENBERG[5]

Citizens of the United States, also Citizens and Residents of the City, County and State of New York being desirous to associate ourselves together for the purpose of forming and organizing a *Benevolent Society, do hereby certify*

That we have pursuant to the Laws of the State of New York, as prescribed in Article III Title 6, Chapter 18 of the Revised Statutes entitled, *"An Act"* for the Incorporation of Benevolent, Charitable, Scientific, and Missionary Societies, passed April 12th 1848, and the Acts amendatory thereof, associated ourselves together for the purpose of forming and organizing a *Benevolent Society.*

That the name by which said society or organization shall be known in law is the:

---

[1] In the *New York City Directory* [=NYCD] for the year 1886-1887, there are eight persons listed by this name with various occupations such as clerk, pedlar, segarmaker, shoes.

[2] He is listed as dealing in clothing at 74 Baxter Street in *NYCD* for the year 1886-1887.

[3] Abram Rubenowitz is written in by hand over an erasure here. Also see page 243, note 17. There is an "Abraham Rubenowitz" listed as a tailor at 9 Forsyth Street (*ibid.*).

[4] Rachmiel Witman is not listed (*ibid.*), although several other persons are listed with the surname "Wittman."

[5] "Henry M.", appearing in the name Henry M. Greenberg, is written by hand over an erasure. The signature that appears subsequently on p. 243 reads "H. C. Greenberg." However, there is a "Henry W. Greenberg" listed in *NYCD* for the year 1886-1887, living on the Lower East Side, who dealt in real estate, but in *NYCD* for the year 1887-1888, the name appears as "Henry M. Greenberg," who dealt in real estate, and was located at a different address in the same neighborhood on the Lower East Side.

Chebrah Machsiḳa Ishiwas Etz Chaim.

That the objects and business of the society or organization are the improvement of the spiritual, mental and social condition of *Hebrew Boys,* to provide for them Teachers and instructions in *Hebrew,* to foster and encourage the study of the *Sacred Scriptures,* the *Talmud,* and the Hebrew language and literature; to hold religious service in accordance with Orthodox Judaism: also to provide teachers and instruction for said *Hebrew Boys* in reading, writing and speaking the English Language; and to perform such other charitable acts and purposes as may be specified in the Constitution and By-Laws of the Society or Organization.[6]

That the number of Directors or Trustees of the said Society or Organization shall be nine.

That the number of Directors or Trustees, for the first year of the existence of the Society or Organization hereby formed shall be as follows,

JULIUS D. BERNSTEIN[7]	who shall act as *President*
MORRIS BERNSTEIN[8]	who shall act as *First Vice Pres*
MOSES HELLER[9]	who shall act as *Second Vice Pres*
FALK BERMAN[10]	who shall act as *Treasurer*
LOUIS SHAPIRO[11]	who shall act as *Secretary*
ELIAS RATKOWSKY[12]	who shall act as *First Trustee*
LOUIS SIEGELSTEIN[13]	who shall act as *Second Trustee*
RACHMIEL WITMAN[14]	who shall act as *Third Trustee*
BARUCH P. LIBERMAN[15]	who shall act as *Fourth Trustee*

[6] See Appendix I and Alexander M. Dushkin, *Jewish Education in New York City* (New York, 1918), Appendix F, pp. 480-483.

[7] The name Julius D. Bernstein does not appear in *NYCD* for the years 1886-1887 and 1887-1888. There are three persons listed in these directories bearing the name of "Julius Bernstein." In the *Jüdische Gazetten,* Jan. 15, 1897, Rabbi Yehuda David Bernstein is referred to as the founder of Yeshivat Etz Chaim as well as a founder of the Rabbi Isaac Elchanan Theological Seminary [Appendix IV]. His name also appears on the Certificate of Incorporation of the Rabbi Isaac Elchanan Theological Seminary Association [Appendix III].

[8] See p. 241, note 1.

[9] The name Moses Heller is not listed in *NYCD* for the year 1886-1887. However, there is a Morris Heller listed as a tailor at 60 Mulberry Street.

[10] Falk Berman is listed as a tailor at 15 Chrystie Street [*ibid.*].

[11] Louis Shapiro is listed as a pedlar at 140 East Broadway [*ibid.*].

[12] Elias Ratkowsky is not listed in the *NYCD* for 1886-1887 and 1887-1888.

That the said nine members shall hold office as such Directors, Trustees and Officers for one year from the date hereof, and shall constitute the Board of Directors or Trustees.

That the business of the Society or Organization shall be transacted in the City of New York.

In Witness Whereof, we have hereunto set our hands and seals this 15th day of September 1886.

MORRIS BERNSTEIN
S. WAXMAN
ABRAM RUBENOWITZ   [*Signed*]
RACHMIEL WITMAN
H. C. GREENBERG[16]

State of New York.
City and County of New York. ss.

On this 15th day of September 1886, before me personally came MORRIS BERNSTEIN, SAMUEL WAXMAN, ABRAM RUBENOWITZ,[17] RACHMIEL WITMAN and HENRY M. GREENBERG,[18] to me severally known, to be the persons described in and executed the foregoing instrument and they severally acknowledged to me that they executed the same, for the uses and purposes therein mentioned.

ADOLPH COHEN
Notary Public
NYCounty

---

[13] Louis Siegelstein, is listed as a pedlar at 71½ Division Street [*ibid.,* for the year 1886-1887].

[14] See p. 241, note 4.

[15] Baruch P. Liberman is not listed in *NYCD* for the years 1886-1887 and 1887-1888. However, there is some biographical data concerning him in the *Hebrew American Directory and Universal Guide* (New York, 1892), p. 139. His full name, given there, is Baruch Pinchas Liberman.

[16] See p. 241, note 5. Here the signature appears as "H. C. Greenberg."

[17] The complete name here again is written in by hand over an erasure.

[18] In the copy of the Certificate registered in Albany the name "Henry M." is written in by hand over an erasure. In the copy of the Certificate found in the Hall of Records the name is not erased but two lines are drawn through "Hyman M." and above it is inserted "Henry M."

APPENDIX III: CERTIFICATE OF INCORPORATION, RABBI ISAAC ELCHANAN THEOLOGICAL SEMINARY ASSOCIATION

State of New York ⎱
City of New York ⎰ ss:

We, the undersigned, desiring to form a corporation pursuant to the provisions of the membership corporation law, all being of full age and two-thirds being citizens of the United States and at least one a resident of the State of New York, do hereby certify and state:

First: The particular objects for which the corporation is to be formed are to promote the study of the Talmud and to assist in educating and preparing students of the Hebrew faith for the Hebrew Orthodox Ministry.

Second: The name of the proposed corporation is the Rabbi Isaac Elchanan Theological Seminary Association.

Third: The territory in which its operations are to be principally conducted is the City, County and State of New York.

Fourth: The town, village or city in which its principal office is to be located is the City of New York in the County and State of New York.

Fifth: The number of its directors is eleven.

Sixth: The names and places of residence of the persons to be its directors until its first annual meeting are:

Name		
SAMUEL SCHATZKIN	1 Canal Street	New York
JEHUDA SOLOMON	134 E. Broadway	" "
ASHER L. GERMANSKY	30 Canal Street	" "
MAX LEWIS	24 Orchard Street	" "
DAVID ABRAMOWITZ	5 Hester Street	" "
MENDEL ZUCKERMAN	162 Henry Street	" "
JULIUS BRAUNSTEIN	272 E. Broadway	" "
SAMUEL SILBERSTEIN	235 Division Street	" "
MOSES H. BERNSTEIN	89 Division Street	" "
JULIUS [YEHUDA] BERNSTEIN	71 Henry Street	" "
MOSES M. MATLIN	172 Clinton Street	" "

Seventh: The times for holding its annual meeting is the first Sunday in January of each year.

State of New York
City, County of New York } ss:

On this 26th day of February, 1897, before me personally came Samuel Schatzkin, Jehuda Solomon, Asher L. Germansky, Max Lewis, Jacob H. Selikowitz, Mendel Zuckerman, Julius Bernstein, Samuel Silberstein, David Abramowitz, Simon Selikowitz, M. H. Bernstein, Moses M. Matlin, Joseph Goldenson, Julius D. Bernstein, to me personally known to be the individuals described in and who executed the same.

ABRAHAM ROSENBERG
Commissioner of Deeds
New York County

[Endorsed]

I, the undersigned, Justice of the Supreme Court of the State of New York, do hereby approve of the within certificate

Dated at New York this 8th day of March, 1897.

MILES BEACH
J S C

Certificate of Incorporation
The Rabbi Isaac Elchanan Theological Seminary Association
(A membership corporation)

State of New York

Office of Secretary of State   March 20, 1897

Filed and recorded

ANDREW DAVIDSON

Deputy Secretary of State

APPENDIX IV: ANNOUNCEMENT OF FOUNDING OF THE RABBI ISAAC ELCHANAN THEOLOGICAL SEMINARY[1]

"THE MORE STUDY THE MORE WISDOM"

Congregation Anshei Emes of Mariampol
44 East Broadway

announces that just as the Yeshiva Etz Chaim and the Machzikei Talmud Torah were organized in this Synagogue years ago so, too, the Yeshiva of the great *Gaon* Rabbi Isaac Elchanan, may his memory be a blessing, is being organized now. The purpose of the Yeshiva is [to enroll] children who can study a page of Talmud with Tosafot. A daily "shiur" will be taught by a Rosh Yeshiva [teacher of advanced Talmudic subjects] and a teacher will give instructions in the language of the land. The founder of the Yeshiva is Rabbi Yehuda David Bernstein, the founder of Yeshiva Etz Chaim.

> By direction of the President
> David Abramowitz, Secretary

[1] *Jüdische Gazetten*, January 15, 1897.

APPENDIX V: FINANCIAL REPORT OF THE RABBI ISAAC ELCHANAN THEOLOGICAL SEMINARY[1]

For the period

July 2, 1901   to   August 19, 1902

Income

Surplus from last year	193.74
Dues from members	950.50
Dues from Ladies Branch	275.00
From Collection Boxes	3196.50
Donations from Congregations	233.50
Gifts from individuals	120.00
From collections on eve of Yom Kippur	116.70
Rabbi Litwin's collections in the "countries"	1140.00
Rabbi Shapiro's collections in the "west"	236.50
	$6452.44[2]

Expenses

To collectors Einhorn and Shapiro	616.00
Seforim, English books, etc.	60.00
Secretary's salary	120.00
Advertisements	115.50
Printing and Postage	69.30
Roshei Ha-Yeshiva salaries (faculty of religious department)	523.00
"Teachers" salaries (faculty of secular department)	240.00
Instruction in English language	100.00
Food, clothing and lodging for students	4398.21
	$6242.01

Total	Income	6452.44[2]
	Expenses	6242.01
	Surplus	210.43

[1] *Jüdische Welt,* August 24, 1902.
[2] This is an incorrect figure; the income totaled $6462.44.

247

Committee
 Abraham Leib Dubowsky
 Samuel Isaac Andron
 Eliezer Zev Eppner
 Baruch Pinchas Liberman, Treasurer
 David Abramowitz, Secretary

𝔓𝔯𝔬𝔤𝔯𝔞𝔪 𝔬𝔣 𝔈𝔵𝔢𝔯𝔠𝔦𝔰𝔢𝔰

on the occasion of the dedication of the

RABBINICAL COLLEGE

ESTABLISHED BY

the Yeshibath Etz Chaim and the Rabbi Isaac Elchanan Theological Seminary

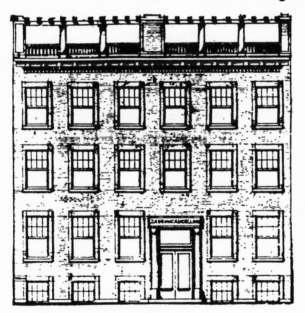

To take place at our new building,
Nine   and   Eleven   Montgomery   Street.

From Sunday, December 5th, 1915   *Kislev* 28th, 5676.
To Sunday, December 12th, 1915   *Teves* 5th. 5676.

THE COMBINED YESHIBOTH.

Some thirty years ago (1886) the Jewish community of this city became conscious of the crying need for a centre of Jewish learning for its growing youth. The demand for educational institutions in which Judaism will go hand in hand with secular learning was felt to be imperative, in order to avoid the clash which was sure to make its appearance in the life of the Jewish child if his education was to be completely secularized. The result was the establishment of "Yeshibath Etz Chayim"—the first school of its kind in this country.

Time has given ample proof of the necessity and great usefulness of this institution. During the last thirty years several thousand Jewish young men have received a thoroughly Jewish training and their general education in the "Yeshibath Etz Chayim" and have taken their position as loyal and devoted Jews and as useful members of the community in every walk of life.

Some ten years later (1895) the need for a truly orthodox rabbinical seminary became apparent. It was realized that in order to preserve traditional Judaism in this country and transmit it to our children as a living force, an institution of higher learning must be founded upon sanctioned Jewish models where the study of the holy Torah, the Talmud, the Codes, Jewish History and Literature shall be most comprehensive and thorough. The chosen few who dedicate their lives to the Torah needed encouragement and support.

The Rabbi Isaac Elchanan Seminary was thereupon founded. It has supplied the rabbinate and Jewish world at large with men of extensive learning and deep piety who have helped to perpetuate traditional Judaism in this country. Among its graduates are many rabbis of profound scholarship who occupy important pulpits and spread the knowledge of and love for the Torah in the various cities of the country.

To facilitate the accomplishment of their joint aims both institutions have recently affiliated and have elected as their "Rosh Yeshiboth" Rabbi B. Revel, A. M., Ph.D., a recognized master of Hebrew and secular learning. This holy work holds forth great promise for Judaism.

The newly erected building on 9-11 Montgomery Street, equipped with all modern appliances, will house the combined institutions.

OFFICERS

Mr. Jacob Hecht .... President
Mr. Harry Fischel .... Vice-President
Mr. Nathan Roggen .... Treasurer

BUILDING COMMITTEE

Mr. Harry Fischel, Chairman
Mr. Nathan Roggen   Mr. Jonas S. Scheff

COMMITTEE ON ARRANGEMENTS

Rabbi M. S. Margolies   Mr. Jonas S. Scheff
Rabbi H. S. Goldstein   Mr. Nathan Lamport
Dr. Theo Hurwitz   Mr. Aaron Kommel
Mr. Jacob Hecht   Mr. H. Robinson
Mr. Harry Fischel   Mr. Peter Wiernik
Mr. Nathan Roggen   Mr. Guedalia Bubelik

PROGRAM

Sunday Afternoon at Three O'clock.

Selections by the Hebrew Orphan Asylum Band.

OPENING PRAYER—Rabbi M. S. Margolies.

GREETING—Mr. Jacob Hecht, President.

PRESENTATION OF THE KEY—Mr. Harry Fischel, Chairman of the Building Committee.

ADDRESS—Rev. Dr. Philip Klein.

ADDRESS—Hon. Geo. McAneny, President of the Board of Aldermen, City of New York.

ADDRESS—Hon. Isadore Montefiore Levy.

ADDRESS—Rabbi Wolf Margolies.

ADDRESS—Rabbi Solomon E. Jaffe.

ADDRESS—Rabbi Herbert S. Goldstein.

ADDRESS—Rev. Harris Masliansky.

BENEDICTION—Dr. H. Pereira Mendes.

Kindling of the Chanukah Lights by Cantor Ruttman.

Sunday Evening at Seven O'clock.
Mr. Nathan Lamport, Chairman.

ADDRESSES by Rabbi A. Alperstein, Rev. Dr. Bernard Drachman, Rabbi Meyer Berlin, Hon. Otto A. Rosalsky, Rabbi J. Kanowitz.

Monday Evening, December 6th, at Seven O'clock.
Mr. Guedalia Bubelik, Chairman.

ADDRESSES by Rabbi Wine, Rabbi B. L. Levinthal, Rev. Dr. Moses Hyamson, Rabbi I. Rosenberg, Rabbi I. Siegel.

Tuesday Evening, December 7th, at Seven O'clock.
Mr. E. Kaplan, Chairman.

ADDRESSES by Rabbi Isakson, Rabbi M. Rabinowitz, Dr. S. Th. Hurwitz, Rabbi J. Levenberg, Rev. Philip Jaches.

Wednesday Evening, December 8th, at Seven O'clock.
Siyyum Hatorah סיום החורה
Mr. Hyman Dolinsky, Chairman.

ADDRESSES by Rabbi Finkelstein, Rabbi N. Hurwitz, Hon. N. Taylor Phillips, Rabbi Inselbuch, Rev. Orliansky.

Thursday Evening, December 9th, at Seven O'clock.
Mr. H. Robinson, Chairman.

ADDRESSES by Rabbi M. Guth, Rabbi Gusik, Rev. Dr. D. de Sola Pool, Rabbi Peikus, Rabbi Eskolsky.

Saturday Evening, December 11th, at Eight O'clock.

Rabbi M. Peikus, Chairman.

ADDRESSES by Rabbi Frankel, Albert Lucas, Dr. S. Friedman, Rabbi Swirnosky, Rabbi Kanarik, Dr. Goldberg.

Sunday, December 12th, 1915, 3 p. m.

INDUCTION of Rabbi B. Revel, A.M., Ph.D., as Rosh ha Yeshibot— Chairman, Rabbi M. S. Margolies.

ADDRESSES by Rev. Dr. Ph. Klein, Rabbi S. A. Jaffe, Rabbi B. L. Levinthal, Philadelphia; Rev. Dr. S. Schaffer, Baltimore; Rabbi M. S. Sivitz, Pittsburgh; Rabbi A. A. Alperstein; Rabbi I. Rosenberg, Paterson; Rabbi I. Siegel, Bayonne; Rabbi J. Levenberg, Jersey City; Rabbi Mayer Berlin.

ALUMNI OF THE YESHIVA—Rabbis Gutterman, Glick, Davidson, Fleischer, Swirin, Kaplan, Kapner, Romanov, Rosenberg, Yerachmelewitz, Pearl, Yarmis; Dr. Rosenberg, Dr. Robinson.

STUDENTS OF THE YESHIVA—Rabbis Esrog, Burock, Kaplan, Rogen, Yalow.

FACULTY

BERNARD REVEL, M. A. (New York University), Ph. D. (Dropsie), President of the Faculty and Instructor in Talmud and Codes.

H. PEREIRA MENDES, M. D. (New York University), D. D. (Jewish Theological Seminary), Homiletics.

BERNARD DRACHMAN, Ph. D. (Heidelberg), Pedagogy.

NAHUM SLOUSCH, Litt. D. (Sorbonne), Mediaeval Jewish History.

SOLOMON T. H. HURWITZ, M. A., Ph. D. (Columbia), Hebrew and Aramaic Philology.

MOSES SEIDEL, Ph. D. (Berne), Bible and Librarian.

Rabbi B. L. LEVINTHAL (Philadelphia), Non-Resident Lecturer in Midrash.

J. D. EISENSTEIN, Lecturer in Midrash.

Rabbi BENJAMIN ARANOWITZ
Rabbi JOSEPH LEVINE } Talmud and Codes.
Rabbi SAMUEL GERSTENFELD

HIGH SCHOOL STAFF

SOLOMON T. H. HURWITZ, M. A., Ph. D. (Columbia), Principal.

GEORGES BACARAT, Ph. D. (Leipzig; Toulouse), Classical and Modern Languages.

DAVID SUSSMAN STERN, M. A. (Columbia), Mathematics.

ISAAC ROSENGARTEN, B. A. (C.C.N.Y.), History.

MAX LIEBERMAN, B. S. (C.C.N.Y.), Public Speaking.

SHELLY R. SAFIR, M. A., Ph. D. (Columbia), Biology.

S. ELIHU POSIN, Ph. C., Phar. D. (Columbia), Chemistry.

REUBEN STEINBACH, Ph. D. (Johns Hopkins), English.

MAXWELL S. HELLER, M. A., LL. B. (New York University), Drawing.

MAX WINKLER, M. A. (New York University), German.

MEDICAL ADVISER

E. DAVID FRIEDMAN, M. D. (Bellevue).

OFFICERS

Chairman, Executive Committee .... Jacob Hecht
Vice-Chairman .... Harry Fischel
Treasurers .... J. S. Scheff, Nathan Roggen
Secretaries .... Lesser Lipnik, Rabbi Saul Silber

RABBINICAL COLLEGE COMMITTEE OF THE UNION OF ORTHODOX RABBIS OF AMERICA AND CANADA

Rabbi M. S. Margolies .... New York
Rabbi S. E. Jaffee .... New York
Rabbi B. L. Levinthal .... Philadelphia
Rabbi I. Rosenberg .... Jersey City
Rabbi E. Silver .... Harrisburg
Rabbi E. Preil .... Trenton

COMMITTEES

Finance

| S. R. Travis | J. S. Scheff | L. Kamaiky |
| J. Robinson | Charles Garfiel | J. D. Cohen |

Property

| H. Fischel | Nathan Roggen | N. Lamport |

Library

| J. Altshul | H. Masliansky | E. Lewin-Epstein |
| | S. Wilner | Dr. S. Friedman |

ORGANIZATION

The Rabbinical College of America is an institution of higher learning devoted to the comprehensive study of Judaism and to the training of rabbis and teachers. It was organized in September 1915, and includes:

(a) The Etz Chaim Talmudical Academy incorporated in the State of New York, September 15, 1886, "to foster and encourage the study of the Sacred Scriptures, the Talmud, the Hebrew Language and Literature, and to afford an elementary school education for Jewish boys."

(b) The Rabbi Isaac Elchanan Theological Seminary, incorporated in the State of New York, February 11, 1897, "to promote the study of the Talmud and to educate and prepare students of the Hebrew faith for the Hebrew Orthodox ministry."

BUILDING

A three-story, modern fire-proof building in the heart of the Jewish section of the City of New York, 9-11 Montgomery St., houses the Rabbinical College of America. The building is divided into:

Ground floor which contains business offices, supply and reading rooms, and laboratory for the high school department.

First floor which contains the offices of the President of the Faculty, a teachers' room and a synagogue.

Second and third floors which contain the study rooms of the College.

LIBRARY

The College possesses a working library of about five thousand volumes of Biblical and Rabbinical literature. The original collection was about twenty-five hundred volumes of Rabbinics brought together by the late Rabbi Gerson Ravinsohn of Cleveland. Since then the library was augmented by the purchase of the collection of books on Hebrew philology of the late Mr. Agib Ricketts of Wilkes Barre, Pa., of the library of the late E. Hausdorf of Baltimore, Md., and by several bequests and exchanges with other libraries. Sectional libraries for the use of the instructors pertaining to the subjects they are engaged in teaching are being assembled. The library possesses also a small collection of manuscripts.

COURSE OF STUDY OF THE ETZ CHAIM
TALMUDICAL ACADEMY

The Etz Chaim Talmudical Academy is the preparatory department of the Rabbinical College. Any Jewish boy of good character, who has a good knowledge of the Pentateuch and the Rashi Commentary and a general knowledge of the other books of the Bible and has completed the primary grades of the Public School, having been prepared to begin the study of the Talmud, is eligible for admission to the Etz Chaim Talmudical Academy.

The course of study includes:
   (a) Bible and Commentaries
   (b) Hebrew Grammar
   (c) Jewish History and Literature
   (d) Talmud

The requirements for graduation are:
   (a) Translation at sight of any part of the Bible.
   (b) Hebrew Grammar (regular and irregular verb and noun forms).
   (c) Jewish History (until the destruction of the Second Temple).
   (d) The ability, upon preparation, to expound a סוגיא of the Talmud and Tosafoth.
   (f) Completion of the 8B work of the Public School.

The grammar school department of the Etz Chaim Talmudical Academy follows the curriculum of studies prescribed by the Board of Education of the City of New York under whose supervision the school is conducted. The 8B work of the public school must be completed to entitle the student to a certificate of graduation, which admits him to any of the high schools of the city. Graduates of the Academy enter the junior department of the Rabbinical College.

HIGH SCHOOL DEPARTMENT OF THE
RABBINICAL COLLEGE

The Rabbinical College conducts a high school department in which the regular high school studies as prescribed by the Board of Education of the City of New York for the city high schools are taught. A laboratory has been instituted to carry on the necessary experimental work in biology, physics, and chemistry.

SCOPE OF STUDIES IN THE RABBINICAL COLLEGE

Junior Department: The course of study in the junior department includes the entire Bible with early and later Hebrew Commentaries, advanced Hebrew and Aramaic Grammar, Jewish History to the expulsion from Spain, Jewish Literature of the Middle Ages, Shulchan Aruch Orach Chaim (first part), and an intensive study of six tractates of the Babylonian Talmud with its important commentaries.

Senior Department: The course of study in the senior department includes the reading of the important Jewish mediaeval and modern commentaries on the Bible, the Targumim, and Halachic Midrashim studied in connection with the Bible. The various versions are consulted. The course in Talmud and Codes comprises the study of both Babylonian and Palestinian Talmuds, Codes, early and later commentaries, annotators, and the responsa literature. The course in Jewish history includes the study of historical texts and documents which are discussed in Seminar. Particular stress is laid on the historical material contained in Talmudic and Midrashic literature. The vast responsa literature is utilized in the study of Jewish history. Research work along these lines is encouraged and provision is made for such work. The course in Jewish literature includes the reading of Jewish philosophical and ethical works. In the course in Midrash and Homiletics the students become acquainted with the most important Midrashic and Homiletic works.

ORDINATION

All candidates for ordination התרת הוראה must be resident students of the College for at least two years. The התרת הוראה is conferred by the College upon its graduates after a written and oral examination proving their intimate knowledge of the Talmud and Codes and their ability to decide religious questions. During the senior year the students are given opportunity to observe and assist in the decisions of religious questions pertaining to א״וח יו״ד ואה״עז. Only those whose religious and moral life is blameless can be candidates for ordination. Mere faithful attendance at the College and pursuit of its courses of study does not entitle anyone to התרת הוראה.

ACADEMIC YEAR

There are two semesters during the academic year, the Fall and Winter term and the Spring and Summer term. The first begins the first Sunday after Simchath Torah and extends until the last Thursday before Pesach. The second begins the first Sunday after Pesach and extends until the last Thursday before Rosh Hashonah. The instruction in the grammar and high school department conforms to the division of the terms established by the Department of Education of the State of New York.

STIPENDS

The Rabbinical College offers stipends to deserving students upon their admission as regular students of the College. The stipends are awarded for a period of one year and amount to three hundred dollars. Students who are awarded stipends shall not accept other employment except by permission of the President of the Faculty.

PRIZES

The following prizes are offered for the year 5678.

1. A prize of fifty dollars for an essay on the following subject:

   An exposition of the Principles of טעם כעיקר in both Talmuds and Codes.

2. A prize of fifty dollars for an essay by a student of the senior class on the subject of מלאכה שאינה צריכה לגופה דבר שאינו מתכון in both Talmuds, the ראשונים and codes.

3. A prize of fifty dollars for an essay on the same subject by a student of the junior class.

4. A Homiletic Prize of twenty-five dollars.

For information concerning admission, courses and stipends, apply in writing to the President of the Faculty, Rabbi Dr. B. Revel, 9-11 Montgomery St., New York City.

EVENTS OF THE YEAR 5677

During the year 5677, the following events of importance in the history of the Rabbinical College took place.

Three of the graduates of the Rabbinical College were appointed to important positions. Rabbi W. Roggen became rabbi of the Jewish community of New London, Conn., Rabbi D. Esrig received a call from the community of Colchester, Conn., and Rabbi Aaron Burack was appointed rabbi of Congregation Ohel Moshe of Brooklyn, N. Y.

On Thursday, Adar 7th (March 1st), a dinner was tendered to Rabbi

Dr. Bernard Revel, President of the Faculty of the Rabbinical College, by the orthodox Jewish community of New York in recognition of the work accomplished by the Rabbinical College during its first year of organization. On this occasion Mr. Samuel R. Travis of New York and Tulsa, Okla., pledged an annual contribution of $5000.

On April 1st, 1917, Dr. N. Slousch of the Sorbonne, Paris, was named instructor in Mediaeval Jewish History at the Rabbinical College. On August 15th, Rev. Dr. H. Pereira Mendes was appointed to the chair of Homiletics at the Rabbinical College. On October 1st, 1917, Rev. Dr. Bernard Drachman became the head of the Department of Pedagogy at the College. On October 15th, Dr. Moses Seidel of Baltimore, Md., was appointed Instructor of the Bible.

DEPARTMENT OF THE BIBLE AND HEBREW PHILOLOGY COURSES OF STUDY FOR THE YEAR 5678

Psalms: A study of the book with the leading mediaeval and modern Jewish commentaries. The versions will be consulted. Both Terms. Second Junior Division.   Dr. Seidel.

Joshua and Judges: A study of both books with leading Jewish commentaries. In connection with this course the geography of ancient Palestine will be studied. First Term. First Junior Division.
Dr. Seidel.

Samuel and Kings: A study of these books with leading Jewish commentaries. Second Term. First Junior Division.
Dr. Seidel.

Hebrew Grammar: Advanced Lecture Course. A history of the development of Hebrew Grammar with readings in Hebrew grammatical literature and a comparative study of the phonology, morphology and syntax of the Hebrew language (a knowledge of one other Semitic Language is required). Both Terms. Senior.
Dr. Hurwitz.

Biblical Aramaic: A study of the grammar with readings of the Aramaic portions of Daniel and Ezra. First Term. Second Junior Division.
Dr. Hurwitz.

Babylonian and Palestinian Judeo-Aramaic: A study of the grammar of the Babylonian Talmud and Targumim with readings. Second Term. Second Junior Division.   Dr. Hurwitz.

The language of instruction in the department of the Bible and Jewish History and Literature is Hebrew.

DEPARTMENT OF TALMUD AND CODES

Babylonian Talmud: An intensive study of the tractates Kethuboth and Gittin with Tosafoth, Rosh, Ran and other early commentaries and the Decisors.

Orach Chaim §§1-135, will be read. *Tur Shulhan Arukh.* Both Terms. Second Junior Division.

Babylonian Talmud: The tractates Sabbath, Erubin and the minor tractates of Seder Moed in conjunction with the corresponding parts of Orach Chaim. Both Terms. Senior.

Yoreh Deah §§1-121 טור ושלחן ערוך together with the study of **Hullin** and commentaries.

Rabbis B. Revel, B. Aranowitz, J. Levine and S. Gerstenfeld conduct the different courses.

In the elementary grades, the tractates Baba Kamma, Baba Metzia and Gittin are studied.

DEPARTMENT OF JEWISH HISTORY AND LITERATURE

History of the Orient at the time of the Redaction of the Babylonian Talmud. Both Terms. Senior.

Dr. Slousch.

The Gaonate and Exilarchate. Both Terms. Senior.

Dr. Slousch.

The Jews in the Diaspora in the Seventh Century—Romans and Byzantine Realms. Both Terms. Junior.

Dr. Slousch.

Midrash: The Halachic and Aggadic Midrashim on the Pentateuch will be read and interpreted. Both Terms. Second Junior Division.

Mr. J. D. Eisenstein.

Hebrew Poetry: Theory of the prosody of Mediaeval Hebrew poetry sacred and secular, with selections from the works of the most representative writers. Both Terms. Second Junior Division.

Dr. Slousch.

Jewish Ethics: The Emunoth we-Deoth of Rabbi Saadya Gaon will be studied in connection with different problems in Jewish philosophy and ethics. Both Terms. Senior.

Dr. Revel.

Homiletics, Junior and Senior Divisions: The composition and delivery of sermons. History, theory and practice. In the synagogue of the College building and New York synagogues, pulpit opportunities are afforded to the students. Both Terms.

Dr. Mendes.

Jewish Pedagogics: Theory and practice, methods of teaching, school management and class discipline. Both Terms.

Dr. Drachman.

POSITIONS HELD BY ALUMNI

Rabbi Aaron Burack, Ohel Moshe Synagogue, Brooklyn, N. Y.
Rabbi N. Ebin, United Hebrew Congregations, Buffalo, N. Y.
Rabbi D. Esrig, United Congregations, Colchester, Conn.
Rabbi B. Fleisher, Beth Hamedrash Hagodol, Brooklyn, N. Y.
Rabbi S. Glick, General Sec'y Union of Orthodox Rabbis of America.
Rabbi H. Guterman, Hebrew Community, Scranton, Pa.
Rabbi M. A. Kaplan, Nachlas Zvi, New York.
Rabbi A. Levy, Brooklyn, N. Y.
Rabbi J. Miller, Kingston, N. Y.
Rabbi A. N. Mosessohn, Principal Rabbi Chaim Berlin School, Brooklyn.
Rabbi B. Pearl, Uptown Talmud Torah, New York City.
Rabbi M. Romanoff, Baltimore, Md.
Rabbi W. Roggin, New London, Conn.
Rabbi Abraham Shapiro, Canton, Ohio.
Rabbi Baruch Shapiro, Seattle, Wash.
Rabbi D. Swirin, United Hebrew Congregation, Wilmington, Del.
Rabbi N. Toxin, United Congregations, Omaha, Neb.

STUDENTS OF THE RABBINICAL COLLEGE OF AMERICA

Altman, Solomon, Brooklyn, N. Y., R. C. H. S.[1]
Baxt, Jacob, New York City.

[1] R. C. H. S.—Rabbinical College High School.

Burg, Joseph, New York City, R. C. H. S.

Cohen, Jeremiah, New York City, R. C. H. S.

Cohen, Saul Jehudah, Toronto, Canada, A. B. (Brandon College, Man.)

Cooper, Israel Leon, Baltimore, Md., Undergraduate, Johns Hopkins.

Damesek, Jehudah, New York City, Rabbinical Diploma.

Feinerman, Louis, New York City.

Forman, Charles, Brooklyn, N. Y., Student C. C. N. Y.

Friedman, Solomon, Cleveland, Ohio, L. L. B. (Baldwin Wallace) Graduate Student, Columbia.

Friend, Israel D., Brooklyn, N. Y., R. C. H. S.

Fuhrman, Moses, Brooklyn, N. Y.

Gimprich, David, New York City.

Gribetz, Louis J., New York City, L. L. B. (St. Lawrence University).

Golner, Moses L., Boston, Mass., Grad., Boston Eng. High School.

Goodman, Isadore, New York City, Student, New York University.

Helfand, Judah, New York City.

Hirschprung, Max, New York City.

Jacobson, Hyman, Baltimore, Md., Undergraduate University of Md.

Karp, Hirsch, New York City.

Kessler, M., Brooklyn, N. Y., R. C. H. S.

Kolatch, Isadore, New York City, R. C. H. S.

Krasner, Joseph, New York City.

Kravitz, Manachem, New York City.

Krixstein, Joseph, Webster, Mass., R. C. H. S.

Leipziger, Nathan, New York City.

Lerner, Aliakum Ch., New York City, R. C. H. S.

Lesser, Joseph, Brooklyn, N. Y., R. C. H S.

Levy, Abraham, New York City, Rabbinical Diploma.

Levy, Simon, New York City.

Lifshitz, Mayer, Brooklyn, N. Y., R. C. H. S.

Mintz, Max, Scranton, Pa., Grad. Scranton Tech, H. S.

Perlberg, Abraham, New York City.

Rakowsky, Joseph, New York City.

Raskas, Joseph R., St. Louis, Mo., Washington University (Undergr.)

Relbag, Leib, New York City.

Robin, Morris J., Kansas City, Mo., R. C. H. S.

Rosen, Hyman, Brooklyn, N. Y., R. C. H. S.

Sachs, Eiser, New York City, Rabbinical Diploma.

Schwartz, Joseph J., Baltimore, Md., Grad. Baltimore City College.

Seltzer, Joseph, New York City.
Shain, Joseph, Boston, Mass., Grad. Boston Latin School.
Shapiro, Moses, New York City.
Siegel, Judah, Chicago, Ill., Student, New York University.
Solomon, Hyman, Montreal, Canada, Grad. High School of Montreal.
Steinbach, Reuben, Baltimore, Md., Ph. D. (Johns Hopkins)
Stern, David Sussman, New York City, M. A. (Columbia University).
Stern, Lipman, New York City, R. C. H. S.
Tannenbaum, David, Denver, Colorado, B. A. (Denver University).
Wolk, Samuel, New York City, R. C. H. S.

APPENDIX VIII: RECIPIENTS OF HONORARY DEGREES
JUNE 1932–JUNE 1968

NAME & TITLE	DEGREE	DATE
Shmuel Yosef Agnon Israeli author and Nobel Laureate	DH Litt	1967a
Dr. A. Adrian Albert Dean, Division of the Physical Sciences, and E. H. Moore Distinguished Service Professor of Mathematics, University of Chicago	Sc D	1968
Dr. James E. Allen Commissioner of Education, State of New York	LLD	1957
George Alpert President, New York–New Haven Railroad	LHD	1959a
Walter H. Annenberg Editor and Publisher, The Philadelphia Inquirer; Overseer, Albert Einstein College of Medicine, Yeshiva University	LHD	1963a
*Rabbi Aaron Mordecai Ashinsky Distinguished rabbi, Pittsburgh, Pennsylvania	DD	1942
*Honorable Simcha Assaf Justice, Supreme Court of Israel; Professor of Gaonic Literature, Hebrew University, Jerusalem	LLD	1951
Rabbi Abraham Noah AvRutick Rabbi, Congregation Agudas Achim, Hartford, Connecticut	DD	1966
His Excellency Nathan Barnes Permanent Representative of Liberia to the United Nations	LHD	1965
*Bernard M. Baruch Adviser to Presidents	LLD	1947

NAME & TITLE	DEGREE	DATE
Charles C. Bassine Chairman of the Board and Chief Executive Officer, Spartans-Korvette, Inc.; Chairman, Board of Overseers, Albert Einstein College of Medicine, Yeshiva University	LHD	1967a
Arthur B. Belfer Chairman of the Board, Belco Petroleum Corp.; Trustee, Yeshiva University	LHD	1968
Rabbi Samuel Berliant Rabbi, Congregation Tifereth Israel, Jackson Heights, New York	DD	1962
Honorable Bernard Botein Presiding Justice, Appellate Division, New York State Supreme Court	LLD	1965
Very Reverend Israel Brodie Chief Rabbi, British Commonwealth	DD	1956
Dr. Detlev W. Bronk President, Rockefeller University	LHD	1965a
Dr. Ralph J. Bunche Under Secretary for Special Political Affairs, United Nations	LHD	1964
Dr. Mary I. Bunting Member, U.S. Atomic Energy Commission; President, Radcliffe College (on leave)	LHD	1965
*Rabbi Aaron D. Burack Professor of Talmud, Yeshiva University	DD	1954
*Honorable Benjamin N. Cardozo Associate Justice, United States Supreme Court	LHD	1935
*Dr. Harry J. Carman Dean Emeritus, Columbia College	LLD	1952
Dr. Ernst B. Chain Nobel Laureate; Head, International Center of Chemical Microbiology, Istituto Superiore di Sanita, Rome	LHD	1961a

NAME & TITLE	DEGREE	DATE
Irwin S. Chanin President, Chanin Management, Inc.; Overseer, Albert Einstein College of Medicine, Yeshiva University	LHD	1964a
*Dr. Pinkhos Churgin President, Bar-Ilan University, Israel	LHD	1955a
Dr. Kenneth Bancroft Clark Professor of Psychology, City College of New York; President, Metropolitan Applied Research Center	LHD	1968
Dr. Joseph G. Cohen Former Dean of Teacher Education, City Colleges of New York	LHD	1961
Honorable Wilbur Joseph Cohen Under Secretary, U.S. Department of Health, Education, and Welfare	LHD	1967a
Dr. James B. Conant President, Harvard University	LLD	1949
Dr. Finla G. Crawford Vice Chancellor Emeritus, Syracuse University	LHD	1962
Dr. Lee Joseph Cronbach Professor of Education and Psychology, Stanford University	LHD	1966a
*Honorable Wilbur Lucius Cross Governor, State of Connecticut	LLD	1943
Dr. Leo M. Davidoff Director of Neurosurgery, Beth Israel Hospital, New York	LHD	1958a
Dr. Lawrence G. Derthick U.S. Commissioner of Education	LHD	1959
Honorable Thomas E. Dewey Governor, State of New York	LLD	1951a
Dr. Rene Dubos Member and Professor, Rockefeller Institute	LHD	1961a

NAME & TITLE	DEGREE	DATE
Freeman John Dyson Professor of Physics, Institute for Advanced Study, Princeton, New Jersey	LHD	1966
His Excellency Abba S. Eban Ambassador from Israel to the United States	LHD	1957
*Professor Albert Einstein Institute for Advanced Study, Princeton, New Jersey	LHD	1934
Dr. Martha Eliot Chief, Children's Bureau, Federal Security Agency	LHD	1952a
Max J. Etra Attorney and communal leader; Chairman, Board of Trustees, Yeshiva University	LLD	1958
His Excellency Levi Eshkol Prime Minister of Israel	LHD	1964
Dr. Alvin C. Eurich President, State University of New York	LHD	1954
Dr. Sidney Farber Professor of Pathology, Harvard Medical School	Sc D	1966a
Rabbi Oscar Z. Fasman President, Hebrew Theological College, Chicago, Illinois	DD	1955
Dr. Benjamin Fine Education Editor, The New York Times	LHD	1949
*Dr. John Huston Finley Editor, The New York Times	LHD	1933
Dr. Joshua Aaron Fishman Distinguished University Research Professor of Social Sciences, Ferkauf Graduate School of Humanities and Social Sciences, Yeshiva University	Pd D	1968
Dr. Arthur S. Flemming Secretary of Health, Education, and Welfare	LHD	1960

NAME & TITLE	DEGREE	DATE
George Frankel President, Frankel Fund, Inc.; Overseer, Albert Einstein College of Medicine, Yeshiva University	LHD	1965a
Max L. Friedman Secretary, Board of Overseers, Albert Einstein College of Medicine, Yeshiva University	LHD	1964a
Charles Frost Chairman, Board of Directors, Bright Star Industries, National Pneumatic Co.	LHD	1959a
Honorable Stanley H. Fuld Judge, Court of Appeals, State of New York	LLD	1962
Sol Furst Chairman of the Board, First Northeast Securities Co.; Trustee, Yeshiva University	LHD	1967
Honorable John W. Gardner Secretary of Health, Education, and Welfare	LLD	1967
Louis J. Glickman Chairman of the Board and President, Glickman Corp.; Trustee and Chairman, Development Committee, Yeshiva University	LHD	1962
Honorable Arthur J. Goldberg Associate Justice, Supreme Court of the United States	LLD	1963
Samuel H. Golding Chairman of the Board, Sterling National Bank and Trust Co.; Overseer, Albert Einstein College of Medicine, Yeshiva University	LHD	1965a
Dr. Jacob E. Goldman Associate Director, Science Laboratories, Ford Motor Co., Dearborn, Michigan	LLD	1961
Rabbi Herbert S. Goldstein Professor of Homiletics, Yeshiva University; Rabbi, West Side Institutional Synagogue, New York	DD	1941

NAME & TITLE	DEGREE	DATE
Honorable Nathaniel L. Goldstein Attorney General, State of New York	LLD	1952a
Benjamin Gottesman President, Yeshiva Endowment Foundation; Trustee, Yeshiva University	LHD	1959
*Dr. Frank Pierrepont Graves Commissioner of Education, State of New York	LHD	1940
*Rabbi Henry Guterman Chief Rabbi, Scranton, Pennsylvania	DD	1958
*Dr. Jacques S. Hadamard Professor, College de France, Paris	LHD	1944
*Honorable Learned Hand Judge, United States Court of Appeals, Second Circuit	LLD	1953
His Excellency Avraham Harman Ambassador from Israel to the United States	LHD	1962
Dr. Gaylord P. Harnwell President, University of Pennsylvania	LHD	1966
Dr. Earl G. Harrison Dean, University of Pennsylvania Law School	LHD	1947
Dr. Jacob I. Hartstein Dean, School of Education, Long Island University	LHD	1962
Professor Louis Henkin Professor of Law and of International Relations and Diplomacy, Columbia University	LHD	1963
His Excellency Yaakov D. Herzog Ambassador from Israel to Canada	LHD	1963
Dr. Maurice B. Hexter Executive Vice President, Federation of Jewish Philanthropies of New York	LHD	1961
*Rabbi Jacob Hoffman Rabbi, Congregation Ohab Zedek, New York	DD	1951

NAME & TITLE	DEGREE	DATE
Dr. Donald F. Hornig Special Assistant to President Johnson for Science and Technology	LHD	1965a
Honorable Hubert H. Humphrey Vice President of the United States	LLD	1965a
Honorable Vincent R. Impellitteri Mayor, City of New York	LHD	1953
Dr. Moses Legis Isaacs Professor of Chemistry, Yeshiva University	Sc D	1967
*Honorable Irving M. Ives United States Senator from New York	LLD	1956
Honorable Jacob K. Javits Attorney General, State of New York	LLD	1955
Dr. Alvin Johnson President Emeritus, New School for Social Research	LHD	1950
Honorable Lyndon B. Johnson Vice President of the United States	LHD	1961a
Rabbi Leo Jung Professor of Ethics, Yeshiva University; Rabbi, Jewish Center, New York	DD	1949
Honorable Harry E. Kalodner Judge, United States Court of Appeals, Third Circuit	LHD	1950
Dr. Joseph Kaplan Professor of Physics, University of California; United States Chairman, International Geophysical Year	LHD	1958
Rabbi Menachem M. Kasher Editor, the Talmudic Midrashic Encyclopedia "Torah Shelemah"	DD	1946
Honorable Kenneth B. Keating United States Senator from New York	LHD	1962
Dr. Barnaby C. Keeney President, Brown University	LLD	1961

NAME & TITLE	DEGREE	DATE
Honorable Robert Francis Kennedy United States Senator from New York	LLD	1967a
Francis Keppel U.S. Commissioner of Education	LHD	1965
Professor Cassius Jackson Keyser Adrian Professor Emeritus of Mathematics, Columbia University	LHD	1942
Rabbi Mordecai Kirshblum Head, Torah Education and Culture Department, Jewish Agency, American Section	DD	1965
Dr. Paul Klapper President, Queens College, New York	LHD	1938
Dr. Marcus D. Kogel Commissioner of Hospitals, City of New York	LHD	1952
Dr. Saul R. Korey Professor and Chairman, Department of Neurology, Albert Einstein College of Medicine, Yeshiva University	LHD	1963a
Dr. Arthur Kornberg Nobel Laureate; Chairman, Department of Biochemistry, Stanford University	LHD	1962a
Dr. Willis E. Lamb, Jr. Henry Ford II Professor of Physics, Yale University	LHD	1965
Rabbi Simon Langer Rabbi, Congregation Orach Chaim, New York	DD	1964
Roy E. Larsen President, Time Inc.	LLD	1957
William L. Laurence Science Editor, The New York Times	LHD	1957
Dr. Paul Felix Lazarsfeld Quetelet Professor of Social Science and Associate Director, Bureau of Applied Social Research, Columbia University	LHD	1966a

NAME & TITLE	DEGREE	DATE
Honorable Louis J. Lefkowitz Attorney General, State of New York	LLD	1967
Honorable Herbert H. Lehman Governor, State of New York	LHD	1933
Professor A. Leo Levin Professor of Law, University of Pennsylvania	LLD	1960
Dr. Samuel Albert Levine Clinical Professor of Medicine, Harvard Medical School	LHD	1959a
Rabbi Jacob Levinson Distinguished rabbi, Brooklyn, New York	DD	1949
Rabbi Bernhard L. Levinthal Member of the Praesidium, Union of Orthodox Rabbis of the United States and Canada; Rabbi, United Orthodox Congregation, Philadelphia, Pennsylvania	DD	1941
Abraham Levitt Philanthropist and builder	LHD	1959a
Honorable Arthur Levitt Comptroller, State of New York	LHD	1968
Honorable Samuel Levy President, Borough of Manhattan, City of New York; Chairman, Board of Trustees, Yeshiva University	LLD	1934
Rabbi Mendell Lewittes Rabbi, Young Israel Center, Montreal, Canada	DD	1963
Dr. Fritz A. Lipmann Nobel Laureate; Professor of Biochemistry, Rockefeller Institute	LHD	1964a
Rabbi Joseph H. Lookstein Professor of Sociology, Yeshiva University; Rabbi, Congregation Kehilath Jeshurun, New York	DD	1949a

NAME & TITLE	DEGREE	DATE
Joseph I. Lubin Partner, Eisner and Lubin; Overseer, Albert Einstein College of Medicine, Yeshiva University	LHD	1966
*Rabbi Yehuda Leib Maimon Minister of Religions, Israel	DD	1951a
Honorable Mike Mansfield Majority Leader, United States Senate	LLD	1966
*His Excellency Jan Masaryk Minister of Foreign Affairs and Vice Premier, Czechoslovakia	LLD	1942
Rabbi Morris Max Rabbi, Queens Jewish Center, Forest Hills, New York	DD	1966
Joseph M. Mazer Treasurer, Hudson Pulp and Paper Corp.; Trustee, Yeshiva University	LHD	1960
Honorable James G. McDonald Former United States Ambassador to Israel	LLD	1951
*Dr. Nelson Prentis Mead Professor of History, formerly Acting President, City College of New York; Professor of History, Yeshiva College (1928-1938)	LHD	1942a
Honorable Samuel Mellitz Judge, Superior Court of Connecticut; Trustee, Yeshiva University	LLD	1954
Feivel Meltzer Israeli author; Visiting Professor of Bible, Yeshiva University	DD	1952a
Jakob Michael Chairman of the Board and President, New England Industries, Inc.; Overseer, Albert Einstein College of Medicine; Trustee, Yeshiva University	LHD	1967

NAME & TITLE	DEGREE	DATE
Rabbi Israel Miller Rabbi, Kingsbridge Heights Jewish Center, Bronx, New York	DD	1967
Dr. J. Hillis Miller President, University of Florida	LHD	1949
Dr. Deane Montgomery Professor of Mathematics, Institute for Advanced Study, Princeton, New Jersey	LHD	1961
Rabbi Benjamin Morgenstern Rabbi, Congregation Sons of Israel, Brooklyn, New York	DD	1968
*Honorable Henry Morgenthau Former Secretary of the Treasury	LHD	1948
Dr. Harold Marston Morse Professor of Mathematics, Institute for Advanced Study, Princeton, New Jersey	LHD	1962
Rabbi Israel Mowshowitz Rabbi, Hillcrest Jewish Center, Jamaica, New York	LHD	1966a
Honorable Abraham J. Multer Member from New York, United States House of Representatives	LLD	1963
Dr. James Madison Nabrit, Jr. President, Howard University	LHD	1967
Dr. Carroll V. Newsom Associate Commissioner for Higher Education, State of New York	LHD	1955
Honorable Richard M. Nixon Vice President of the United States	LLD	1957a
*Dr. Mordecai Nurock Former Chief Rabbi of Latvia; member of the Latvian Parliament	DD	1946
Dr. Ewald B. Nyquist Deputy Commissioner of Education, State of New York	LHD	1960

NAME & TITLE	DEGREE	DATE
Dr. Severo Ochoa Nobel Laureate; Chairman, Department of Biochemistry, New York University School of Medicine	LHD	1965a
Albert Parker Senior Partner, Parker, Chapin, and Flattau, Attorneys; Vice Chairman, Board of Overseers, Albert Einstein College of Medicine, Yeshiva University	LLD	1964
*Dr. Enoch George Payne Dean, School of Education, New York University	LHD	1943
Dr. James Alfred Perkins President, Cornell University	LHD	1968
Dr. Harry Polachek Technical Director, United States Navy Applied Mathematics Laboratory, David Taylor Model Basin, Washington, D.C.	LHD	1964
*Rabbi Moses Aaron Poleyeff Professor of Talmud, Yeshiva University	DD	1959
Dr. Isidor I. Rabi Higgins Professor of Physics, Columbia University	LHD	1964
His Excellency Major General Yitzhak Rabin Ambassador from Israel to the United States	LLD	1968
Dr. Emanuel Rackman Rabbi, Congregation Shaaray Tefila, Far Rockaway, New York	DD	1961
Charles H. Revson Chairman of the Board, Revlon, Inc.; Overseer, Albert Einstein College of Medicine, Yeshiva University	LHD	1966a
Honorable Abraham A. Ribicoff Governor, State of Connecticut	LHD	1955a
Nelson A. Rockefeller President, Rockefeller Brothers Fund	LLD	1958

NAME & TITLE	DEGREE	DATE
Dr. Julius M. Rogoff Professor Emeritus of Endocrinology, University of Pittsburgh Medical School	LHD	1952a
Mrs. Franklin D. Roosevelt Chairman, Committee on Human Rights, United Nations Economic and Social Council	LHD	1952
Honorable Otto A. Rosalsky Judge, Court of General Sessions, New York; Trustee, Yeshiva University	LLD	1934
Gustave G. Rosenberg Chairman, Board of Higher Education, City of New York	LHD	1960
Rabbi Leonard Rosenfeld Executive Vice President, Jewish Education Committee of New York	DH Litt	1968
Rabbi Isaac Rubinstein Chief Rabbi of Vilna	DD	1944
Dr. Albert B. Sabin Distinguished Service Professor, University of Cincinnati	Sc D	1966a
Dr. Jonas E. Salk Commonwealth Professor of Experimental Medicine and Director, Virus Research Laboratory, University of Pittsburgh Medical School	LHD	1959
Dr. Shelley Ray Saphire Director, Yeshiva University High Schools	LHD	1963
Samuel Leib Sar Dean of Men and Professor of Bible, Yeshiva University	DD	1953
Dr. Bela Schick Former head of the Department of Pediatrics, Mount Sinai Hospital, New York	LHD	1952a
David Schwartz Chairman of the Board, Jonathan Logan, Inc.; Overseer, Albert Einstein College of Medicine, Yeshiva University	LHD	1965a

NAME & TITLE	DEGREE	DATE
Dr. Joseph J. Schwartz European Director, American Jewish Joint Distribution Committee	LHD	1949
Dr. James A. Shannon Director, National Institutes of Health	LHD	1962a
Chaim Moshe Shapiro Former Minister of Religious Affairs and Social Welfare, Israel	DD	1959
R. Sargent Shriver Director, U.S. Peace Corps	LHD	1964a
Charles H. Silver President, Board of Education, City of New York; Trustee, Yeshiva University	LHD	1955a
Rabbi David L. Silver Rabbi, Congregation Kesher Israel, Harrisburg, Pennsylvania	DD	1960
Honorable Edward S. Silver Surrogate, Kings County	LLD	1966
Dr. Abe Silverstein Director of Space Flight Programs, National Aeronautics and Space Administration	LHD	1960
*Dr. David Eugene Smith Professor Emeritus of Mathematics, Columbia University	LHD	1936
Max Stern President, Hartz Mountain Products Corp.; Vice Chairman, Board of Trustees, Yeshiva University; Founder, Stern College for Women	LHD	1955
*Honorable Adlai E. Stevenson Former Governor of Illinois	LLD	1953a
Dr. George D. Stoddard Commissioner of Education, State of New York	LLD	1946
*Honorable Harlan Fiske Stone Chief Justice of the United States	LLD	1944a

NAME & TITLE	DEGREE	DATE
Dr. Charles Hard Townes Nobel Laureate; Institute Professor, Massachusetts Institute of Technology	Sc D	1967
Dr. Ralph Winfred Tyler Director, Center for Advanced Study in the Behavioral Sciences, Stanford, California	LHD	1966a
*Siegfried Ullmann Vice Chairman of the Board, Minerals and Chemicals, Philipp Corp.; Overseer, Albert Einstein College of Medicine, Yeshiva University	LHD	1963a
Honorable Robert F. Wagner Mayor, City of New York	LLD	1962
Dr. Selman A. Waksman Professor of Microbiology, Rutgers University	LLD	1948
Honorable Earl Warren Chief Justice of the United States	LLD	1961a
Jack D. Weiler Chairman, Board of Overseers, Albert Einstein College of Medicine, Yeshiva University	LHD	1962a
Dr. Abraham Weiss Professor of Rabbinics, Yeshiva University	DH.Litt	1967
Dr. Abraham White Associate Dean and Chairman, Department of Biochemistry, Albert Einstein College of Medicine, Yeshiva University	LHD	1959a
Dr. Eugene Paul Wigner Thomas D. Jones Professor of Mathematical Physics, Princeton University	LHD	1963
*Dr. Lewis A. Wilson Commissioner of Education, State of New York	LHD	1951
Honorable W. Willard Wirtz Secretary of Labor	LLD	1966a

NAME & TITLE	DEGREE	DATE
Professor Rachel Wischnitzer Professor of Fine Arts, Stern College for Women, Yeshiva University	LHD	1968
Dr. Harry Austryn Wolfson Nathan Littauer, Professor of Hebrew Literature and Philosophy, Harvard University	LHD	1950
Herman Wouk Author and Visiting Professor of English, Yeshiva University	LHD	1955
Dr. Solomon Zeitlin Horace Stern Professor of Rabbinic Law and Lore, Dropsie College	LHD	1965
Dr. Harry M. Zimmerman Director of the Laboratory and Chief Pathologist, Montefiore Hospital, New York	LHD	1957

NOTES

1. *An asterisk indicates the person is deceased.

2. The title given refers to the individual's affiliation at the time the honor was awarded.

3. Abbreviations: DD   —Doctor of Divinity
DH Litt—Doctor of Hebrew Letters
LHD   —Doctor of Humane Letters
LLD   —Doctor of Laws
Pd D   —Doctor of Pedagogy
Sc D   —Doctor of Science

4. The letter "a" following a date indicates the honor was awarded at a convocation other than commencement.

5. Summary of Honorary Degrees, June 1932–June 1968:

DD	29
DH Litt	3
LHD	110
LLD	42
Pd D	1
Sc D	5
Total	190

APPENDIX IX: DIVISIONS OF YESHIVA UNIVERSITY

Yeshiva College for Men
Stern College for Women
Erna Michael College of Hebraic Studies
Teachers Institute for Women
Rabbi Isaac Elchanan Theological Seminary
Bernard Revel Graduate School
Harry Fischel School for Higher Jewish Studies
James Striar School of General Jewish Studies
Albert Einstein College of Medicine
Sue Golding Graduate Division of Medical Sciences
Wurzweiler School of Social Work
Ferkauf Graduate School of Humanities and Social Sciences
Belfer Graduate School of Science

Bibliography

BIBLIOGRAPHY

Primary sources and personal interviews, to the extent that they are available, were used almost exclusively in creating an integrated narrative. The author has interviewed extensively the early instructors and students of Etz Chaim and RIETS now living. Contemporary Yiddish and Hebrew newspapers and periodicals, as well as autobiographical and biographical materials, were read exhaustively.

The difficulties encountered in the search for material were multiple. There are almost no primary sources available for the study. The absence of firsthand studies on Jewish education between 1885 and 1915 reflects the paucity of the facilities and the lack of a professional attitude toward Jewish education. Most disappointing of all, however, is the absence of minutes of the proceedings of the business meetings of the school. Such minutes had undoubtedly been kept since the very early days of Etz Chaim and RIETS but seem to have been lost in time. It is known that Mr. Eleazar Lipnick, Secretary of Yeshivat Etz Chaim since the turn of the century and later Secretary of the Rabbinical College of America, had recorded complete notes until 1917 or thereabouts. However, when Mr. Lipnick migrated to Palestine, sometime before 1920, it is supposed that he took the minutes with him. Mr. Lipnick is now deceased, and all efforts to locate the minutes were unsuccessful. There is no trace of them today, and they have probably been lost or destroyed.

The contemporary newspapers and periodicals offer the only clue to the growth and development of the Rabbi Isaac Elchanan Theological Seminary. The *Jüdisches Tageblatt, Die Jüdische Gazetten, Die Jüdische Welt*, and the *Jewish Morning Journal* were studied extensively. Every issue of one or the other of these newspapers that were published between 1887 and 1919 was read. Anglo-Jewish publications, mainly the *Jewish Messenger*, the *American Hebrew*, and the *Hebrew Standard*, were also read at great length, and hundreds of biographies and autobiographies were consulted. The Hebrew newspapers, *Ha-Ivri* and *Ha-Yehudi*, and the Hebrew periodicals, *Ha-Shiloah*, and *Ha-Tzefirah*, were also examined.

Abramowitz, Duber. Foreword to *Bet Vaad le-Ḥakhamin. (Hebrew)* New York, 1903, I. 1ff.

Abrams, Norman B. "Bet Midrash Lemorim," *Nir: Annual Student Publication of the Teachers' Institute.* New York, 1926.

Adler, Cyrus. *I Have Considered the Days.* Philadelphia: Jewish Publication Society, 1941.

———. *Jacob H. Schiff, His Life and Letters.* Garden City: Doubleday, Doran and Co., Inc., 1928.

———. ed. *The Jewish Theological Seminary of America, Semi-Centennial Volume.* New York: Lord Baltimore Press, 1939.

Antin, Mary. *The Promised Land.* Boston: Houghton Mifflin Company, 1912.

Aron, William. "Einstein: The Jew and His Judaism," *Hadoar,* April 9, 1965.

Benderly, Samson. "Jewish Education in the United States," *Jewish Education,* January-March 1935, VII, No. 1.

Ben Horin, Meir. "Solomon Schechter to Judge Mayer Sulzberger, Part II. Letters From the Seminary Period (1902-1915)," *Jewish Social Studies* April, 1965, XVII, No. 2, p. 76.

Bentwich, Norman. *Solomon Schechter.* Philadelphia: Jewish Publication Society, 1948.

Berkson, Isaac B. *Theories of Americanization.* New York: Teachers College, Columbia University, 1920.

Berlin, Meir. "Autobiographical Sketch," in *Talpioth,* January, 1952. V, Nos. 3-4, p. 392.

———. *Fun Volozhin biz Yerushalayim* II. (Yiddish) New York, 1933.

Berman, Jeremiah J. "Jewish Education in New York City, 1860-1900," *YIVO Annual of Social Science 1954,* New York, IX, p. 272-74.

Berman, Myron. "A New Spirit on the East Side: The Early History of the Emanuel Brotherhood, 1903-1920," *American Jewish Historical Quarterly,* September 1964, LIV, No. 1, pp. 53-77.

Bernstein, Bernard. "A Message," *Hedenu,* New York: Student Organization of the Rabbi Isaac Elchanan Theological Seminary, 1936.

Blaustein, David. *Helpful Thoughts, Our Brethren of the Tenement and the Ghetto.* New York, 1899.

Blaustein, Miriam. *Memories of David Blaustein.* New York: McBride, Nast and Co., 1913.

Borowitz, Eugene B. "The Typological Theology of Rabbi Joseph B. Soloveitchik," *Judaism,* Spring 1966 XV, No. 2, pp. 203-210.

Cahan, Abraham. *Bleter Fun Mein Leben.* (Yiddish) New York: Forward Association, 1926.

Chipkin, Israel S. "Twenty Five Years of Jewish Education in the United States," *American Jewish Year Book,* 1936. Philadelphia: Jewish Publication Society.

Churgin, Pinkhos. "Horav Dr. Dov Revel ve-Yezirato," *Horeb, VI,* November 1941, pp. 1-8.

———. "The Man of Wide Horizons," in *Talpioth,* January 1952, V, Nos. 3-4, 389-91.

Cohen, I. "Yeshiva Rabbi Isaac Elchanan," *Aspaklaria,* Adar, 1907.

Cowen, Philip. *Memories of an American Jew.* New York: The International Press, 1932.

Davis, Moshe. "Jewish Religious Life and Institutions in America," in *The Jews, ed.* Louis Finkelstein. Philadelphia: Jewish Publication Society, I, 1949.

———. "Biographical Sketches," *The Emergence of Conservative Judaism: The Historical School in Nineteenth Century America.* Philadelphia: Jewish Publication Society, 1963.

———. "Raishit ha-Hinuk ha-Ivri ha-Gavoa be-America," *Yesodot ha-Hinuk ha-Yehudi be-America* (Hebrew). ed. Zvi Scharfstein. New York: Teachers Institute, Jewish Theological Seminary, 1947.

———. *Yahadut America be-Hitpathutah.* (Hebrew) New York: Jewish Theological Seminary, 1951.

Deinard, Ephraim. *Kohelet America.* (Hebrew) St. Louis: Moinester Press, 1926.

Drachman, Bernard. *The Unfailing Light.* New York: Rabbinical Council of America, 1948.

Dropsie College for Hebrew and Cognate Learning Register, 1963-1964. Philadelphia, 1963, p. 64.

Dushkin, Alexander M. *Jewish Education in New York City.* New York: Bureau of Jewish Education, 1918.

Eduth le-Yisroel: Jubilee Volume in Honor of Rabbi Israel Rosenberg. New York: Ezras Torah Fund, 1949.

Eideinu: Memorial Volume Published by the Students of the Rabbi Isaac Elchanan Theological Seminary in Memory of Rabbi Solomon Polachek. New York, 1928.

Einbinder, Ph. "Fifty Years Since the Founding of the First Yeshiva in America," *Jewish Daily Forward.* (Yiddish) Sept. 11, 1936, p. 9.

Eisenstadt, Ben Zion. *Israel's Scholars in America.* (Hebrew) New York: Rosenberg, 1903.

———. *Anshei ha-Sheim be-Artzot ha-Brit.* (Hebrew) St. Louis: Moinester Press, 1933.

Eisenstein, Judah David. "Yeshiba," *Jewish Encyclopedia.* New York: Funk & Wagnalls Co., Inc., 1906, XII, p. 600a.

———. *Otzar Zikhronotai.* (Hebrew) New York: J. D. Eisenstein, 1929.

Elberg, Simha, ed. *Sefer ha-Yovel ha-Pardes.* (Hebrew) New York, 1951.

Engelman, Morris, ed., *In Memoriam-Rev. Dr. and Mrs. Philip Klein.* New York: Ference Press, 1926.

Engelman, Uriah Z. "Educating the Jewish Child," *Jewish Affairs.* New York, 1946, I, p. 26.

———. *Hebrew Education in America.* New York: Jewish Teachers Seminary and People's University Press, 1947.

Feuchtwanger, O. *Righteous Lives.* New York: Bloch Publishing Co., 1965.

The First Decade: A Progress Report. New York: The Albert Einstein College of Medicine, 1966.

The First Fifty Years: A Brief Review of Progress. New York: Board of Education, 1949.

Fischel, Harry. *Forty Years of Struggle for a Principle.* New York: Bloch Publishing Co., 1928.

———. *Continuation of Biography of Harry Fischel known as "Forty Years of Struggle for a Principle."* Unpublished.

Friedlander, Israel. *Past and Present.* Cincinnati: Ark Publishing Co., 1919.

Gamoran, Emanuel. *Changing Conceptions in Jewish Education.* New York: The Macmillan Co., 1924.

Ginzberg, Louis. "The Rabbinical Students," *The Maccabean,* February 1946, X, p. 41.

———. "The Jewish Primary School," *The Jewish Exponent.* Philadelphia, 1907, p. 5.

Goldberg, Nathan. "The Jewish Population in the United States," in *The Jewish People: Past and Present.* New York: Central Yiddish Culture Organization, 1948, II, 25 and 105.

Goldman, Alex. *Giants of Faith.* New York: Citadel Press, 1964.

Goldman, Solomon, "The Portrait of a Teacher," in *Louis Ginzberg Jubilee Volume.* (English section) New York: The American Academy for Jewish Research, 1945.

Goldstein, Israel. *A Century of Judaism in New York.* New York: Congregation B'nai Jeshurun, 1930.

Gordon, Hirsch L. "The Meitscheter Illui," *Eidenu: Memorial Volume Published by the Students of the Rabbi Isaac Elchanan Theological Seminary in Memory of Rabbi Solomon Polachik.* New York, 1928.

———. "The Meitscheter Illui," *Hadoar,* March 5, 1965.

Grinstein, Hyman B. *The Rise of the Jewish Community of New York.* Philadelphia: Jewish Publication Society, 1947.

———. "Teachers Institute for Men—Bet Midrash le-Morim," *Alumni Review of Yeshiva University.* New York, 1962, fall issue.

Handlin, Oscar. *The Uprooted.* Boston: Little, Brown and Company, 1952.

Hapgood, Hutchins. *The Spirit of the Ghetto.* New York: Funk & Wagnalls Co., Inc., 1902.

Hartstein, Jacob I. "A Half Century of Torah in America," in *Hedenu.* New York: Students' Organization of the Rabbi Isaac Elchanan Theological Association, 1936, p. 22.

———. "The Yeshiva Looks Back over Fifty Years," *Jewish Education,* April-June 1937, IX, p. 53.

———. "Yeshiva Rabbi Isaac Elchanan." *Hadoar* (Hebrew), March 19, 1943.

———. "Yeshiva University," in *American Jewish Year Book.* Philadelphia: Jewish Publication Society, 1946.

———. "The Yeshiva as an American Institution," *Jewish Education,* March 1947, XVII, No. 26.

Hebrew American Directory and Universal Guide. New York: Gordon Publishing Co., 1892.

Hershman, Elias. "Immigrant M. Hurewitz, True Founder of Y.U.," *Commentator* (Undergraduate publication of Yeshiva College), Mar. 12, 1956.

Hidushe ha-Illui mi-Meitschet. Preface. New York, 1947.

Hilquit, Morris. *Loose Leaves From a Busy Life.* New York: The Macmillan Company, 1934.

Hirschprung, Mordecai. "Short History of the Rabbi Isaac Elchanan Theological Seminary," *Jewish Morning Journal,* May 14, 1925.

Hoenig, Sidney B. *The Scholarship of Dr. Bernard Revel,* New York: Yeshiva University Press, 1968.

Hoffman, Ben Zion. *Fuftzig Yahr Cloakmacher Union.* (Yiddish) New York: Cloak Operators Union, Local 117, 1936.

Honor, Leo L. "Jewish Education in the United States," in *The Jewish People: Past and Present.* New York: Central Yiddish Culture Organization, II, 1948.

Hurwitz, Solomon Th. "The Jewish Parochial School," *The Jewish Teacher,* I, December 1917, p. 217.

Illowy, Henry. *Sefer Milḥamot Elohim.* (Hebrew) Berlin: M. Poppelauer, 1914.

Jacobs, Joseph. "United States," *Jewish Encyclopedia.* New York: Funk & Wagnalls Co., Inc., 1906, XII, 373.

James, Edmund J. and others. *The Immigrant Jew in America.* New York: B. F. Buck and Co., 1906.

The Jewish Communal Register of New York City 1917-1918. New York: Kehillah of New York City, 1918.

Joseph, Samuel. *Jewish Immigration to the United States from 1881-1890.* New York; Columbia University, 1914.

Jung, Leo. "Bernard Revel," in *Eidenu: Memorial Publication in Honor of Dr. Bernard Revel;* New York Students' Organization of the Rabbi Isaac Elchanan Theological Seminary, 1942, pp. 6-14.

Karp, Abraham J. "New York Chooses a Chief Rabbi," *Publications American Jewish Historical Society,* XLIV, March 1955, No. 3, 162ff.

Kevod Ḥakhamim. Issued on the Occasion of the 70th Birthday of Rabbi Bernard L. Levinthal. (Hebrew) Philadelphia, 1935.

"Klein, Philip" in *Universal Jewish Encyclopedia* VI. New York: Universal Jewish Encyclopedia Co., Inc., 1942, p. 415b.

Konovitz, Israel. "Be-Raishit ha-Ḥinukh ha-Ivri be-New York," *Sefer ha-Yovel Shel Agudat ha-Morim ha-Ivrim be-New York,* ed. Zvi Scharfstein. New York, 1944.

———. "Matzav ha-Ḥinukh ha-Ivri be-America," *Luaḥ Achiever,* I (1918) p. 39.

Lebeson, Anita L. "The American Jewish Chronicle," in *The Jews.* Philadelphia: Jewish Publication Society, I (1949).

Lederhendler, Sampson. "The New York Yeshibath," *New Era Illustrated Magazine,* VI, No. 4 (March-April 1905), 344-47.

———. "The Religious Unrest," *New Era Illustrated Magazine,* VI, No. 3 (February 1905), 289-96.

Lestchinsky, Jacob. "The Economic Development of the Jews in the United States," in *The Jewish People: Past and Present.* New York: Central Yiddish Culture Organization, 1946, I.

———. "Jewish Migrations 1840-96," in *The Jews,* ed. Louis Finkelstein. Philadelphia: Jewish Publication Society, IV, 1949, 1225.

Levinson, Jacob. "In Memory of Rabbi Meir Bar-Ilan (Berlin)," *Talpioth,* V, Nos. 3-4, January, 1952, 389-391.

Levit, Ezekiel. "What We Need," *Jüdisches Tageblatt,* Feb. 5, 1903.

Lichtenstein, Aharon. "Joseph Soloveitchik," in *Great Jewish Thinkers of the Twentieth Century,* Simon Noveck, ed. Washington: B'nai B'rith Department of Adult Jewish Education, 1963, pp. 281-97.

Lifschutz, E. "Jewish Immigrant Life in American Memoir Literature," *YIVO Annual of Jewish Social Science,* V. New York, 1950.

Lisitsky, Ephraim. *Eleh Toldot Adam.* Jerusalem: Mossad Bialik, 1956.

Lookstein, Joseph H. "Dr. Revel and Homiletics: A Page of Yeshiva Memoirs," *Hedenu.* New York: Students Organization of the Rabbi Isaac Elchanan Theological Seminary, 1936, p. 62.

Margolis, Isidor. *Jewish Teacher Training Schools In the United States.* New York: National Council for Torah Education of Mizrachi-Hapoel Mizrachi, 1964. pp. 135-87.

Matt, C. David. "Rabbi Bernard Louis Levinthal," *Jewish Exponent.* Philadelphia, May 17, 1935.

Mirsky, Samuel. "Dedication," *Talpioth,* March 1952, VI, Nos. 1-2, p. 1.

New York City Directory. New York, for years 1886-1887 and 1887-1888.

"The New York Theological Seminary," *London Jewish Chronicle,* June 22, 1906, p. 21.

Rabinowitz, Chaim R. "Ha-Rav Yosef Dov Soloveitchik ke-Darshan," *Hadoar,* May 12, 1967, Vol. 47, No. 25, pp. 467-69.

———. "60 Shana le-Shevitot be-Yeshivat Rabbeinu Yitzchak Elchanan," *Hadoar,* June 14, 1968, Vol. 47, No. 30, pp. 552-554.

Raisin, Max H. "Ha-Yehudim ve-Hayahadut be-America," *Ha-Shiloah* (1898), IV, 169ff., 468ff., 566ff.

Revel, Hirschel, "Bibliography of the Writings of Rabbi Dr. Bernard Revel," in *Eidenu: Memorial Publication in Honor of Dr. Bernard Revel.* New York Students' Organization of the Rabbi Isaac Elchanan Theological Seminary, 1942, pp. 21-26.

———. "Rabbi Dr. Bernard Revel," in *Eidenu: Memorial Publication in Honor of Dr. Bernard Revel,* 15-18.

———. "Bibliographia Shel Kitvei ha-Rav Dr. Revel," *Horeb,* VI, November 1941, pp. 200-204.

Reznikoff, Charles, ed. *Louis Marshall: Champion of Liberty.* Philadelphia: Jewish Publication Society, 1957.

Ribalow, Menachem. "Obituary of Dr. Revel," *Hadoar,* Dec. 6, 1940, p. 81.

Riis, Jacob A. *How the Other Half Lives.* New York: Charles Scribner's Sons, 1897.

——. *The Battle With the Slums.* New York: The Macmillan Company, 1902.

Rischin, Moses. *The Promised City.* Cambridge: Harvard University Press, 1962.

Rivlin, Moshe. "Yeshiva Rabbi Isaac Elchanan," *Ameriḳaner,* Apr. 4, 1927.

Rosenfeld, S. "Ha-Das ve-ha-Ḥinukh," *Ha-Shiloaḥ* (Hebrew), Berlin, 1897, pp. 263, 274.

Rosengarten, Isaac. "A Pioneer in American Jewish Orthodoxy," *The Jewish Forum,* April 1925, VIII, No. 3, 145-47.

Rothkoff, Aaron. *Vision and Fulfillment: The Life of Rabbi Dr. Bernard Revel.* Unpublished Doctoral Dissertation. New York: Yeshiva University, 1966.

——. "The Meitsheter Illui," *Jewish Life,* November-December 1967, 29-35.

Safir, Shelley R. "Beginnings and Early Life of Yeshiva College," *The Jewish Forum,* April 1954.

——. "Ten Years of the Talmudical Academy," *Tenth Anniversary Souvenir Journal of the Talmudical Academy Alumni Association.* New York, 1926.

Sar, Samuel L. "Rabbi Berlin as President of the Rabbi Isaac Elchanan Theological Seminary," *Der Mizrachi Weg* (June, 1952), XVI, No. 9, p. 6.

——. "The Rabbi Isaac Elchanan Theological Seminary and Yeshiva College," *Orthodox Union,* 1942, IX, 12.

Scharfstein, Zvi. *History of Jewish Education in Modern Times.* New York: Ogen, 1947, II, 190.

——. "Le-Toldot ha-Ḥinukh ha-Yehudi be-Artzot ha-Brit," *Sefer ha-Shannah* (Hebrew). New York: Histradrut Ivrit of America, 1944, VII, pp. 538-55.

Sefer ha-Yovel shel Agudat ha-Rabbanim ha-Ortodoḳsim. New York: Oriom Press, 1928.

Shimoff, Ephraim. *Rabbi Isaac Elchanan Speḳtor.* New York: Yeshiva University, 1959.

Shurin, Aaron. *Keshet Gibborim.* Jerusalem: Mossad Harav Kook, 1964.

Taḳanot Agudat ha-Rabbanim. Philadelphia: Joseph J. Shur, (no title page, unnumbered pages).

Ten Brave Years (1955-1965). New York: Albert Einstein College of Medicine, 1966.

Waxman, Nissan. "Rabbi Shlomo Poliachek: A Portrait," *Talpioth,* Vol. VI, Nos. 1-2, March 1952, pp. 3-34.

Weekly Bulletin of the Department of Health. New York, April 17, 1915, IV, 16, p. 129.

Weinberger, Moses. *Sefer ha-Yehudim ve-Hayadult be-New York.* (Hebrew) New York: Dr. Morris Wechsler Printer, 1887.

Wiernik, Peter. *History of the Jews in America.* New York: The Jewish Press Publishing Co., 1912.

Wilansky, Dena. *Sinai to Cincinnati.* New York: Renaissance Book Co., 1937.

Zuroff, Abraham. "My Father-in-Law," in *Talpioth,* Vol. VIII, Nos. 3-4. April, 1963, pp. 245-48.

INDEX

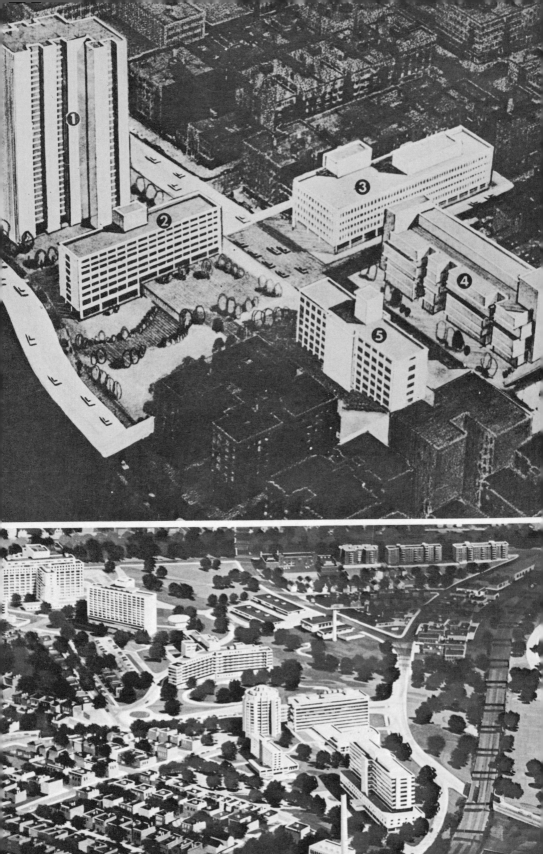